# Indigenist Mobilization

**DISLOCATIONS**

**General Editors:** August Carbonella, *Memorial University of Newfoundland,* Don Kalb, *Central European University & Utrecht University,* Linda Green, *University of Arizona*

The immense dislocations and suffering caused by neoliberal globalization, the retreat of the welfare state in the last decades of the twentieth century, and the heightened military imperialism at the turn of the twenty-first century have raised urgent questions about the temporal and spatial dimensions of power. Through stimulating critical perspectives and new and cross-disciplinary frameworks that reflect recent innovations in the social and human sciences, this series provides a forum for politically engaged and theoretically imaginative responses to these important issues of late modernity.

*For a full volume listing, please see back matter*

# Indigenist Mobilization

## Confronting Electoral Communism and Precarious Livelihoods in Post-Reform Kerala

Luisa Steur

berghahn
NEW YORK • OXFORD
www.berghahnbooks.com

First published in 2017 by
Berghahn Books
www.berghahnbooks.com



**Library of Congress Cataloging-in-Publication Data**

Names: Steur, Luisa, author.
Title: Indigenist mobilization : confronting electoral communism and precarious livelihoods in post-reform Kerala / Luisa Steur.
Description: New York : Berghahn Books, 2017. | Series: Dislocations ; Volume 20 | Includes bibliographical references and index.
Identifiers: LCCN 2017010905 (print) | LCCN 2017016279 (ebook) | ISBN 9781785333835 (eBook) | ISBN 9781785333828 (hardback : alk. paper)
Subjects: LCSH: Adivasis—Political activity—India—Kerala. | Dalits—Political activity—India—Kerala. | Agricultural laborers—Political activity—India—Kerala. | Adivasi Gothra Maha Sabha (Organization) | Land reform—India—Kerala. | Communism—India—Kerala. | Kerala (India)—Politics and government.
Classification: LCC DS432.A2 (ebook) | LCC DS432.A2 S74 2017 (print) | DDC 323.154/83—dc23
LC record available at https://lccn.loc.gov/2017010905

**British Library Cataloguing in Publication Data**

A catalogue record for this book is available from the British Library

ISBN 978-1-78533-382-8 (hardback)
ISBN 978-1-78533-383-5 (ebook)

Index by Sanne Bongers

# Contents

## Part V: Conclusion

# List of Figures

# MAP

**Figure 0.1** Map of Kerala

# ACKNOWLEDGMENTS

This book would have been meaningless without the solidarity, generosity and intellectual confrontation from friends spread out over many places. I thank all those who took me into their lives and politics in Kerala: Jain Vasudevan and his family, thanks to whom I have come to admire the lived, genuine history of Communist struggle in Kerala; Sunny Kapicadu, whose radical courage and charisma, combined with gentle friendship, always makes me feel the pulse of history; I. Ambika, Meera Moorkoth, and K. C. Bindu, who were all three so much more than translators—through sharing their own experiences, struggles, and insights they also provided deep companionship and made me better understand some of the manifold gendered oppressions that exist in Kerala (and beyond). I also thank the people of Kottamurade, who shared their time with me and taught me that some of Kerala's most piercing commentators can be found among people without any formal education.

Without an academic community beyond Kerala, however, what I learned would not have materialized into book form. I thank all my mentors (especially Judit Bodnar, Prem Kuman Rajaram, and Jan Breman) and my former fellow students at the Central European University (CEU) in Budapest, from where I undertook the research and much of the writing that this book is based on. I feel lucky to have been part of an academic community where the drive to gain radical, politically-relevant historical insight was so present. Apart from CEU, there have been various other academic communities where I have been made to feel at home and that I have learned from, in particular Philip McMichael and his students at Cornell University, Crispin Bates and his students at the Center for South Asian Studies (Edinburgh), and fellow Marxist anthropologists of the Anthropology and Political Economy Society (APES) and the IUAES Commission for Global Transformation and Marxian Anthropology that we later founded. My ties to Dalit and Adivasi activism in India were strengthened further through my postdoctoral engagement with David Mosse's "Caste Out of Development" research project. It is thanks to my assistant professorship at the University of Copenhagen that I finally, however, managed to complete this book. Throughout all this time, my managing editorship of *Focaal: Journal of Global and Historical Anthropology* provided me with a steady intellectual heartbeat and—thanks to coeditors—with comradeship. Perhaps, then, it is here most of all that I should mention the companionship and radical inspiration I got from Don Kalb.

Finally, I thank my parents and siblings who have helped me out in many ways without which this book would not have come about. I also am deeply grateful to Jean Blaylock, who has always been generous and supportive towards me and my projects (including this book), and to Carmel Christy, with whom, even in difficult times, I always rediscover a more alive version of myself. I also thank Sylvain Ropital, my love, who shares with me the greatest joy: our son Tristan Steur-Ropital.

I dedicate this book to the memory of Connie Steur (1957–2014), my aunt who was a homecare nurse in the Netherlands and who worked for several years among Baka (indigenous) communities in Western Africa. Her joyful dedication to the happiness of those around her and to a more just and beautiful world was unique, and she is very much missed.

# PART I

## INTRODUCTION

– Introduction –

# Research and Activism in, on, and beyond a Capitalist World System

In January 2003, a large group of landless people gathered in an area of depleted forestland, the Muthanga Wildlife Sanctuary, in one of the hilly northern districts of Kerala, and started settling there. Most of them had taken everything they owned with them, but that just meant a few pots to cook in and some plastic bags with clothes and memorabilia. They were planning to claim a piece of land to call their own at Muthanga, for despite many government promises that agricultural workers were to own at least the plot of land their homes stood on, this had never materialized for them. At this event, their claims were not, however, phrased in terms of their poverty or the government's broken promises to agricultural workers: they were presented in the language of indigenous, or *Adivasi*, rights, the aim being to reclaim the land and lifestyle of their ancestors. The Adivasi Gothra Maha Sabha (AGMS), the movement leading the land occupation, did not give out statements about the need for these people to become emancipated, full citizens of Kerala—even less so about the need for them to be uplifted into the mainstream of society. Their statements were about autonomy and cultural pride. One and a half months later, however, the occupiers were evicted from the area by a massive police force that left little intact of the new life participants had hoped for.

When I first arrived in Kerala in August of 2003, it was not only the participants in the occupation who were still deeply impressed by the events: the whole of politically active Kerala (which is almost to say the whole of Kerala) was still debating the issues it had raised. Was Kerala, a society that prided itself on being progressive, that had seen the most radical land reforms in the whole of India, where everyone had the chance to a decent wage, education, and healthcare, losing out to globalization? Was it corrupted and no longer supportive of general well-being? Or had its model of development never been supportive of this group of people, of Adivasis? Was identity politics then the way forward—was it a good thing? Was it dangerous?

I became interested in this debate and how it could shed light on the more general question of why, in the last decades of the twentieth century in many regions of the world, people who earlier struggled for emancipation, social integration, and even socialism turned to more culturally and autonomy-oriented indigenist politics. I wanted to understand, in other words, how peasants and workers had become indigenous people. This question has attracted attention in Latin America—certainly in areas where there is a strong continuity between socialist and indigenous organizing—but less so in India. By studying how and why the shift happened in Kerala, a state once known as one of the greatest success stories of democratic socialism in the world, I want to sharpen our understanding of the mechanisms producing the global rise of indigenism. I hence situate my research on the new indigenist movement that arose in Kerala in the course of the 1990s in the capitalist world system, and try to see what the social processes unfolding in Kerala indicate about this global complex of relations. And I do so in light of the urgency of transcending the capitalist world system. I seek to recognize sources of praxis that may do more than create bastions of socialism in the peripheries of global capitalism. I also, however, want to take praxis beyond the image of "500 years of indigenous resistance" as islands of hope representing people who have somehow refused to become part of the world's proletariat and now are miraculously going to push back the power of centuries of accumulated capital. If anything, it is in the synthesis of indigenist and socialist thinking and action that I see a space of hope, and it is therefore precisely at this intersection that I have undertaken my research in, on, and beyond the capitalist world system.

My aims in this book are threefold. First, to break the reifying boundaries between people supposedly "in" and people supposedly "outside" the capitalist world system and, worse, the mapping of this division onto culturally or regionally holistic divides. Chapter 1 and 2 of this book are dedicated to deconstructing such reifying categorizations, which have historically stood in the way of more relational, contextual, and historical readings of how people come to be known as indigenous or not. Secondly, rather than speak of "indigenous resurgence," where indigenous people who were previously struggling for their emancipation as peasants or workers instead turn to their indigeneity for inspiration, my aim is to be clear that the rise of indigenism is a formal rather than a substantive phenomenon and that what hence needs explanation is not why indigenous people rebel but why they have started doing so under an indigenist political program. In chapters 3 to 6, I answer precisely this question. My final aim is to consider what all this can mean for praxis—for the possibility of human intervention in the capitalist logic we seem locked in that creates islands of wealth among cyclically returning wide-scale violence, dispossession, and hunger. After having tried to read history against the grain and come up with a more realistic interpretation of the world-historical processes that have led to the rise of indigenism, I hence return in chapter 7 to indigenism as a social movement, to ask how it may contribute to a different world system. These three aims emerge from my engagement with Marxian theory and methodology, which this chapter will briefly elaborate on.

## Marxian Anthropology and Indigenous Studies

I work loosely within a Marxist intellectual tradition and this leads to certain emphases. Foremost among those is taking seriously class—that power-laden and historically determined social relationship of humans to each other—as a major driving force behind the totality of relations in the world system. The analytical emphasis on class is not the same as some popular understandings of class analysis as postulating that history, culture, gender, race, the state, nations or the family—to name but a few key sites of the reproduction and accumulation of relations of power—do not matter. The latter are all key mechanisms through which class relations are produced and reproduced and without which contemporary capitalism would not function. The prediction by some Marxists that in capitalism eventually such super-structural phenomena would melt into thin air as a proletariat and a bourgeoisie polarize into pure forms has been amply refuted. Class struggle in and beyond a capitalist world system has to take place along shifting historical axes of inequality of gender, race, or nation and in confrontation with the various key institutions that deepen a capitalist logic. As simultaneous development and underdevelopment represents the dynamism of capitalism, capitalist colonialism is moreover another crucial axis of class struggle (Krishna 2009). Class struggle need not—perhaps cannot—ever take place in pure form. What a Marxist perspective does is relate various historically developed social forms to class relations to thereby understand the role they play in the larger anticapitalist struggle. One such social form, to which I turn now, is the notion of indigeneity.

## The Clay-like Qualities of Indigeneity

> "Would it not make more sense to try to understand peoplehood for what it is—in no sense a primordial stable social reality, but a complex, clay-like historical product of the capitalist world-economy through which the antagonistic forces struggle with each other" (Wallerstein 1987: 387).

Before we can ask what explains the rise of indigenism, we need to ask what "indigeneity" stands for: how it can be understood in historical context as a particular sociological phenomenon rather than as a given, primordial reality. For if we understand indigenous peoplehood as primordial and stable, we need not wonder at all why so many people today revolt against threats to their livelihood as indigenous people since that would be the only possible basis for them to do so. If, however, we see indigeneity as expressive—in various, contested ways—of a particular historical relationship, we can understand it does not simply, once and for all, map onto substantive categories of people or particular coherent geographical regions. If we moreover acknowledge how under particular circumstances it can also become the key site of resistance against the same historical processes that formed indigeneity into an axis of dispossession, it becomes all the more clear that in this capacity it is a political project rather than simply the name of a given group of people.

It is not always easy to retain a dialectical notion of indigeneity as, in Wallerstein's words, a "clay-like historical product." Despite the emphasis many scholars put on relational analysis, this often becomes a dialogical analysis of the relationship between different categories rather than a dialectical analysis of the meaning of categories through a focus on what their relationship to each other in wider historical context is. Pierre Clastres (1977: 185–86) for instance claims that if "the history of peoples who have a history is the history of class struggle, [i]t might be said, with at least as much truthfulness, that the history of peoples without history is a history of their struggle against the state". This elegantly juxtaposes the meaning of the categories of the working class and indigenous people but only by suggesting a misleadingly binary image of the role of class struggle and the state in the actual joint historical formation of each category.

In the history of the capitalist world system, indigenism has come to stand for the struggle on behalf of an original society to confront its subordination to this system. We should not ignore, however, that by the time this original society is constituted as such—as an "imagined community" (Anderson 1983)—it is already an integral part of the capitalist world system.

Indigenous people sometimes maintain distinct ways of life, some of which lean more towards a kin-based mode of production, but almost everywhere today the surpluses of this production are siphoned off as accumulated global capital that in return gains ever greater leverage over these (and other) people's lives. Many people struggling in the name of indigenism are even more obviously part of global capitalism as they do not own any means of sustaining themselves except their own body and are fully dependent on selling their labor power as agricultural laborers, construction workers, mine workers, etc. Many of those who hold dear an indigenous way of life spend their productive lives working under direct supervision from managers of capital, subjected to dealing with whatever more "efficient" production process these come up with. Other people considered indigenous meanwhile suffer from not having their labor power appropriated by global capital and finding themselves disemployed—first having been violently made dependent on being employed, only to then be turned into a reserve army of labor. Since this is a much more widespread reality for people identifying as indigenous than self-sufficient slash-and-burn agriculture in isolated forests is, it makes sense to see indigeneity not as a relational position that is actually outside of the capitalist world system but, according to Wallerstein's vision, as a particular historically evolved axis through which the appropriation of social labor by a capitalist world economy is organized as well as contested. By this I do not mean to portray indigenous people as "simply disappearing into the vast underclass of the capitalist periphery" (Lee 2006: 457). But I do want to contest the essential difference that much current scholarship rehearses between indigenous people and the rest of the working world. Pierre Clastres's contrasting of people "with" and "without" history is unhelpful in understanding present realities, even if the phrase of "people without history" is meant ironically. Through the case of the Adivasi Gothra Maha Sabha in Kerala, this book will describe the complexities of an indigenist struggle led by people who are as much part of the capitalist world system as so-called working classes are. Where it is becoming increasingly popular, not just in the rhetoric of social movements but also in academic analysis, to distinguish what James C. Scott (2009) calls "state-repellent" peoples versus state subjects, I want to think beyond this dichotomy of indigenous people and working classes. And I want to disrupt this common-sense dichotomy particularly where it is a product of capitalist governmentality. In chapter 1, I prepare the ground for this by discussing the notion of the tribe-class divide as it historically evolved, with particular attention to how it did so in Kerala. In chapter 2, I follow this up by tracing the more contemporary ways in which the notion of indigenous people as a politically distinct category developed in Kerala.

Let me briefly introduce here the context of the contemporary debate on the conceptual difference, if any, between indigenous and working people. Since it seems that in the past decades, the most counterhegemonic challenges to the present world system have been emanating from its margins rather than from within its core—from people identifying as indigenous rather than as workers (with the grand exception of China)—it is not surprising that increasingly from around the 1970s, we have seen a passionate effort in social science to rethink history from the margins. This includes steering clear of Eurocentric, nation-centric, and state-centric views and their tendency to posit the formal working class in core states and its struggle with capital as the main engine of history.

The Subaltern Studies school that emerged in the early 1980s[1] is a major such intervention from India. Its original program was to rewrite history beyond the teleology of the Indian nation-state and hence with much more attention to the role of peasants, tribals, and women in shaping and resisting what became known as India. Inspiration came from within the Marxist tradition and particularly the work of Gramsci[2] and E. P. Thompson (1970), both of whom were admired for their ability to hold in dialectical tension dimensions of social life—domination and resistance, culture and economy, elite and subaltern—that orthodox Marxism had by then reduced to sterile disjunctions. As Sumit Sarkar (1997) argues, Subaltern Studies scholars posited the notion of the subaltern to help avoid the pitfalls of economic reductionism while retaining a necessary emphasis on relations of power. The notion helped analyse collectivities of protest and transformation without positing them in terms of fixed and reified identities.

Around the same time, Eric R. Wolf (1982) promoted a similar critical turn in US anthropology with the publication of his seminal *Europe and the People Without History*. In it, Wolf sought to tell a relational world history of an expanding capitalist core and the populations and regions it incorporated, which from an imperial perspective looked "static" and "without history." Wolf worked within a Marxist (or, his preference, "Marxian") tradition and the difference he tried to make in understanding the history of capitalist expansion was to emphasize "the world as a whole, a totality, a system, instead of as a sum of self-contained societies and cultures" (1982: 385). Paying due attention, as the Subaltern Studies school did, to the "autonomous" (not predetermined) development of non-European/nonhegemonic classes and communities, Wolf emphasized mutual (though unequal) conditioning within an evolving common social formation—the capitalist world system.

A similar effort in more relational historical theory was meanwhile taking place among European Marxist anthropologists (e.g. Meillassoux 1981), who were rethinking the essentialist distinctions current in the mode of production debate. Orthodox Marxism had seen the rise of capitalism in Western Europe and its subsequent hegemony over places like South Asia as caused by essential differences between the European or feudal mode of production and the Asian mode of production. The latter had supposedly dominated the history of Asia and, unlike feudalism, entailed an absolute incapacity for innovation. Rethinking this debate led to different explanations of Europe's dominance, namely as resulting from uneven and combined development.

This post-1968 generation of scholars working to revitalize Marxist theory and critique its creeping dogmatism worked in tandem with a generation of political activists pursuing similar aims in terms of struggling for socialism but against Stalinism. Their aims differ significantly from the contemporary activist-intellectual project that latently builds on relational-historical Marxism but frames the exercise as one of criticism of (rather than critical engagement with) Marxist theory. As Sumit Sarkar (1997) has noted, on the trail of the Subaltern School there came a tendency toward "essentializing the categories of 'subaltern' and 'autonomy' in the sense of assigning to them more or less absolute, fixed decontextualized meanings and qualities" (1997: 304). We can see this move towards emphasizing the autonomy of indigenous people clearly for instance in the work of James Scott. In the 1970s and 1980s, Scott's work already emphasized how state subjects—the Malaysian peasants struggling with the polarizing effects of the Green Revolution—have myriad ways of retaining a sense of autonomy under a surface of symbolic compliance. In *The Art of Not Being Governed* (2009), Scott then proceeded to map class struggle on the one hand and struggle against the state (for autonomy) on the other onto distinct geographical areas and types of peoples. Though he admits that his analysis of Zomia—upland

Southeast Asia—is based on more distant history and that the distinction may be approaching an end, the argument that emerges is popular in contemporary indigenous studies. According to this view, indigenous "state-repellent" peoples and state subjects are related in that they produce each other. They are not, however, related as part of a totality across which an accumulation of power—affecting them both—takes place. Indigenous, highland societies are moreover seen as emerging through a conscious choice to avoid the state. What is thereby ignored is the role of the state itself in defining indigeneity within its sphere of influence for its own interests.

Though Scott explicitly proposes a relational analysis, the relationality lies in that it connects categories and studies the organization of social labor within these categories. He does not study the ways in which social labor is mobilized and appropriated across these categories. If we look at indigenous people from the latter perspective, we see that most indigenous areas and people are seeing their social labor alienated and its value flowing towards an ever-expanding pool of global capital, managed through state power. Hence indigeneity becomes a particular axis of inequality, similar to ethnicity, gender or race in constituting a way in which social labor is organized and appropriated in a global division of labor. It moreover, necessarily, becomes an axis along which the struggle against this division of labor will take place. I see indigeneity not as a category outside of a capitalist world system but precisely one produced in as well as against it and hence in many ways continuous with other such categories. Indigeneity is not, to come back to the epigraph of this section, a stable social reality but, like peoplehood, "a clay-like historical product of the capitalist world economy through which the antagonistic forces struggle with each other" (Wallerstein 1987: 387). And like race and ethnicity, indigeneity has increasingly attained not just a global form but also a global content. Yet precisely because indigenism has come to stand for the fight against the capitalist world system as such (though it has originally also stood for the struggle to impose such a system and often still functions as such), it is easily essentialized as coming from outside of the system.

At a "tactical level of power" (Wolf 1990: 587), indigenism can be seen as indigenous people's struggle to have to live "within, and also against, their own histories and their own cultures, and simultaneously within and against the histories and cultures that others try so intensely to impose upon them" (Sider 2003: xiii).[3] At a more "structural level of power" (Wolf 1990: 587), indigenism is likewise best seen as a struggle both against and within global capitalism. For this provides a more realistic perspective on what the struggle is about and what kind of alliances it can form. Indigeneity cannot only be an inspiration for others, an object through which to remind the world of the relative newness of the state and capitalism in world history—it also needs to be a position that can concretely ally with other struggles. This is not to deny, therefore, that indigeneity reflects a particular history but to open up this particularity to wider alliances. A question that follows from this perspective is, why do indigenous people increasingly struggle as indigenous people while there are potentially many other identifications open to them?

## Framing Movements: From Class to Indigeneity

It takes the deconstruction of reified notions of indigeneity to realize that what is usually presented as the recent "rise of indigenous societies" is in fact largely a formal shift in political subjectivity—a question of a different framing of political initiatives. Hence we can ask why this shift took place. In finding an answer, however, there are few sources to rely on because most existing arguments on why we have seen a rise of indigenism in the last quarter of the twentieth century either essentialize indigenous people or ignore the existence of alternative political projects, notably socialist ones, in which indigenous people were engaged. Marc Becker (2008) is among the few authors who explicitly acknowledge the continuities between socialist and indigenist political initiatives in terms of people's life histories and the trajectories of social movements. In his case, in Ecuador, he has done so as a historian, describing the process through time in detail, though without, as sociologists would, signaling key causal mechanisms for shifting ideological forms. Studies that do discuss causal mechanisms, on the other hand, usually fall into the categorical trap of considering "workers" and "indigenous people" to be necessarily different people and of ignoring the variety of forms of political mobilization (other than indigenism) that indigenous people were involved in. As an alternative to this, I have sought to focus on changing—rather than a priori different—forms of political subjectivity and mobilization while indeed connecting these changes to wider global processes.

There are researchers who have looked at the wider global processes underlying the rise of indigenism. They have tended to focus on the more immediately visible, organizational linkages involved. Ronald Niezen's (2003) *Origins of Indigenism,* for instance, argues that the rise of indigenous movements has been the product of new transnational strategies of organizing and funding and the political possibilities created with the democratization of authoritarian and colonial regimes. Niezen emphasizes the organizational efforts of indigenous people, particularly through the UN Working Group on Indigenous People, and demonstrates that it was a lot of work to create a feeling of commonness and sameness in a category of people ("indigenous people") among whom in fact "the clearest expression of human diversity can be found" (2003: 2). Capitalist conditioning of the rise of indigenism only figures in Niezen's work in a reference to "the destructive and assimilative forces of environmental degradation, state domination, and ethnic rivalry … changing the world's cultural landscape" (2003: 142), functioning as a threat against which indigenous people start organizing. Deborah Yashar's work in Latin America on "why indigenous movements have emerged now and not before" and why they have organized "along ethnic lines to promote an explicitly indigenous agenda" (2005: 5) likewise argues that the neoliberal restructuring that took place in Latin American countries from the late 1970s onward posed a threat to the autonomy and economic viability of indigenous communities, which people had creatively managed to maintain under previous corporatist citizenship regimes. This threat motivated indigenous people to organize.

I argue that while transnational organizing and new communication technologies have played a role in the consolidation of an international indigenous movement, it was not merely the threat of capitalism that conditioned the rise of indigenism. For the threat of capitalism—as if an outside force—does not explain why social conflicts have stopped being framed as class struggle and have instead been reinterpreted and enacted as concerning "indigeneity"; why people used to see their poverty or oppression as a result of how they were relationally positioned vis-à-vis richer people but over time have instead come to see this as the result of discrimination directed at them for being of indigenous background; why social movements of the past are reinterpreted as not actually having been about left versus right, peasant and worker versus capitalist, or poor versus rich, but about nonindigenous oppressing indigenous people (see also Nelson 2003: 123). To understand these shifts in the language and forms of resistance, it is necessary both to analyze how older forms became ineffective or unfeasible and to study how political shifts are embedded in people's changing everyday experiences of making a living, in turn shaped by changing capitalist dynamics (cf. Harvey 2003). Such a focus leads me to argue in the second part of this book that the rise of indigenism is not only about an indigenous criticism of globalization or of greater possibilities for communication and organizational resources available to indigenous people but also about the ideological disintegration of the kind of socialist movements indigenous people had been part of earlier, together with political-economic changes that dispossessed many people of the material basis of perceiving themselves as worker-citizens.

## Global Systemic Cycles and Critical Struggles

> "Viewing social movements as units of analysis … risks cultural and historical abstraction. We invert this procedure, viewing struggles as units of observation, not in comparative relation to one another, but in relation to a shared political-economic conjuncture. We view them as expressing this historical moment, and their cognitive engagement is precisely with the terms or claims of this neo-liberal conjuncture" (McMichael 2010: 5).

"Critical struggles" is the dialectical approach Philip McMichael advocates of contextualizing social movements in relation to global processes, including understanding their position and structuring within the world system. But it is also about making the dialectical countermove of studying social movements to see what they tell us about the current conjuncture in the world system. A critical struggles perspective aims hence to be both realistic and liberating—it studies social movements through the lens of existing theories of global capitalism but then is attentive to how social movements may change our understanding of existing global structures. The critical struggles approach should be kept in mind as a counterweight to the structural determinism of the theories capturing the systemic forces behind the rise of indigenism, which I turn to now.

Jonathan Friedman has consistently called for studying indigenous movements not just within their particular national contexts but also as part of a dynamic and multiplex global system that constitutes a field of analysis that must be "our central focus for understanding" (1999: 391f). Friedman's "global systemic anthropology" is hence aimed at understanding "both the world and the cultural identities and derivative discourses that are generated by the structures of that world" (Friedman 2000: 648). What is nowadays called "globaliztion," according to Friedman, should not be seen as a new era but rather as a cyclically returning historical phase. The fact that from the mid-1970s capital is increasingly exported from the post–World War II centers of global hegemony—especially of course from the United States—is symptomatic of the kind of economic crisis accompanying a period of "hegemonic decline," when costs of reproduction in the core lead to capital fleeing elsewhere while no new global hegemon has yet emerged (Ekholm-Friedman and Friedman 2003). Periods of hegemonic decline are also characterized by "double polarization": vertically in terms of class stratification of astounding proportions (ibid.: 10), but at the same time horizontally as modernist identification (e.g., that of citizenship) declines and is substituted by all kinds of "rooted" forms of identity (ibid.: 7). The rise of indigenous movements can be seen as an expression of a "transformation-fragmentation" process of identification in the world system that follows the "disintegration of homogenizing processes that were the mainstays of the nation state" (Friedman 2000: 650).

These global systemic cycles, however, can be found throughout the last 5000 years of history, so we need to further specify the present cycle and India's position in it. David Harvey argues that the present cycle of world history is characterized specifically by a neoliberal counter-reaction to the gains made by working classes over capital in the post–World War II period. Neoliberalism is the political process accompanying a more structural shift that Harvey (2003) has characterized as a move from "expanded reproduction" to "accumulation by dispossession" as the dominant mode through which capital reproduces itself. Kalyan Sanyal (2013) argued that in a postcolonial capitalist context such as India, this process does not simply swell the ranks of the unemployed—the reserve army of labor—but leads to a much more literal creation of a surplus population, of people that are not only dispossessed but altogether excluded from "the circuit of capital" and basically have no way of subsisting anymore. According to Partha Chatterjee (2008), under conditions of electoral democracy, the Indian government, though subservient to corporate/financial capital in its economic policies, is then driven to try to "reverse the effects of dispossession" through the generation of "governmental policies" to enable certain populations that are made surplus to subsist. Such welfare policies are usually extended in rather ad hoc, random and exclusionary ways to the denizens of "political society" who hence become encouraged to spend their political energies on competing against each other on the basis of categorical identities.[4]

Some "absolutely marginal groups"—mostly Adivasis, according to Chatterjee (2008)—do not even pose enough of a potential threat to be invited to join the competition for benefits and are presumably those most likely to become attracted to the Naxalite path of armed isolation. Adivasi groups in post-reform Kerala, unlike some Adivasi groups in central and north-eastern India, are not, however, "absolutely marginal" in Chatterjee's sense of falling outside of political society. There are moreover remarkable differences between the politics of a movement like the AGMS and those political formations primarily shaped by—and aimed at—governmental policies for Scheduled Caste and Scheduled Tribe populations, which do absorb the political energies of many subaltern groups in other parts of India (e.g., see Lerche 2008). As I will demonstrate in detail in this book, structural shifts in global capitalism and political governance certainly play a role in the rise of indigenism in Kerala but need to be understood in more complex ways than elsewhere in order to make sense in the particular context of Kerala.

To return to a critical struggles perspective it is necessary to not only grasp social movements' positions in world-historical processes but also to read the world through struggles for social change. Such a perspective cannot rely on the past as a finished product, in which struggles that never managed to put their stamp on history have no further meaning or consequence. In light of contemporary changes, "the content of pastness necessarily constantly changes" even though "since … pastness is by definition an assertion of the constant past, no one can ever admit that any particular past has ever changed or could possibly change" (Wallerstein 1987: 381). The rise of indigenism may well signal a disintegrative process in the global system, but it is also important to see how indigenism itself intervenes in these processes and thereby also unsettles established histories. A closer study of indigenism in light of the struggles that preceded it reveals that it need not be just the symptom of declining hegemony in the world system. The meaning of acquiring a piece of land, for instance, can signal a back-to-the-land trend typical of the demise of national developmentalism in periods of hegemonic decline, but it can also be read as the completion of a land reform that never happened for all social classes, coupled with an awareness of the difficulty of making a living of farming under neoliberal conditions and the need for a broader alliance that can confront global capital's grip on agriculture. Indigenism can signal disintegration when looked at from a global systems perspective but integration when studied more closely in terms of what people are trying to accomplish on the ground. It indeed signals the collapse of the alternative of the Soviet Bloc and its sponsoring of socialist politics in certain pockets but it also signals an opening for international, space-making socialism of the kind that refuses to be locked into desperate national bastions. The analysis in this book thus moves within this dialectical tension between a historical-realist and a praxis-oriented perspective.

From this critical struggles approach, a struggle such as that led by the AGMS should also be considered a historical force in itself, not merely a site where we can capture the nature of inevitable structural changes. Satheese Chandra Bose and Shiju Sam Varughese make a similar argument when they suggest that instead of perceiving certain identities as outliers of developmental modernity—which is often the case with Adivasis vis-à-vis the Kerala model of development—we had better "bring into analysis their engagement with the multiple/alternative registers of development which shape Kerala modernity differently" (2015: 8). Reading capitalist change and modernity through the lens of social movements introduces the human element of will and hence indeterminacy. It opens up the possibility that as the future unfolds under the influence of these movements, they may well force us to reinterpret the past they grew out of. "Critical struggles" are about keeping in mind Marx's famous call to philosophers to start changing, rather than merely understanding, the world. This does not mean that social scientists should drop their pens but that there is a relational interconnectedness of intellectual and material processes and that hence our understanding of the world is a product of social change, but at the same time, as McMichael emphasizes, helps produce social change. Hence though we need theories that capture the coherent logic of large-scale processes, there is no neutral and complete theory that explains the world independent of history as it evolves and as we are part of it. This book certainly foregrounds a theoretically informed contextualization of the rise of indigenism, against a tendency in indigenous studies to focus entirely on the messages and intentions of indigenous movements and treat the context of their struggle as the all-too-well-known structure of oppression they resist. On the other hand, this is no dry, objectivist exercise but rather an effort to understand the world as part of changing it.

## For a Dialectic of Discovery and Interpretation

The theoretical intervention outlined above builds on a particular methodological approach to connecting global and local processes, which I will lay out here. This approach follows a "place-making perspective" that does not, as classic anthropological "thick descriptions" do, collapse space and place by analogy (Gupta and Ferguson 1997:7) but instead sees peoples, cultures, and places as relational constructs shaped in time and space. The question is, if not through analogy, then how to connect the local and the global? One way is through an "ethnography of global connection" (Tsing 2004), akin to multi-sited fieldwork (Marcus 1995), which traces the global empirically according to the "travels" of goods, people, ideas, organizations or corporations. Against this empiricist emphasis that refuses to engage with the global as a totality and traces the global only inductively, I propose a historical-realist, dialectical methodology as more suitable to yielding insights that can inform political praxis. I will take Anna Tsing's (2004) method of global connection as a starting point because it exemplifies how despite the desire to move away from the determinism attributed to Marxism, the solution of purely inductive theorizing in fact ends up reproducing the parameters of the status quo.

Tsing's methodology is explicitly aimed at avoiding the universalism of globalization theories, which she finds Marxist approaches particularly complicit with. She argues that "rather than assume we know exactly what global capitalism is, even before it arrives, we need to find out how it operates in friction" (2004: 12). Hence theories that grapple with a whole, a universal, or a capitalist world system need to be "destabilized" by tracing exactly how "universals" travel and create the ruse of universalism. This method would, according to Tsing, open up the notion of globalization beyond the inevitable and unauthored process it supposedly is in Marxist theory. In fact, actual Marxist theorists of global-local connection, such as Immanuel Wallerstein or Terrence Hopkins, are equally convinced that methodology is even more crucial than theory. As Lukacs (1923) before them claimed, Marxism's most important intervention lies not in defending a particular theory but in working with a dialectical method. The difference with Tsing is that this method is used to build on and sharpen existing theory, rather than ignore it. Existing Marxist theory is a starting point but never an endpoint.

In the context of Tsing's rejection of Marxist (or any noninductive) theory, we may recall, in the earlier postmodern turn towards the constant deconstruction of "grand narratives," Eric Wolf's (1990) intervention:

> We need to be professionally suspicious of our categories and models; we should be aware of their historical and cultural contingencies; we can understand a quest for explanation as approximations of truth rather than truth itself. But I also believe that the search for explanation in anthropology can be cumulative; that knowledge and insight gained in the past can generate new questions, and that new departures can incorporate the accomplishments of the past. (587)

Mere description and interpretation are thus not enough: anthropologists also need to provide explanations. It was frustrating to see that with the postmodern turn so much explanatory work done in anthropology was merely deconstructed without being reconstructed: new generations of anthropologists were always inventing the wheel. Hence Wolf (1990: 588) worried that "[a]s each successive approach carries the ax to its predecessors, anthropology comes to resemble a project in intellectual deforestation".

A contemporary source of anthropological deforestation comes, I think, in the guise of methodological empiricism in face of the global. It is often said—with echoes in Tsing's work—that understanding global capitalism is boring, that it brings nothing new, and that what is instead interesting is exactly how people, things, and ideas travel through global networks, assemblages, and chains. Hence comes the methodology of "global connection", focusing solely on how the global is constituted in and by the local and refusing the dialectical countermove of studying how the local is constituted in and by the global. Tsing does not see this problem as she actually claims to be doing both: she says she not only studies how "minorities have accommodated themselves to global forces" but also studies global forces as "congeries of local/global interaction" (2004:3). We are then still left to continue with the unlikely assumption that these minorities' constitution preceded the history of the modern world system. Tsing does not engage in what Terence Hopkins (1978) called "concretization": the effort of taking seemingly concrete things like an ethnic group, a local practice or material fact as abstractions that only make sense because of the actual "concrete" whole that they are part of. Since this whole is the "totality" of social relations, and the method of concretization can in that sense be called "totalizing", it has become easy to rhetorically dismiss it. An advantage, however, is that it can guide a quest for the conjectures where political praxis is possible. Without a theory of the totality of social relations, we can—as Tsing does—discover agency everywhere, and everywhere to an equal extent, since there is no concept of the structure this agency is supposed to defy.

Tsing sees the shift from class politics to indigenism as having happened because of the way "indigenous voice" traveled through a process of "friction"—both grip and tension—through different settings, eventually forming different "traveling models" of indigenism. This is similar to how Eva-Maria Hardtmann (2003), inspired by George Marcus's multi-sited fieldwork, describes her practice of doing fieldwork on Dalit movements as "following the field". The field, in this interpretation, is understood as a relational network that can be traced not just along material objects but also according to plot lines, themes and symbols, and actors and their life histories. Such fieldwork that branches out in various directions and unpacks supralocal influences into various threads indeed opens up "the global." Initially inspired by Tsing's work—as well as that of Hardtmann—I too sought to see indigenism in Kerala not as a homogeneous place-bound phenomenon but as a complex and varied set of political articulations that travel to places where the dominant themes of the "model" (Tsing) or "plot" (Marcus/Hardtmann) have some purchase, but then often become transformed. I was also interested in how these travels encounter what Tsing calls "gaps" (2004: 175)—"conceptual spaces and real places into which powerful demarcations do not travel well." Burawoy (2000), building a Marxist approach to "global ethnography," similarly calls for attention to "disconnections", which are equally important to think with as positive connections are.

My problem with Tsing's methodology, however, is that it does not go beyond providing descriptions of how things happened: the friction-ridden travels of indigenous voice cannot provide explanations of why indigenism arose in Kerala at a particular point in world history. Why did global discourses of indigenism start resonating with local history and experience in Kerala in the 1990s and not earlier? Tracing the "travels" of indigenous models in Kerala does not provide the answer here and would ignore how the local is produced by—and not just "adapts to" or "is in dialogue with"—the global.

The need to go beyond a methodology of tracing direct empirical connections became even clearer to me from the fact that such transnational connections were not all that strong in the case of Kerala. C. K. Janu, the leader of the main indigenist movement in Kerala, whom we will meet frequently in the pages of this book, did travel abroad in the late 1990s, and, through the media, indigenist notions originating in other contexts (e.g., the globally circulating speech by Chief Seattle) did, of course, enter Kerala. Yet, as I came to see it, this transnational influence merely provided the language and symbols—the dressing—for a more structural shift in political mobilization that was at once more locally and more globally produced. In refusing to go beyond ethnographic theory, Tsing leaves the process generally denoted as "globalization" or "neoliberalism"—but better theorized as an ongoing process of capitalist transformation—unpacked. While Tsing claims to want to undermine globalization's universal pretentions, it remains an unchallenged and apparently uninteresting "background" or "discourse" in her description of the global rise of indigenism. She thus provides no answer to the question of how exactly the capitalist world economy conditions political mobilization in different places around the world at different, but connected, times: how the local, all the way down to people's political subjectivities, is shaped by the global as much as our understanding of the global is reshaped by emergent political subjectivities.

A dialectical relational-historical perspective suggests that indigenism, locally perceived as the quest on behalf of an original society to confront its subjugation to the world system, at the same time signals a disintegrative relational process unfolding in those regions, and among those population groups, where the increased mobility that capital won for itself since the late 1970s is destroying local regimes of labor in favor of "accumulation by dispossession." In this book, I will demonstrate that this argument needs refinement in terms of what is happening in those areas where it is not an alliance of finance capital and the state that is physically dispossessing people of their land but where, as in the case of Kerala, the mobility of global capital is gradually putting such pressure on local economies that the kind of livelihoods and public provisions characterizing a previous phase of global capitalism became largely impossible or overshadowed by private capital.

By studying the political economy of Kerala and how it has changed in recent history, I am not simply looking at "local conditions" that explain why traveling models of indigenism stick or not, but at globally produced local processes, not authored by a handful of activists or capitalists, but by a complex totality we need to try to understand in its systematic qualities. I can agree with Tsing and others that this does not mean the process is "unauthored," but precisely because there are so many authors involved we need structural relational analysis. A description of globalization's main plots and actors necessarily has to be complemented by a more theoretical understanding of the totality of unequal social relations involved. The systematic qualities of this totality are not unaffected by indigenist politics: having an idea of the structuring forces of the capitalist world economy also gives us the chance to see where and how indigenism actually intervenes in it. What I aim for thereby is not just the discovery of what Tsing calls "agency" but the search for praxis, the kind of agency that confronts the structural logic of capitalism. And this in turn can only be discovered through the dialectic of moving from the local (ethnography) to the global (theory) and back. I thus share Tsing's worry about the determinedness of capitalism—its power to exert limits and put pressure on what is possible at a particular point in time—but my methodological answer is not to retreat into empiricism to the neglect of theory. Rather my answer is a commitment to a dialectical method that constantly moves between using and adjusting theories, that helps understand the world, what's happening in it, and how human action may strategically intervene in it. As Michael Burawoy puts it: "By throwing up anomalies history is continually forcing the reconstruction of Marxism, leading, in turn, to the reconstruction of history but also of possible futures" (2009: 150).

## A Glimpse into Fieldwork: Reflexivity and Academic Labor

For the reader to be able to situate my research, I would like to offer a glimpse of the particular experiences and relations that shaped it. Since I grew up in different countries of the global South, "development" was an obvious interest of mine as a young student. Yet I became more interested in the global structures producing underdevelopment and the ways in which local people had resisted these than in becoming a development practitioner. Hence my attraction to Kerala, where so-called development clearly had been achieved not through development aid but rather through political struggle. Arriving in Kerala and visiting the Communist headquarters in Trivandrum for the first time in 2003, I received "red salutes" to welcome me as "a comrade from the Netherlands." I had some side thoughts about the ritual performance of the salutes and my own ritual acceptance of them, but undeniably they also made me feel connected, part of an ongoing historical struggle. Soon I became closely befriended to Jain Vasudevan, a journalist for the Communist daily, the Deshabhimani, who adopted me into his family and taught me a great deal about the Communist movement in Kerala. Becoming less of an outsider, I also, however, started to feel the consequent restrictions on exploring the challenge posed to the Communist movement by the Adivasi Gothra Maha Sabha as my Communist friend's family history and work was entirely bound up with unconditional loyalty to the Communist Party. Neighborhood gossip about my improper gender behavior (walking about alone as a woman) moreover had the potential of affecting his family's reputation. Hence we decided I would undertake my actual fieldwork, in 2005–2006, disconnected from my initial network in Kerala. In this, the two female research assistants I found, recently graduated from the Department of English at Kozhikode University, were invaluable. Though they would hate to describe themselves as "feminist" (understandable, considering the matriarchal forms of feminism prevalent in Kerala), they were certainly radical in their criticism of existing gender norms in Kerala. Apart from helping with translation, they thus also greatly helped me in sharpening my thoughts on gender relations in Kerala.

My research assistants were also unique in that they accompanied me despite the caste and particularly gender taboos in Kerala on unmarried, educated young women hanging out in poor people's colonies, outside the vigilance of family networks.[5] There was one colony, in Wayanad—the district where the AGMS emerged—where we returned to almost weekly, often several days a week, during the year of fieldwork I did (and with return visits later on). We befriended the woman active in running the kindergarten (*anganwadi*) there, and people saw that we kept on returning to the colony. Thus those people of the colony who initially had seemed suspicious of our presence seemed after a while to appreciate the interest we took in their stories. Though most adults of the colony had hardly attended school, we soon discovered this made their views more unpredictable and interesting than those of more educated Malayalees. Most people, moreover, had enough confidence to interview me back about what my interest in their colony was all about and what could be in it for them—questions I usually answered by explaining I was writing a book on the movement they took part in, that there was nothing directly in it for them perhaps, but that I was doing my best to make sure their struggles would not be forgotten. Of course this was all perhaps a bit too immaterial for many, so I took the slightly risky step of sponsoring the acquisition of a television and antenna for the woman we were closest to in the colony—the only setup I could think of that might contribute something at least semipublic to the colony.[6] After many visits to the colony, I started to feel so comfortable with the people there that it was a shock to see photos reminding me of the embodied difference between us: standing beside them I looked like a white giant almost twice their size.

In breaks from fieldwork with my research assistants among AGMS activists and Adivasi workers in Northern Kerala—in the colony I just described, but also in other colonies and at several land occupations—I traveled throughout Kerala, and sometimes over its borders, to meet activists of other political groupings, scholars working on Adivasi issues, bureaucrats in charge of implementing Adivasi development plans, cultural producers of purportedly Adivasi art, journalists who had been reporting on the AGMS, politicians active for the Adivasi cause, environmentalists and landlords with distinct views on "the tribal question," social workers in charge of Adivasi welfare, and tourism promoters interested in using the potential in Adivasi culture to attract more tourists to "God's own country" (as the Ministry of Tourism has branded Kerala). I moreover spent several months with Dalit-Adivasi activists in Central Kerala, one of whom, Sunny M. Kapicadu, hosted me in his family home and became a good friend. Sunny's critique of the Keralese variant of Marxism as a cover-up for upper-caste dominance helped me greatly in sharpening my thoughts. Together my research assistants, my Communist friends and my Dalit activist friends all had a tremendous, critical impact on my research, though their views were often conflicting. Their influence is not random—it is a reflection of the kind of informants and research assistants I sought. Despite the sympathy I have for each, I never seriously considered following reflexive experiments such as explicitly combining activism and ethnography or coauthoring my text. I think anthropologists have a distinct, critical role to play where they are not part of the social movement(s), and social networks, they study (e.g., see Edelman 2001). Not coauthoring, I preserve some of the intellectual freedom that a relative outsider has.

As a final methodological note, I must point out that fieldwork relations are not the only relations that shape anthropological research. I was lucky to be able to pursue most of the research that this book is based on as a PhD student at the Central European University in Budapest, a private but not profit-oriented international university where narrow political and economic interests had little leverage over the content of my work.[7] The space for such academic freedom has, however, been narrowing in Europe. Within academia, one's position and career are ideally structured such that no particular political movement, state imperative, corporate interest or kinship network has leverage over the contents or conclusions of research projects. However, with the "global marketing of knowledge production" since the 1980s, many countries have seen a shift away from this ideal of academic knowledge production toward a conception of the university as a transnational business corporation where research activities are defined in terms of commercial interests and entrepreneurial outcomes (Shore 2010: 27f). In the process, we see a replacement of "professional relationships based on collegiality and trust with a regime of measurement, performativity and surveillance," creating entirely contradictory incentives and ultimately "schizophrenic academic subjects" (ibid.). A critical awareness of (and struggle against) such processes that threaten to replace critical anthropology with "anthropreneurship" is hence a necessary complement to more fieldwork-centered reflexivity. For the racism that many anthropologists of the colonial period have been criticized for, and that indigenous people in particular have suffered from, was not due to a general ignorance of anthropologists at the time. Rather, it was the outcome of powerful mechanisms that tied anthropologists' careers to the compromises they made with the institutions endowing them with their professional status. Unfortunately, such mechanisms have in many ways only gotten a greater grip over anthropologists' careers since the formal end of European imperialism.

## Conclusion

Certain times and places make it easier for the researcher to stick to the kind of theoretical and methodological approach sketched in this chapter than others. In places where "liberal-culturalism" reigns (see Steur 2005), where indigeneity has become fixed as a coherent and fiercely defensive identity discourse (as in the United States), my research project would have been difficult. Outside of these centers of liberal culturalism, in regions that have known strong socialist movements that continue to disrupt culturalist discourses on indigeneity, my project is a much more likely one. In Latin America, for instance, one could, in the last quarter of the twentieth century, find a lot of blurring of indigenous and class politics. The Zapatista rebellion is a case in point: some anthropologists, such as June Nash (2001), have been impressed by the Mayan cosmologies it apparently based itself on, whereas others, such as Neil Harvey (1998), see it as a continuation of the struggle for land and democracy that socialist groups had historically been waging in the region. Just over the border, in Guatemala, there was an explicit controversy on indigenous versus class interpretations of the civil war. As Diane Nelson (2003) describes, the war was no longer interpreted, as it was in the 1980s, as a "class war with ethnic components" but was now claimed, by so-called *culturales,* to have been a racist war perpetrated by right and left against the indigenous Maya. Or, to move further south, in Bolivia some have emphasized how Evo Morales was the country's first indigenous president, while others have pointed out that Morales himself had identified above all as a Trotskyite unionist (e.g., cf. Gordon 2009 and Postero 2006).

The Confederation of Peasant Trade Unions of Bolivia confronted the tensions between class and ethnicity head-on by stating in 1983, "We refuse to accept and will never accept class reductionist ideas which transform us to the status of mere 'peasants' … Nor do we accept ethnic reductionism which transforms our struggle into a confrontation between 'Indians' and 'whites'" (Yashar 2005: 179). I have written this book in the spirit of such refusal and emphasize that where I use words such as "workers" or "indigenous people", these should always be taken to signify contingent and relational rather than primordial identities. Sitting in the crossfire between, on the one hand, indigenist groups who refuse to accept Marxist thinking can be anything but hypocritical, and, on the other hand, socialists who choose to consider indigenist activists as opportunists or even racists, is not too comfortable. Yet, I felt I had to use my position as a sympathetic outsider, moving between indigenist and Communist activists, to try to contribute to a political space beyond the common sense[8] that helps to fix the indigenist and the Marxist positions into a deadlock. Kerala is a rather unique ground to study the tensions between indigenism and Marxism precisely because the active confrontation of the two in Kerala tends to lay bare the complexities involved perhaps even more clearly than in Latin American settings.

I must, then, add a few words here about Kerala's "exceptionalism" and the question of what lessons we may learn from the Kerala experience. As Ritty Lukose puts it, Kerala is without doubt "part of India" (2009: 23ff.) and differences it has with the rest of India have developed precisely because of particular historical processes that have unfolded within the Indian peninsula in its interaction with the wider world. "Local history" or "tradition" in Kerala includes the many overseas influences that have shaped and become part of Kerala for at least two centuries as much as it does the matrilineal inheritance forms and extremely rigid caste system that have characterized Kerala in the nineteenth century. Kerala is thus not an exception but a particular relational conjunction in a wider historical trajectory. Kerala is particularly interesting for my research because of the degree to which a Communist program of land reform, wage protection, and other social rights was implemented, the extent to which the ideology of Communism is part of many people's common-sense understanding of the world in Kerala, and the fact that the Communist movement managed to gain power in Kerala within an overall democratic framework. However, the state government, even when in Communist hands, is much more social-democratic in its policy-making than the formal Communist label suggests. It has confronted the challenges of capitalist crisis without immediately creating the stark levels of class polarization and poverty that have developed in other parts of India (see Sandbrook et al. 2007), but liberalization has nevertheless intensified the relational production of what Charles Tilly

(2001) would call "categorical inequalities". Recent reform has led to the steady dismantling of the historical architecture of the Kerala model and created economic and social problems that are probably better termed "hazards" than "challenges" (Oommen 2010). As this book will show, projects for local social democracy do not hold out against the onslaught of neoliberalism indefinitely. The need for a global confrontation with capital remains.

The most notable quality of Kerala to the study of the rise of indigenism is that modern indigenism has only recently emerged in the state. Since it is not yet a well-oiled or institutionalized program, the variety of interpretations of indigenism and indigenous identity are striking. In addition to this, "accumulation by dispossession" (Harvey 2003) is a more subtle process in Kerala than elsewhere in India. This adds to making an explanation of the rise of indigenism based on primordial identities or an abstract "threat to indigenous livelihood" unsatisfactory—it forced me to move along the theoretical and methodological lines sketched in this chapter, in order to reach a better explanation for the rise of indigenism. The degree to which Kerala's indigenist movement incorporates a variety of political strands and constantly veers into counterhegemonic directions—in the interest of working-class rather than landed Adivasis, in the interest of broad alliances confronting social inequalities rather than in the interest of exclusive communities—also forced me to consider the possibility that indigenism is not just a reaction to global forces but also a reincarnation, by other means, of past struggles for emancipation. Hence I was guided towards certain explanations and openings not just by my theoretical and methodological insights, but also by what I encountered in Kerala itself. Eric Wolf's work shows how history is constantly in the process of creating "hidden histories" (Schneider and Rapp 1995). This is particularly so when it comes to failed or fragile attempts at socialist solidarity or complex relational understandings of indigenous identity. I therefore think that the traces of the complex interrelation of socialist and indigenist politics that were so clearly visible in Kerala also may help scholars studying the rise of indigenism in other contexts become more sensitive to articulating such hidden histories.

## Notes

1. The first Subaltern Studies volume came out in 1982, edited by Ranajit Guha, who also was editor of the five subsequent volumes. Contributions were mostly concerned with "peasant revolt" and "rebellious hillmen".
2. Gramsci's prison notebooks, written between 1926 and 1937, were edited and published in English in 1971 by Quintin Hoare and Geoffrey Nowell Smith.
3. Note that there is still a seed of essentialism in Sider's formulation in posing a dichotomy between one's "own" culture and that of "others", though for Sider culture is not a particular bounded and coherent structure but rather the way in which people make sense of the contradictions of everyday life. We may thus read "others" as potentially including indigenous others.
4. The dichotomy that Chatterjee hereby creates—of a "political society" where material benefits are supposedly attained purely in informal and ad hoc manner and a "civil society" that is the institutional domain of liberal-bourgeois activism—has been much criticized (see Steur 2015). For an insightful critique of Chatterjee's concept of 'political society' in the light of the history of Kerala see Mannathukkaren 2010.
5. Such behavior was bound to lead parents to hasten their search for a proper groom (before the young woman's reputation was beyond repair) and hence was in some ways all the more risky for women who strongly valued their freedom.
6. That this was a somewhat risky step was apparent from the issues it gave rise to: some women were very happy that the television in the colony stopped many of the colony's people from watching television at the nearby shop and, in the process, getting further indebted to the shopkeeper. The shopkeeper, obviously, was less pleased. My friend who had the television in her possession, moreover, had decided that she would only put it on after school hours—something many people agreed with her on but others were angry about. And soon the clay ridges around my friend and her neighbors' houses were crumbling because so many people were always gathering there to watch television.
7. For a concrete and critical analysis of the global political context in which the Central European University was founded see Guilhot 2007. Compare this, however, with the commitment to a classical liberal (and far from neoliberal) vision of knowledge production promoted by Yehuda Elkana (2009), CEU's rector during most of my PhD.
8. In this book I use "common sense" and "good sense" in the way Gramsci coined these concepts (Hoare and Nowell Smith 1971).

# PART II

## ADIVASINESS AND ITS DISCONTENTS

– Chapter 1 –

# THE "TRIBE" IN WORLD TIME

The trajectory of the making of the notion of the tribe is a dense accumulation of hidden assumptions shaping the beliefs of our time, carried on from ideas dominating our past. The understanding of who and what Adivasis are has thereby become what Gramsci would call common sense. The aim of this chapter is to disturb this common sense, to demonstrate its historical construction and thereby deconstruct the hegemonic premises sustaining its coherence. I do this in order to open up space for a more critical and conflicted understanding of the tribe in the context of the political interventions and struggles occurring in its name. If we want to consider the possibility that indigenism, a politics centering on "Adivasiness," may hold a transformative, counterhegemonic vision in Kerala today, it is important to first understand the historical challenges it faces in this respect because of the problematic historical baggage the notion carries. By examining the notion of the tribe, this chapter also takes a critical look at the history of anthropology, a discipline that has played a major role in legitimizing the conceptual and political divisions the notion draws.

This chapter is not about who or what tribes really are or what their real social history is. It is not about correcting mistaken theories about the historical origins of particular tribes, though engaging in this type of debate from a sensitivity, developed by Eric Wolf (1982) and further by, for instance, William Roseberry (1989), to how today's tribes are the dialectical product of an expanding world system, would certainly be a welcome exercise in the case of Kerala. A good example of such work on the area of Bastar in the central Indian state of Chhattisgarh is Nandini Sundar's (2008) historical-anthropological account of how the idea of tribes as isolated and outside of politics and history was essentially a product of colonialism and postcolonialism. Sundar provides an alternative social history of political relations in Bastar and demonstrates in vivid detail that when it comes to processes of dispossession in the area, the present phase of economic liberalization is but one moment—a blip perhaps—in a long history initiated by the colonial wave of lawmaking that produced the penal code, the forest act, and the land acquisition act.

A critical alternative history for tribes in Kerala would be quite distinct from the history of tribes in a region like Bastar, and it would certainly deepen our understanding of present-day conflicts in Kerala. Unfortunately, however, it goes beyond my research project. What this chapter provides is merely one crucial ingredient to destabilizing hegemonic tribal history in Kerala and hence thinking critically about recent shifts in political identification, namely a study, through secondary sources, of how the notion of the tribe as such emerged. Such tracing of the idea of the tribe allows us to start to see the way "common sense" knowledge about tribes has been shaped and to try to think beyond this. Moreover, it provides the historical background to the kind of conceptual references that a politics that presently bases itself on the notion has to negotiate with.

This chapter will start with a discussion of the tribe's trajectory in the capitalist world system—in "world time" as Walton (1984: 181) calls it. We will see that the "tribe" originally started as a concept through which various philosophers argued about their understanding of the modern world: the tribe was assumed to be everything modern class society was not. If class was progressive and rational, the tribe was primitive and innocent; if modern society was polarizing and alienating, tribal society was egalitarian and organic. As the British Empire took on a more proactive role in ruling the Indian subcontinent, the notion of tribe, however, became entangled in the colonial effort to govern the territory's population. Although the ethnographic exercises of trying to finalize the category of the tribe and who belonged to it were full of contradictions, the label nevertheless came to play a major role in determining the limits within which political debate concerning these "tribals" could take place. Moving on to a discussion of the tribe in post-Independence India, we see how debates on "the tribal question" were still heavily shaped by the ethnographic state, which determined the boundaries within which the tribe could be signified: those who attempted to deconstruct these boundaries often failed to become recognized as having participated in the debate on the question at all.

The second part of this chapter moves to a more detailed consideration of how the practice of anthropology has historically contributed to understandings of the concept of the tribe in Kerala. As I demonstrate, the production of ethnographic knowledge of a particularly isolating and essentializing kind has remained largely uncontested in anthropological work on Kerala, despite the fact that radical social movements in Kerala have historically focused on science as a site for emancipation. Only with the rise of the Adivasi Gothra Maha Sabha (AGMS, lit. Indigenous Clans Grand Council) did academia take notice of relevant realities outside of the dominant paradigm of tribal ethnography—and still mostly in disciplines other than anthropology. I hence end this chapter with a brief overview of literature (and films) in disciplines that have responded to the rise of the AGMS in ways that complement its agenda. In presenting some of the most significant knowledge produced in response to the debates that have arisen around the AGMS, I also acknowledge these as sources this book draws on in trying to produce a relevant intervention from anthropology that does not succumb to the ruling ethnographic paradigm.

## The Tribe in an Expanding World System

> "The continuing study of colonial regimes should be more than a neo-abolitionist denunciation of a form of power now safely consigned to history." (Cooper and Stoler 1997: 35).

I now turn to the history of the notion of the tribe in the context of the (un)making of class relations within the capitalist world system. This history has a continuing influence in shaping the lenses through which "the tribe" is seen today. Divorced of this kind of "structuring" perspective (Abrams 1982)—one that sees the past as continuing into the future by forming the material on and through which future decisions are made—the study of the history of the tribe may indeed, as Stoler and Cooper warn, run the danger of becoming a "neo-abolitionist denunciation" of past ideas and practices (1997: 35). In historically deconstructing the concept of the tribe, I do not want to presume a linear evolution of the notion itself any more than I want to follow the Hegelian belief in the necessary rationality of history that is such a considerable part of the concept's problematic intellectual baggage. Instead I have tried to consider the historical-intellectual trajectory of the notion of the tribe as "that of its various fields of constitution and validity, that of its successive rules of use, [and] that of the many theoretical contexts in which it developed and matured" (Foucault 2007: 5). In order to pursue a genealogy of the notion of the tribe, with a study of the historical processes producing it, I have adopted a critical agnostic stance vis-à-vis the Hegelian certainty of progress and instead, from a structuring interpretation of history, have seen the past as setting limits and exerting directional pressure on the present but also offering many moments of contingency.

It would of course have been satisfactory to *not* start out with European debates when discussing historical development in India and to instead "provincialize" Europe (Chakrabarty 2000) by starting with a discussion of the actual history of some of the peoples figuring in this book—peoples who have so persistently been denied history. Yet the problem is that the historical studies that exist on this subject are all heavily formed by European concepts. All that is possible for an anthropologist like me, who needs to rely on secondary historical sources and on what people tell me about the past *in the present,* is hence to deconstruct these dominant concepts. What this does is not so much give the "true" history of tribes in India but reveal the relations of power that have shaped the way we think about this history. As I discussed in the previous chapter, if you take a dialectical rather than a dialogical approach to the study of tribes, the state and capital cannot be conceived of as external forces to the process of how these entities emerged. Perhaps before the intensification of capitalist incorporation of the northeastern regions of India in the eighteenth century, one might ignore the determining effects of the capitalist world system and argue for a dialogical perspective. Yet to take a dialogical rather than a dialectical view of tribes in the modern history of Kerala—a period intensely shaped by global capital—would certainly unduly reify the boundaries between tribes and nontribes as substantive and self-generated.

## *Imperialist Inventions of the Tribe: "I Know One When I See One!"*

In this section I discuss how the notion of the tribe is the historical product of a transnational project of capitalist expansion that was hegemonic in its ability to set the terms in which struggle against it took place. The process includes two major moments: on the one hand, the drastic class polarization happening within the core of the empire and, on the other hand, the intensified exploitation of its periphery. These two moments were closely interconnected, in the first place economically, but also in terms of how theories emerging in one context traveled to the other to fulfill a connected but reconstituted role there. The notion of the tribe was closely connected in Europe to an idea that became hegemonic in the mid-nineteenth century: that society was progressing towards a rational endpoint. In order to conceptualize what this rational end point was, we saw the birth of what Adam Kuper (1988) has called "the illusion of primitive society"—captured by the notion of the tribe—as its conceptual opposite. In this very meaning, the "tribe" gained an important function in the colonies as a way to divide and manage local populations (Li 2009).

Adam Kuper (1988) is right to stress the flexibility and adaptability of the notion of "primitive society," and with it the "tribe," as key to its survival over time. The notion of progress away from tribality was both part of the language of the bourgeoisie, who used it to legitimize their restructuring of society, and part of socialist utopian thinking, which saw tribal society as an ideal to return to. The category of the tribe could be used to mobilize certain populations for capitalist production, just as it could be used in other contexts to argue for a paternalist protection from such exploitation (Li 2009). The hegemonic function of the tribe lay primarily in how it prevented tribal struggles to be framed as another form of class struggle and vice versa. The notion of the tribe contributed to making it almost unthinkable that people considered to have entered the era of modern class society could form an alliance with those seen as its historical remnants to jointly contest the process of capitalist expansion that was affecting their lives.

To the contemporary anthropologist doing research on people who happened to be known as tribes in India, it can be rather puzzling why these groups are so often equated with "indigenous people" and "forest dwellers" when there seems to be no actual relation between being indigenous and living in a tribal community and where such people can be seen more often than not living outside of the forest just like "mainstream" others. Conceptually it is assumed that tribal communities can be distinguished according to certain criteria such as the organization of the community on the basis of direct reciprocity and equality, the fact of being the first people settled in a certain area and the act of living in forests (or jungles). These criteria, however, did not just originate in the empirical realities of the Indian subcontinent but primarily were shaped by preoccupations with the changes that European societies were undergoing. Similar to how Dumont's classic work on caste, *Homo Hierarchicus* (1972), was intended primarily as a commentary on what was going on in Western society, the notion of the tribe initially took shape as an obsession with what was supposed to be its mirror image: modern class society in Europe.

Since forests and tribal social organization (conceived as anything from mechanical solidarity to matriarchy) were not what Western modernity was, both could become linked with another opposite of a society fully immersed in "historical progress": antiquity. As Wilmsen (1989: 10) remarks, tribes were paradoxically "permitted antiquity while denied history." Colonial officials—often with a training in anthropology—failed to appreciate how the isolation they saw some groups living in was a product of the colonial regime itself and how these groups had diverse socio-political trajectories by which they had arrived at their contemporary situation (Sumit Guha 1999: 201). They insisted on depicting tribals as isolated and forests as primordial, both relics of a time before history (Sumit Guha 1999: 199). I will refer to such theories here mostly as "social evolutionist" since this was a dominant and virulent current in the upsurge of philosophizing on the tribe in Europe of the 1860s and 1870s (Kuper 1988). The logic of social evolutionism relies heavily on a Hegelian interpretation of history as the unfolding of "reason"—a faculty of every human mind and hence universal—through the dialectic of contradiction and synthesis not just in the human mind but equally in historical reality. Social evolutionism, however, adds to a Hegelian interpretation of history a fixing of time periods in space by mapping them onto certain distinct peoples and/or territories. Social evolutionism proposed not only that human history consisted of certain stages of evolution but also that the distinct communities "found" (in fact constructed) in the world were reflections of these different stages.

European industrializing nations were immediately recognized as the most advanced and the signpost of the level to which reason had progressed in human history. Just as tribal peoples exhibiting a lack of historical progress were identified in the colonies, similarly "backward," "primitive," and "degenerate" people were, however, identified in Europe itself among autochthonous working classes (Sumit Guha 1999: 14). The urge among many nineteenth-century academics to mobilize the notion of tribality to help define and defend modern capitalist society should be read against the background of the perceived threat from a growing tide of socialist mobilization since the French revolution. According to Sumit Guha (1999: 14), this tide forced the bourgeoisie in Europe to look for a better and more potent ally than the religious orthodoxies espoused by the church to combat the rising popularity of the notion that all men (and perhaps even women) were equal. The addition of a racial element to the tribal-primitive-forest-dwelling brew made for an all the more potent combination defining all that was progressive about capitalist society and making it clear that tribal society was a "dark" reality to be avoided. Indeed, ethnographic publications in 1848 seemed obsessed with proving "in the name of science" that the natural equality of men was false (ibid.).

The socialist challenge, however, is ambiguous. If we look at Marx's own writings, we can see that the Communist Manifesto (1848), for instance, avoids the essentialism of mapping historical eras onto particular, apparently isolated, communities but nevertheless demonstrates the clear conviction that there are particular "stages of development" that societies pass through and that historical progress along these stages is "inevitable." It moreover explicitly describes the Western proletariat as the most "advanced" of all oppressed peoples so far and the bourgeoisie as having played a progressive role in society. It seems, as Wilmsen (1989: 20) argues, that Marx in any case "shared the basic tenets of his contemporaries with respect to a prehistoric era set in polar opposition to our own." On the other hand, Wilmsen adds that unlike most other nineteenth-century thinkers, Marx considered contemporary foragers "products of historical contingencies, not of a natural essence or an evolutionary stasis" (ibid: 21). From a reading of the *Ethnological Notebooks* Marx compiled near the end of his life, Gailey (2006) argues that Marx confronted social evolutionists and their evolutionary racial typologies with a historically specific and analytical reading of different forms of precapitalist class society. In contemporary manifestations of such precapitalist societies, Marx did not see vestiges of the past but evidence of resistance to the penetration of state-associated institutions (ibid: 16). Marx moreover, according to Gailey, admired the absence of private property and the classless division of labor characteristic of primitive societies that he envisioned a Communist society would achieve through "dialectical return" toward a more technologically developed form of "primitive Communism" (ibid.). Yet in all this, the notion of the tribe also in Marx's writings fulfilled its usual role of signaling, even if in a more positive light, the opposite of modern class society. In that sense it also set the trend for the gross neglect by intellectuals in the core of generically socialist or even explicitly Marxist initiatives later in the twentieth century among people caught under the definition of "tribe."

During the second quarter of the nineteenth century, under pressure from competition with other emerging imperial powers, the British ruling class saw it necessary to move from the extraction of wealth primarily through trade to a more minute organizing of relations of production in the Indian subcontinent through taxation. As colonial rule in India hence shifted from "a regime of sovereign power to a regime of governmental power" (Gidwani 2008: 7), the notion of the tribe gained a concrete function. Simply put, "there were no 'tribes' in India until the European perception of Indian reality constructed them and colonial authorities gave them their administrative sanction" (Devalle 1992: 51). Racist European ideas of what primitive tribal society was thus received new credibility and confirmation in the colonies, from where these ideas again reverberated back to the core (Cooper and Stoler 1997: 12). Being at the center of exercises to either legitimize capitalism or envision its transcendence in Europe, the "tribe" as attached to actual population groups in India was central to efforts to isolate these groups from other subaltern populations, either for their protection or that of the colonists.

Through the lenses of social evolutionary theory, colonial officials came to see certain social groups in India as childlike peoples, unable to quite grow up. These groups were often also considered unorganized and "wild", in fact completely opposed to the "civilized peace" that colonial rule was supposed to bring (Skaria 1999: 155). These "tribes" logically had to be indigenous and live in the forest since colonial officials understood that tribal organization characterized the earliest humans (the "savages"). They also assumed their way of life was more "primitive" than other economic systems, which had led these groups of people to be driven into the forest when they "came into contact" with more agricultural communities who started claiming plains lands for themselves and obviously had the power to do so since they were more "advanced". This same theoretical framework was also used by British officers to legitimize their rule over predominantly "barbarian," feudal communities in South Asia, on the one hand through the claim that British rule would entice them to reach a higher stage of development but also because the "noble savages" found in the forest needed protection by enlightened British rule from their "barbarian" neighbors in the plains. Social evolutionism, while fixing and isolating population groups into particular niches simultaneously mystified this effect of colonial rule as evidence of the essentially primordial and isolated nature of tribes.

Views on tribes in India were also supported by another grand narrative of historical development: the "Aryan race theory" that gained popularity in nineteenth-century Europe. Formulated initially by German comparative philologists in the 1840s and 1850s as part of the discovery of the Indo-Aryan family of languages, the Orientalist Max Muller took up the concomitant "Aryan invasion theory" to claim Indian civilization was based on the invasion of Aryan peoples from the north sometime around the second millennium B.C. According to historian Romila Thapar (2008), reference to an Aryan people in old religious texts that Muller based his theory on were always about social status and language rather than race. Nevertheless, the theory was taken up by British officials who read Aryan descent as a marker of racial distinctiveness of the more "developed" caste groups who supposedly shared a common descent with the British, as opposed to the darker-skinned Dravidian race from which most lower castes and tribes descended.

When the 1857 uprising, claimed by Indian nationalists today as the country's first "war of independence," spread to the population groups in Central India whom British officials considered tribal (Hardiman 2004), they felt confirmed in their ideas about these groups as "wild people," unable to grasp the British civilizing mission.[1] With it, the need to distinguish tribes from those communities embodying a "higher"—more hierarchical, easily controllable, and taxable—feudal "stage of development" became all the more urgent. Tribes were to be left alone since they had proven themselves "wild" and "primitive" and beyond possible reform into a useful labor force. Feudal society, meanwhile, was to be the prime target of the white man's burden to "civilize" colonial subjects and make them give up their cruel, barbaric practices such as *sati* and child marriage. The great "peasant/tribe divide" (Li 2000), a preoccupation of colonial rule in many colonies, translated in India into the "caste/tribe" distinction, with the census—first held in 1871—as its most symbolic battleground. In interpreting the 1857 rebellion as an "anthropological failure" rather than as a political or economic event, the following years saw the colonial state take on an increasing "ethnographic character" (Dirks 2003: 148).

Tribals and nontribals came to be treated as two entirely different categories of subjects, largely resulting, as the famous missionary-turned-ethnographer Elwin Verrier claimed, "from a desire to quarantine the tribes from possible political infection" (1959: 45). The distinction was linked to the romantic ideals developing in England at the time around the emerging dichotomies of nature and culture. Most colonial officers projected these ideals onto tribes as yet uninfected by the cruelties of human character that market society brought about.[2] But at the same time the distinction was driven by a realist concern to "divide and rule." Hence emerged "rigid … conceptions of the tribal as being clearly differentiated from the rest of society," even where so-called tribals and nontribals lived in the same area (McMillan 2005: 116) and where in practice, tribals were often directly targeted for recruitment into the labor force serving the needs of

British plantation-owners (Phillips 2003). British policy also stressed that tribals required a different sort of administration, even though it was unclear how this was to be practically organized where they did not live in socially homogeneous areas.

The "tribe" came to define a disparate group of what were commonly known as *jatis* (occupational/endogamous castes) as part of British officers' exercise to "render fluid and confusing social and political relationships into categories sufficiently static and reified and thereby useful to colonial understanding and control" (Cooper and Stoler 1997: 11). Colonial officers often either turned into ethnographers themselves or sought the help of European ethnographers—and Indian collaborators—to engage in such categorizing exercises. Though it is debatable to what extent the discipline of anthropology and anthropologists in the field initially facilitated—or, on the contrary, also at times were a major irritant to—colonial rule, there was a clear link between anthropology and colonial administration in that many colonial officers received at least some training in anthropology and started using its cloak to "scientifically" validate their social mapping exercises (Kuper 1996: 99).

It was particularly in the making of the first population survey that anthropology gained a major role in colonial rule. The colonial survey exercise started by drawing on the conviction that religion was the primary fault line in the subcontinent and its history. Since it was believed that Hinduism was "the antithesis of Islam," the primary distinction to be made in the first, 1871–72 all-India census was that between Hindu and Muslim. This happened despite the fact that the myriad of religious practices and ideologies existing in the Indian peninsula at the time—some of which have since come to reside under the label of "Hinduism"—were perplexing enough that a report on the 1871–72 census admits there is no definition of the term "Hindoo"since it encompassed everything from "the agnostic youth who is the product of Western education" to what he tellingly described as "the semi-barbarous hill man, who eats, without scruple, anything that he can procure, and is as ignorant of the Hindoo (*sic*) theology as the stone which he worships in times of danger or sickness" (Plowden 1883: 20). Hence the early censuses still talked rather loosely of tribes and castes, the only clear distinction in this regard being the "Criminal Tribes" category reserved for migrant and irregular population groups judged an urgent threat to the general peace and order.[3] As Susan Bayly (1999: 181) observes of late-nineteenth-century European ethnologists, they were still very uncertain about "whether India was a homogeneous caste society, or a composite of casteless 'tribes,' 'pre-Aryan' untouchables, and 'caste-fettered' Hindu 'Aryans.'"

By the 1881 census, however, the idea that "caste" was what defined Hinduism, and that the tribe was outside of the Hindu fold, had taken root, and yet another connotation was added to the tribal/aboriginal/jungle complex: that of being "nature worshippers" of "animalistic" religiosity. "Aboriginal religion" temporarily became a separate category in the census. This too, however, was far from clear-cut since despite the separate religious category for tribes in the 1881 census, there is also mention of "Christian tribes" as well as constant complaints about the impossibility of distinguishing "lower" forms of Hinduism from tribal religions. In subsequent censuses, the tribe was no longer a religious category and instead became a category unto its own ("aboriginal and jungle tribes") even though no economic way of life, religion, or other characteristic in fact united the category. As Crispin Bates (1995: 117) succinctly argues, the "tribe" came to function largely as a "dustbin category" into which all that was unorthodox and difficult to fit elsewhere was thrown.

Tribal groups were mostly deemed neither Hindu nor Muslim or Christian, but no legal consensus ever took shape that would exclude tribal groups from any particular religious affiliation.[4] Considering the vagueness of the notion of who would constitute a tribal, debates on the categorizations of the census commissioners, despite all their supposedly scientific paraphernalia, often boiled down to the idea that "I know one when I see one" (MacMillan 2005: 117). Under pressure from influential communities seeking to also be legally seen as tribal (or to leave the list and be considered something else), the list of tribes in the census of India has undergone all kinds of changes in the century following its introduction, but the vagueness of criteria for inclusion remains, as does, paradoxically, the general belief that the census denotes absolute and unchanging historical truths about a community's place in society.

The complexity of what determines whether someone is tribal was augmented by the fact that colonial efforts to distinguish particular communities inevitably had different spatial expressions and thus interacted with mapping efforts to distinguish and control particular territories. A primary fault line in this regard was to mark off what were termed "forest" lands from agricultural/"revenue" areas, placing the former under the control of a Forest Department officially set up in 1864. These forestlands were often deemed "zones of anomaly" in need of a distinctive regime of administration for constituting an "impenetrable hilly jungle" (Sivaramakrishnan 1999: 36). Major tribal rebellions encouraged colonial administrators to pay additional attention to containing the effects of colonial expansion because the influx of exploitative state officials, moneylenders, and landlords was usually the cause behind class polarization and revolt in tribal areas. This also led the colonial administration to try to codify the "customary" land rights prevailing in tribal areas and prohibit the transfer of land to nontribals in a paternalist effort to single out tribes for protection from the potentially dispossessing effects of participation in the market (Li 2009).

At times, liberal humanitarian concerns regarding tribes—aligned with the need to maintain order—contradicted other major concerns of imperial political economy, notably the extraction of forest produce (particularly tropical hard wood) for the global economy (see Sumit Guha 1999). Over time, as the military power of the state increased and pacification was more feasible, the idea of forests as pristine wild areas in need of protection however trumped the need to protect the invisiblized people living from and sometimes in them, and became a convenient trope to evict people from areas rich in natural resources. Equally applicable to those tribes not living in or from the forest in the first place, the rhetoric of progress that placed the dark-skinned "savage" at the bottom of the civilization hierarchy and the industrious white man at its top then helped organize the coercive labor practices necessary for the colonial economy and legitimized these as ways to "uplift" these "depressed" people (Phillips 2003: 129).

The repeated emphasis that the people categorized as tribal, no matter how proletarianized and made part of the capitalist system, were clearly a different kind of people initially worked to keep capitalist processes of class formation at bay, but soon turned into a mechanism that prevented public recognition of such processes actually going on. As historian Sumit Sarkar (1983) has argued, the most militant outbreaks against British rule tended to be of tribal communities—and he emphasizes that the notion of the tribe "should not convey a sense of complete isolation from the mainstream of Indian life" as "the tribals were and are very much a part of Indian society as the lowest stratum of the peasantry subsisting through shifting cultivation, agricultural laborers, and, increasingly, coolies recruited for work in distant plantations, mines, and factories" (44). Yet the official insistence on the essential difference between tribes and people marked by class or caste, repeatedly rehearsed in surveys and colonial policies, contributed to the fact that the national liberation movement that was growing in the subcontinent hardly built alliances into areas considered tribal or acknowledged tribal workers and peasants as part of the struggle for independence. As we will see, also after Independence, the trope about the essential difference between tribal and nontribal people survived even as capitalism continued to upset existing distinctions between social groups.

### *"At the Stroke of Midnight," the Ethnographic State Lives On?*

"At the stroke of midnight hour, when the world sleeps, India will awake to life and freedom." I remember a Communist friend of mine from Kerala playing a tape for me with this historic Independence speech by Jawaharlal Nehru and having to fight his tears as these famous words filled the car. It is a sentence that probably every Indian knows and by which a generation of artists and writers have been inspired. But as Srirupa Roy (2007: 25) remarks, it also perfectly captures the predominantly constitutionalist and negotiated character of the transition "at the stroke of midnight." It is thereby symbolic of what allowed "the most pernicious inheritance of colonialism" to be "the colonial role—persisting long after direct colonial rule—in fashioning the oppositional terms for the construction of the idea of a national community" (Dirks 2003: 274). In its very Constitution, the newly independent nation-state was to make a paradoxical exercise of basing the fundamental rights of citizenship on the individual, yet requiring the identification of particular castes and tribes to be Scheduled for a host of protective, affirmative, and developmental initiatives.[5] Though intending to break with colonialism and its ethnographic interventions, the new, supposedly secular, Indian state often returned to treating the tribe as a category of essential difference and backwardness—a more benign version of the category of caste that stood for the evils of ancient and colonial India that the modern, independent nation was to overcome. There was, however, as Anupama Rao (2009: 2) observes, a gradual shift in governmentality from one "characterized by the culturalization of politics and enumerative technologies such as the census" towards a new phase "organized around the political technology of the franchise and procedures of representative government." Indeed, many of the popular democratic challenges launched after independence tried to politicize caste and tribal exclusions as questions of social inequality rather than cultural particularity.

Challenges to the ethnographic state and its role in shaping society in the Indian peninsula had in fact started long before Independence.

As Vivek Chibber (2003) has demonstrated, the continuity of India's pre- and post-Independence economy and society had been conditional on the dismantling of the more radical movements that had figured in earlier phases of the struggle for independence and had threatened to challenge the relations of production and trade that locked India in its fixed position in the capitalist world system and reinforced existing local divisions. Crispin Bates (2007), in retelling the history of India with specific attention to subaltern struggles, provides a detailed account of how Bolshevik and other trade unionist or socialist urban movements—as well as radical antifeudal uprisings in the countryside—were systematically opposed by Gandhi, who preferred to stand "assiduously aloof from these widespread symptoms of activism among the poor and industrial workers" and who choose Nehru to lead the Congress party precisely because he saw in him a leader who would not upset existing relations within Indian society but could help the people "release some steam" (142). Whereas the momentum for Independence had been built up by a coming together of militant workers, peasants, students, Hindus, and Muslims, after 1942 Congress was busy condemning any further militancy and instead promoting Gandhi's faith in nonviolence (Sarkar 1983: 421f.). The labor movements that did exist did not seek connection to workers or peasants in areas known as tribal. Rather than initiating a process of confronting and transforming existing relations of power as they had been fixed ideologically and legally under colonial rule, the run-up to independence saw the taming of such energies as the indigenous ruling class prepared itself for the task of translating the pressures of global capital onto Indian society.[6]

The relative continuity of the structure of governance after Independence is also reflected in the lack of scrutiny in mainstream Indian academia of the ideological constitution of scientific knowledge generated under colonialism (Philip 2003: 161). Where existing ethnographic fault lines were challenged, it was usually in favor of the creation of the new cultural category of the Indian nation. Some nationalists argue that colonial categories had been fixed by the British colonizers in order to lock India in its "backward" condition and make sure the nation would remain forever divided. They hence simplified the divisive pressures arising in the process of organizing the necessary consent and coercion for India to further integrate into global circuits of capital as a matter of conscious conspiracy. After Independence, instead of the challenge that militant popular movements had launched of addressing the structure of Indian economy and society, Nehruvian social democratic modernization was about paying lip service to radical change while in fact containing mass movement in favor of "the strong capitalist element behind Congress" that was "becoming nervous about the security of its property" (Sarkar 1983: 420). "Development" as understood by Nehru was a continuation of evolutionary models in updated form[7] and envisioned as a process of alleviating poverty. It was not about confronting the social relations that continued to deepen economic inequality in India and that created modern forms of poverty worse than anything seen before India's incorporation into the world system (Davis 2001). If it could be called socialist, the Nehruvian variety was of a strongly modernist character with little affiliation, except in rhetoric, to romantic or radical socialism.[8] It centered on a rationally planned economy and secular values that were to replace the backwardness of traditional workplaces and religious prejudices. Large-scale development projects and, above all, mega-dams became India's "temples of the future" (Khilnani 1997), drowning out the more radical efforts to democratize and politicize differences within Indian society. Political differences were rendered technical and legal.

In *Castes of Mind,* Nicolas Dirks (2003) demonstrates the continuing hold of the "ethnographic state" over the way politics is practiced and imagined in India today, particularly with regard to caste. Surprisingly, he hardly mentions the notion of the tribe, though this supposed discovery of the British continued to determine the imagination of how the people falling under its label were to be ruled as much as the discovery of caste did. Unlike caste, which in the modernist visions of Nehru and Ambedkar (though not in Gandhi's), was seen to be a sign of backwardness and feudal cruelty, the tribe was generally imbued with positive associations. Though a sign of a primordial stage of history—a "zero level" (Singh 1989: 8) in terms of progress—the tribe was not an evil to be rooted out. Instead, Indian leaders were swayed to see tribes much as European thinkers had defined them. If capitalist society was admittedly creating conflict, inequality, and pollution, tribal societies were the opposite of all this: innocent, egalitarian, and in harmony with nature.

Jawaharlal Nehru had, as a chronicler put it, a "very soft corner for the tribals" and "did not want any change to be forced on the tribals" even though he also held to the opinion that change was "necessary" and "inevitable" (Das Gupta in Kumar Suresh Singh 1989: 110f). As Singh claims, Nehru's socialism tried to steer a course between the "anthropological" approach that "sought to treat the tribals as museum specimens to be kept apart, for study and observation" and the "assimilation" approach which aimed to force development and "civilization" onto the tribes. Inspired in part by the Soviet Union's approach to what were there called "national minorities" (ibid: 9), Nehru wanted to encourage the preservation of the tribal "civilization of song and dance" (Nehru 1952 in Singh 1989: 3). He wanted to protect tribal "identity" belonging to an "original Communist" stage and wanted tribes to develop "in their own way" (ibid.). There was little room in the debate on the tribal question for envisioning the notion of the tribe as one among various interrelated expressions of historical social inequality. Solving the tribal question as defined by ethnographic conventions did not demand a restructuring of the Indian economy of the kind that had been called for by the popular movements that had fought for Independence. Instead, it could suffice with designing policies towards select population groups, towards "the tribes or tribal communities or parts of or groups within tribes or tribal communities" which according to the procedures laid out in article 342 of independent India's Constitution had been "deemed to be Scheduled Tribes" (Constitution of India, 1950). Since knowing who was part of a tribe or tribal community was assumed to be fairly unproblematic and since the exercise of Scheduling for the purpose of being targeted with the state's protective, affirmative or developmental efforts was left to anthropologists, the heat of the debate was about what approach ought to take priority.

One of the most vocal proponents of the integration approach was G. S. Ghurye, a Sanskrit scholar and professor of sociology at the University of Bombay who held a PhD in anthropology from the University of Cambridge (Sinha 2004: 74).[9] Though the title and intentions of his book *The Aborigines—So-called—and Their future* (1943) suggest otherwise, Ghurye saw tribes in much the same way the British had: as a lower, primitive form of life in need of civilization. Yet such was to be provided not by the white man but rather by wider Hindu society, of which tribes, Ghurye believed, had always been a "backward," "loosely assimilated" part (Ghurye 1943: 21). As a puritan Brahmin, Ghurye believed integration would expose tribes to better methods of cultivation, temper their "sexual license," (ibid.: 68) and cure them of their drunkenness. Ghurye and his student M. N. Srinivas (e.g., 1962) put forward many arguments that seemed to put the ethnographic state in its place—arguments against the view that so-called tribes had been isolated, for an understanding of tribal poverty as inseparable from the history of colonial exploitation, and for a dynamic rather than a static view of tribal cultures. Yet such arguments kept intact an idea of the tribe as denoting not a particular discursive and historically constituted relationship but an essential holistic entity on a continuum of backwardness and civilization. Ghurye's arguments were systematically geared toward arguing for a united modern India that, when truly accomplished, would automatically leave behind the problems of poverty, exploitation, and moral degradation that the British had introduced to India.

Ghandi's approach to the tribal question was close to Ghurye's, though he generally concentrated his political energies on the issue of eradicating untouchability—the blot on an otherwise harmonious, organic division of labor of which *Harijans* (sons of God, as he preferred to call those most oppressed by the caste system[10]) were as much part as those whose calling happened to be studying the *vedas*. Launching anticolonial as well as antiuntouchability campaigns from his native Gujarat, Gandhi seems to initially have had no idea that it was not just in North-Eastern hill states but also in his own Gujarat that the British had classified many groups as "jungle tribes" (Hardiman 2004: 136). It was only during the launching of the non-cooperation movement that he learned of their presence and started sending out volunteers to mobilize them. By that time, to Gandhi's annoyance, a protest movement consisting of thousands of Bhils (one of the so-called tribes in Gujarat) had already taken the initiative of fighting for what they called "Gandhi raj" (ibid.). When the British eventually moved against the protesters, opening fire on a peaceful crowd and leaving at least 1,000 people dead, Gandhi's engagement with his tribal followers remained lukewarm. It stayed that way even when, during the civil disobedience movement of 1930–31, many tribals joined the struggle by disobeying forest laws. Along with Gandhi, the nationalist movement largely failed to appreciate tribals' own initiatives in the struggle for independence—an attitude that carried over in many aspects of post-Independence tribal development policy.

Nehru was influenced by the nationalist approach to the tribal question, yet was also closely attentive to the argument for the protection of tribals, perhaps advocated most explicitly by Verrier Elwin, a self-taught anthropologist who from 1928 until his death in 1964 lived in (tribal) Gond and Baiga communities and wrote a great number of monographs about them. Elwin was also Nehru's chief Advisor on Tribal Affairs for the North-Eastern Frontier Agency for a decade (Sinha 2004: 75). Originally he had come to India as a Christian missionary, but during the struggle for Independence he had become a devoted follower of Gandhi. On Gandhi's advice he went to work in tribal areas, only to eventually turn resolutely away from what he came to see as Gandhi's "bourgeois and Puritan doctrine on the free wild people of the forests" (in Ramachandra Guha 1999: 105). Elwin's efforts after Independence henceforth focused on protecting tribals and keeping them apart from Hindu society to help preserve their cultural distinctiveness. Almost anyone commenting on Elwin's work has noted he was a romantic, and his own words leave little doubt about it. Doing his best to document the various art forms, rituals, and cosmologies of the tribal communities he lived with, he lamented that in matters of art the "great days of the Indian tribesman are gone; all we can do now is search in the debris for traces of inspiration and scraps of beauty" (Elwin in Ramachandra Guha 1999: 307).

Confronted with the violence and hopelessness experienced by those losing out in the process of further incorporation into capitalist, often Hindu, networks of exploitation and dispossession, it is logical that Elwin—unlike Ghurye, who did not easily set foot outside his university office—saw integration into Hindu society as the problem rather than the solution to tribal poverty. Elwin did not, however, defend tribals purely in culturalist terms: often, he spoke rather of his role as that of "the true Dinabandhu [friend of the poor]," who "lives among the poor … learns to love them as people" and no longer thinks of them "as 'masses' to be uplifted with a vague and too-often sterile enthusiasm" (in Ramachandra Guha 1999: 183). Elwin's strong, lived commitment to Adivasi communities did, however, at times make him willfully blind to changes that would interfere with his celebration of them as peoples uncontaminated by civilization: at the very time that he was praising the Gonds in his writings for being all that Gandhi's Puritanism was not, a Gandhian-style movement of renouncing liquor-drinking, meat-eating, dancing, and singing was sweeping through the Gond community. According to Hardiman (2004), the movement was moreover initiated by certain Gonds themselves in defiance of members of their own community, local landlords, and liquor dealers. Elwin's resistance to Ghurye and Gandhi's line on the tribal question hence often ended up deepening essentialist colonial ideas attached to the notion of the tribe. A number of anthropologists today still see themselves as following in the footsteps of Elwin and consider it a radical position to defend the fact that tribes have a rich culture of their own. This could, however, be seen as simply social evolutionism on its head.

Between Nehru and Elwin on one side and Gandhi and Ghurye on the other, the ethnographic notion of the tribe carried over into independent India. It remained a notion of cultural distinctiveness and essential difference, now justified either as respecting cultural uniqueness or as necessary for targeted efforts to redress economic and educational disadvantage (McMillan 2005: 126). Some scholars, such as Beteille (1998), have objected that the Scheduled Tribe—the legal category by which people in need of either such protection or development are identified—is merely intended to implement policy and does not pretend to pass judgment on the substantive history or present-day lifestyle of the groups denoted as such. This argument, however, is hardly tenable. Despite the randomness with which certain groups were historically determined Scheduled Tribes or Scheduled Castes[11] and despite the adjustments of the list to correct for mistakes or simply to take into account new realities,[12] the power of the connection between Scheduled Tribe status and substantive identity claims is such that I usually only hear people without formal education make a distinction between "who we are" and "what the government calls us."

Interestingly, the person perhaps most directly responsible for the contemporary importance of Scheduled Tribe status in India was also someone whose views generally transcended integrationist and romantic answers to the tribal question. Precisely for this reason, however, Dr. Ambedkar is hardly ever acknowledged as having taken part in the debate on the tribal question. Most scholars and politicians recognize the fact that the majority of people classified as tribes are organized, as almost everyone in India, into castes (*jatis*), negotiating their position in particular regional endogamous caste hierarchies. Yet few thereby recognize the importance of what Amebdkar called "the annihilation of caste" for the so-called tribal question. Ambedkar explicitly talked of how the poverty and exclusion experienced by "what are called the aboriginal tribes in India" was produced by the same set of norms oppressing what we would today call "Dalits" (Ambedkar 2002: 270). He talked of the caste mentality of "indifferentism" (ibid.) towards anyone not belonging to one's caste, which constantly hampered efforts of creating solidarity among the oppressed to overturn the deepening of caste inequality under capitalism. Ambedkar was strongly against Gandhi's efforts to reform (and thereby protect) the caste system and bourgeois property relations, and envisioned what in Maharashtra was known as a *bahujan* (majority) alliance that would bring together all the victims of the ruling structures.

As Anand Teltumbde (2010: 14) has shown, Ambedkar was committed to a "caste-class experiment" and started his political trajectory by forming the Independent Labor Party (ILP) precisely on this basis. This ILP was the first political party in direct opposition to Congress and for the elimination of caste, while the Communist Party in fact grew out of Congress and was generally reluctant to emphasize the need to abolish caste (ibid.). It was only when "the entire political climate was becoming communalized" in the 1920s in negotiations with the British administration that Ambedkar reluctantly floated a caste-based platform, the Scheduled Caste Federation (SCF), only to return to his initial strategy with the founding of the Republican Party of India "as soon as [the SCF's] utility was over" (ibid.).

At times, the challenges for Ambedkar of maintaining a broad anti-caste alliance in the face of the politics of divide and rule proved too much. This, in combination with the fact that Ambedkar was trained as a lawyer (with a MSc from the London School of Economics and a PhD from Columbia), contributed to his eventual retreat into efforts at reform from above, institutionalized through the Constitution rather than forced from below—a retreat that ironically, as Teltumbde (2010) points out, most of his followers now see as his main political contribution to the Dalit cause. Ambedkar was not naïve or silent, however, about his turn to reform from above. At the time of the adoption of the Constitution, which had been drafted under his primary supervision, he explicitly stated, "On 26th of January 1950, we are going to enter into a life of contradictions. In politics we will have equality and in social and economic life we will have inequalities" (quoted in Omvedt 1993: xi). He warned that, "We must remove this contradiction at the earliest possible moment or else those who suffer from inequality will blow up the structure of political democracy" (ibid.). Rather than blowing up the structure of injustice, his constitutional efforts had contributed to providing the legal measures, primarily in the form of what are in India called "reservations" for Scheduled Castes and Scheduled Tribes (i.e., reserved quotas in education, civil service, and seats in parliament and other elected bodies), for the formal equality of communities fixed ethnographically and economically in relations of marked inequality. The competition for the status of Scheduled Tribe that has been the outcome of this measure is perhaps the most telling legacy of Ambedkar's temporary retreat at the time from more radical challenges to the ethnographic state.[13]

A second type of challenge against the ethnographic state on the tribal question—again usually not recognized as such—are the various agrarian revolts in which people categorized as tribal played a leading role but that have later become labeled as two apparently exclusive categories: either tribal or, more usually, "Naxal." Though Naxals are now mostly known as educated urban activists trying to spread Maoism to the countryside, the original revolt at Naxalbari, which they derive their name from, was an outgrowth of local organizing by sharecroppers and landless workers from various backgrounds—tribal, lower-caste, and Muslim—supported by the Communist Party of India (Marxist), or CPI(M), and its peasant union (Frankel 2005: 378). The revolt continued when the CPI(M) withdrew its support in order to enter the United Front government. "Direct action" against landlords charged with evicting tenants or hoarding uncultivated lands was started in March 1967 and initially succeeded without any violence. On 23 May, however, a policeman and nine demonstrators died in a clash. It is telling how when the death of the demonstrators is described, they are generally referred to as tribals (e.g., Ray 1988: 98), whereas when the agitation subsequently took on the characteristics of an armed struggle, the demonstrators are generally referred to merely as peasants and a clear distinction is made between tribals and extremists (ibid: 99; see also Frankel 2005: 378).

The shift towards ignoring the tribal background of the Naxalbari peasants partly reflects the fact that China had discovered the events as a "Spring Thunder," and radical students and workers' organizations started to ally with Naxalbari, against the line of the CPI(M) in power. From September 1967 onwards, these "radicals," charging the CPI(M) with suppressing the agrarian revolutionary struggle, left the party in large number in Andhra Pradesh and West Bengal and became collectively identified as "Naxalites," gradually overshadowing the role that people called tribals had played. In the course of time, Naxalbari was remembered as a Maoist revolt that had "used" tribals or—at best—had "exploited the dynamism of tribal … sentiments" and the "unsettled tribal question" (Fic 1970: 419). The idea fit the urban activists' claiming of the leadership over the movement but it also fit the movement's opponents, from the CPI(M) to Congress, all eager to condemn the "extremists" while claiming the moral high ground in defending "innocent tribals." Naxalbari hence forms a typical moment in which a movement set to confront various axes of inequality outside of the legal categories set by the state eventually becomes reinterpreted so that tribals remained in their role of primitive Others. Though posing a major democratic challenge to the postcolonial state, the Naxalite movement could not prevent its participants from falling prey to essentialist ethnographic lenses of interpretation.

## Vicissitudes of the "Tribe" in Kerala Studies

Kerala occupies a particular position in the historical trajectory of the tribe in India. Contributing to this particularity is the fact that the percentage of Kerala's population classified as Scheduled Tribes (STs) hovers around a mere one and a half percent—a much smaller percentage than is for instance the case in India's North-Eastern states. Though concentrated in the hilly Eastern districts of Kerala, most of these STs live intermingled with and depend on other non-ST groups. The "congruence between tribal areas and tribal peoples" (McMillan 2005: 124), which is already problematic elsewhere, is largely absent in Kerala. In fact, we could have expected that for these reasons, there would be less essentialist notions of tribes in Kerala. All the more so considering the historical importance of the Communist initiatives in the 1930s and 1940s at organizing Adivasi workers in Kerala's rubber and tea plantations to confront the backbone of colonial (and later Congress) political power (Baak 1997). Yet despite all this, academic knowledge production in Kerala has had great difficulty moving beyond the essentialist ethnographic paradigm.

The essentialist paradigm is particularly problematic since so-called tribes in Kerala are in fact extremely heterogeneous, their commonality lying in having become defined as tribal rather than in the livelihoods they pursue or in their position in society. The Kurichiya, for instance, generally live from farming their land, which until recently was owned and managed in large matriarchal joint families. They often claim upper-caste status and celebrate Thalakkal Chandu as the "Kurichiya hero" of the historical struggle of 1800–1805 against the British attempt to take possession of Wayanad (S. Menon 2007: 332). The Kattunaikans, by contrast, are mostly people who used to live by collecting forest products. They are most affected by the colonial establishment of protected forest reserves, managed today by the Indian Forest Department. The Paniya and the Adiya, on the other hand, are "wage hunter-gatherers" (Breman 2006). About the origins of the Paniya in particular, the wildest theories have been launched, the most bizarre of which is probably the idea held by the European planting community of the beginning of the twentieth century in Wayanad who thought the Paniyas were "of African origin and descended from ancestors who were wrecked on the Malabar coast" (Thurston 1909, vol 7: 57). What is clear is that both Paniyas and Adiyas—whose *jati* names literally mean "worker" and "slave", respectively—have been bonded laborers for generations and still are generally landless agricultural laborers.

Essentialist ideas about so-called tribes also had political-economic functions. Certain communities in Wayanad became closely interconnected with the plantation industry that the British set up in area and plantation managers were eager to mobilize these communities as so-called tribal labor[14] since tribals would have no need for decent wages but were, supposedly, desperately in need of being civilized. When by the 1920s plantations had been established all over Wayanad, there was even a competition for labor between these private employers and the Forest Department and the latter started to mimic ethnographic studies of the organization and segmentation of tribal groups in the hope of controlling labor patterns (Philip 2003: 94). How certain communities living in the hilly areas of Kerala were distinguished and how some of them came to fall under the same category of the tribe was thus related to how officers and managers encountered and used these communities but was overall framed by the reigning ethnographic perspectives through which these powerholders viewed the world. It is to this history of how "tribes" have been conceptualized in Kerala, therefore, that I briefly turn now.

### *The Anthropological Tribe in Kerala: A Happy People without any History?*

Anthropology in Kerala has not been the site of dynamic change or politicization. Written work still often comes in the form of tribal ethnographies, systematically detailing,[15] in encyclopedic fashion, the social structure, religious beliefs and practices, material culture, marriage and death rituals, and sometimes the political organizing or historical deeds of particular tribes, usually self-admittedly based on a few days or at most a week or two of interaction with the tribe. Usually, the work is directly commissioned by the government and prefaced by a government official lauding the anthropologist's work. Though the overt racist methods used in early tribal ethnographies—such as the cataloguing of nasal indices—have lost appeal,[16] more subtle forms of racist methodology persist, for instance in the fact that observations of "culture" or "behavior" are seldom linked to social relations of power. Anthropologists in Kerala, almost never of tribal background themselves, have shown no interest in a paradigmatic break with the past of their discipline that incarcerated tribes in a primordial definition. Many of them seem to remain content to substitute racism with romanticism while relying on their colonial predecessors as if the conditions under which those produced their knowledge mattered nothing for its validity.

In the early colonial period there was little conceptual clarity on the usage of the terms "caste" and "tribe" in Kerala (as in the rest of India). One of the earliest colonial documents on Kerala, the *Malabar Manual* of 1887, by William Logan,[17] refers to the Nairs, today known as one of the dominant, upper-caste communities in Kerala, as a tribe

(1887: 214). For some of the groups who eventually ended up on the list of Scheduled Tribes, the term "jungle tribe" is used, yet the use of the term was rather indeterminate as Logan, for instance, talks of "jungle tribes and other servile castes" (1887: 37). In another instance, Logan treats the term "tribe" as if referring to all population groups in the Indian subcontinent, arguing that "it is probably correct ... that in 'early times' the present almost innumerable subdivisions of castes did not exist and that a large number [of these sub-castes] are mere repetitions of castes in another tribe and language" (1887: 109). When mentioning "aborigines" (1997: 147), Logan interestingly does so in reference to Cherumas, whom today are considered Dalits (and are a "Scheduled Caste").

After the turn of the century, works documenting Kerala society were still repeating the view that the castes who nowadays identify as Dalit were the aborigines of the area. Later works, however, developed a more rigid conceptual division of castes and tribes and gradually increased the emphasis on the difference between these groups. One such work is Thurston's (1909) *Castes and Tribes of Southern India*, consisting of seven volumes describing the ethnographic particularities of each *jati* and *gotra* found in Kerala. Thurston was a British administrator but also Superintendent of Ethnography and chair of the Madras Museum. A more bounded notion of "hill tribes" as denoting the aborigines of Kerala emerges in his volumes as well as a certain obsession—common in physical anthropology in Europe at the time—with measuring people's noses, skulls, and other physical exteriors in order to substantiate racial theories that saw such measures of body-parts as a guide to the status of their owners (Shah 2007: 1808). Elaborate tables of average, maximum, and minimum stature and nasal index form the introduction of Thurston's book, accompanied with description of various tribes, such as for example the "jungle Chenchus" who "still exhibit the primitive short stature and high nasal index, which are characteristic of unadulterated jungle tribes" (1909: xlvii). Among subsequent Malayalee ethnographers, such as Anantha Krishna Iyer, considered the "father of South Indian ethnology" and one of the erstwhile collaborators of Thurston, anthropology became less obsessed with the physical measurement of skulls but continued to confirm social evolutionist hierarchies. Anantha Krishna Iyer, himself a Brahmin, published widely on how in his home region of Kerala he found "Negroid features in the types among the hillmen and the agrestic serfs, and Dravidian features among the people of the plains, and fine Aryan characteristics among the people of the higher castes" (1925: 49–51).

It was only when this type of racial anthropology got discredited in Europe after the holocaust that nasal indexing and the general emphasis on people's physical exteriors was finally abandoned, also in Kerala. Later ethnographies, such as A. D. Luiz's (1962) *Tribes of Kerala,* shifted from a preoccupation with the physical to the cultural aspects of the different tribes. As such, they continued to produce a more enlightened and supposedly more indigenous form of knowledge that however continued to place Adivasis at the bottom rung of civilization and outside of history. Interestingly, the sixties in Kerala were also a period of great Communist-led turmoil in the field of science, as scientific knowledge was being popularized on a massive scale through various literacy and science movements. Yet such popularization was mainly concerned with the dissemination of scientific information, with an emphasis on the physical sciences (Zachariah and Sooryamoorthy 1994). Little recognition of the importance of social science or of the need for more critical or dialectic methods of generating scientific knowledge entered into the mainstream of academia. The fact that academic science was made available in Malayalam—rather than Sanskrit or English—was already such a break with the past that it was enough to be considered revolutionary. The firm belief in the possibility of rational explanation, of cause and effect, was moreover considered progressive in relation to earlier religious dogma or superstition; the fact that all this science allowed for little popular input or other than Modernist political imagination was not considered as contradicting Communist ideals (ibid.).

Keralese anthropology in the Cold War period hence reflected the staunchly modernist attitude to science that dominated both the capitalist West and communist East. In Kerala this was a juncture in which the problem of racism in anthropological knowledge could remain largely unexplored. So much so that an Englishman like J. B. S. Haldane, whose more than dubious scientific contribution was to support the efforts to unite Darwinian evolutionary theory with Mendelian genetics, was invited to inaugurate the Kerala Science Literary Society in 1962 because of his supposed exemplary commitment to science and to sharing it with the general public (Zachariah and Sooryamoorthy 1994: 57). The field of anthropology in Kerala managed to stay aloof both of the campaign against racial anthropology waging in the West, and the attack on bourgeois anthropology in the East. Moreover, as in most Third World countries, anthropology was a marginal discipline of little interest for its apparent irrelevance to the grand goals of the postwar "developing" world: eradicating poverty and producing what in Kerala is known as *vikasanam* (development).[18]

Indirectly, the Communist movement did, however, have some transformative impact on anthropology as it enabled some persons of lower-caste background to enter academia, that utmost bastion of upper-caste power. A. Aiyappan, a scholar of Izhava descent—from an erstwhile untouchable caste—became an important new such voice in anthropology and was appointed vice-chancellor of Kerala University in 1969. Unlike his upper-caste predecessors, he spent considerable time with ordinary people, showing interest in their hopes, aspirations, and dilemmas and refusing to reduce these to a particular reified generality of their community background. His writings repeatedly reveal his desire to confront the inequalities he encountered (and knew all too well from his own background). Yet he still opens his ethnography of the Paniya (Aiyappan [1973] 1992)[19] with a strangely exoticizing sentence: "Paniyas are a happy people without any history." The sentence is strange because in fact Aiyappan's monograph pays detailed attention to the exploitation of the Paniya and the historical development of their condition. Aiyappan moreover is already remarkable in focusing his ethnography on the Paniya, a group of proletarian, "black" Adivasis not generally considered worthy of elaborate study. In studying the Paniya, Aiyappan even comes to the conclusion that "there is no sociological reason" why certain tribes would not be considered castes. Yet he is hesitant to confront the paradigm of tribal ethnography and its biases explicitly and sometimes, as in the monograph's opening sentence, even reproduces some of its most evolutionary stereotypes.

In the 1980s, we find new attempts to critique the categorical essentialization of castes and tribes in the study of Kerala, though again these stop short of confronting the established paradigm. Brian Morris's (1982: 55) *Forest Traders: A Socio-Economic Study of the Hill Pandaram* argues that even regarding the so-called primitive hunter-gathering tribe he focuses on, "in economic terms there seems to be no essential difference … between a caste and a tribe." Morris moreover argues that "forest communities have not, within historical times at least, been 'isolates' from the wider Hindu culture" (11). He adds that in South India there is generally no substantive sociological distinction between so-called tribes and castes and suggests that talking about a certain "tribe can be taken as the same as talking about a particular 'community'—merely as a descriptive tag for a group of people who see themselves as forming a cultural unit" (38). An explicit intellectual confrontation with the oppressive legacies carried on in the notion of the tribe is, however, avoided. Hence whereas other communities have come to be understood in more relational and dynamic terms—a clear break with the essentialist paradigm being, for instance, the work by Osella and Osella (2000) on the strategies of upward mobility of the (becoming) Izhava community—Adivasis continue to be taken as communities preeminently suited for the reifying kind of ethnographies that cut them loose from the development of the rest of Kerala.

The epistemological understanding of Adivasis as separate, isolated historical remnants that is reproduced in the genre of the tribal ethnography thereby continues to lend academic respectability to the now common-sensical lenses through which tribal people are seen in Kerala. I realized this when, in 2005, I interviewed P. R. G. Mathur, one of the most celebrated anthropologists of Kerala and author of the 1977 *Tribal Situation in India,* a volume containing classical ethnographies of a large number of so-called tribes. Asking him what he knew about the AGMS, he complained of C. K. Janu's "lack of commitment to the issue of unwed Adivasi mothers"—a term generally referring to the phenomenon understood as "outsiders" sexually abusing Adivasi women and abandoning them as soon as they become pregnant.[20] According to Mathur, Janu ought to have "committed suicide" over this issue.[21] He assumed "unwed Adivasi mothers" were "hapless victims"and worried about the "racial mixing" that would spell "the end of the Adivasis." I could not help but hear an echo of Thurston's anxiety that "the purity of blood and ethnological characters of various jungle tribes are unhappily becoming lost as the result of contact metamorphosis from the opening up of the jungles for planter's estates, and contact with more civilized tribes and races, both brown and white" (Thurston 1909, vol 1: xlvii). Coming with all the authority of Kerala's most prominent living anthropologist, I realized how mainstream anthropology in Kerala continued to feed the Othering ethnographic portrayals of Adivasis—and particularly Adivasi women—that I daily encountered in blogs and media and that I could hear ordinary people I spoke to rehearse.

Representing tribal people as threatened, innocent remnants of a better past offers the anthropologist the role of documenting these lost cultures and their problems to thereby help preserve them but deprives the people living under this sign of any contemporary relevance. The paradigm of the tribal ethnography hence helps introduce a political schism between Adivasi activists and a majority of people in Kerala—certainly those educated into the main script on tribal innocence. The consequent deafness to Adivasi activists' actual political interventions is intense enough that when politicians strategically decide to show a different attitude, this tends to have a strong emotional impact on activists. An example of this is the sympathy that activists felt—almost despite themselves—towards the Congress party when, in 2003, Congress Chief Minister A. K. Anthony was prepared to negotiate directly with C. K. Janu. The impact was so strong that for a time it made the AGMS leadership more positively inclined towards Congress than towards the CPI(M), despite the strong historical antagonism between Congress and most subaltern activists and despite the fact that earlier that year A. K. Anthony had been the one who ordered the forceful eviction of a major land occupation organized by the AGMS.

The impact of ethnographic knowledge is also pronounced in the more mundane politics of communities' competition for status and benefits in Kerala. How direct a role colonial ethnographic knowledge plays in this became particularly clear to me when I spoke with people from a community of small farmers identifying as Kunduvadians. This group had previously been on the Scheduled Tribe list but had become reclassified as an OBC (Other Backward Class) when their local leader—purportedly behind everyone's backs—had lobbied the government to remove their community from the ST list: he had been eager to sell his land to set up a cinema but was not permitted to do so as long as he had the status of being an ST.[22] The Kunduvadians were now trying to get back on the list as the agricultural crisis—and subsequent drop in ticket sales—had confirmed to them the need to seek other venues of mobility and access the educational benefits reserved for Scheduled Tribes. One of the men who had been active in this endeavor to become readmitted to the list, explained to me in detail how they had argued for their right to be on the Scheduled Tribes list to KIRTADS, the governmental body in Kerala that is the first institution on the way to modifying centrally ordained tribal status. They had two telling pieces of evidence of their Adivasi belonging. The first was the fact that many of them suffered from the hereditary disease of sickle-cell anemia. As certain other tribes also had a high incidence of sickle-cell anemia and in line with the obsession about race and genetics in colonial accounts of tribal groups, sickle-cell anemia had thus somehow become evidence of tribal belonging. The second piece of evidence was a book carried around with great care, containing a detailed description of the community as tribal and pictures of their tribal forefathers. The book, which was to be sent to the prime minister in Delhi as conclusive evidence, turned out to be C. Gopalan Nair's (1911) *Wayanad: Its Peoples and Traditions,* another meticulous documentation by an upper-caste colonial ethnographer of different castes and tribes in Northern Kerala.

The place within anthropology in Kerala where a cautious move away from the enduring colonial academic tradition of knowledge production related to tribes is taking place is, however, on the edges of the discipline, particularly in applied anthropology. Vineetha Menon (2009) has in connection to the tribal question breached the topic of knowledge and power and introduced a Foucauldian perspective. This allows her to question dominant forms of knowledge in contemporary state practices, to which applied anthropology, she argues, can be a corrective. She hence shows how a notion such as the *oorukoottam* (people's gathering), often taken as a primordial tribal institution, is in fact "a new composition of tribal people, but using a traditional nomenclature," mobilized by the government of Kerala in its decentralized planning campaign (2009: 110). Leaving behind arguments on tribal haplessness and innocence, Menon argues that people agree to the institution for strategic reasons. For the discipline of anthropology in Kerala, this is almost a revolutionary step in that it moves resolutely away from taking state-produced knowledge on tribes for granted. Yet, it is at the same time limited in that there is no questioning of the complicity of anthropology in producing this knowledge historically. Hence Menon notes that the "identity perception" of Adivasis is now in motion but she ignores its complexities in the past, arguing these identities used to be "simple and elementary" (ibid.: 112). For critical anthropology to not just follow the (political) facts as they develop but actually contribute to the challenging of inequalities substantiated and managed through common-sense knowledge, it will need to go a step further and realize that tribal—or other—identities were never "simple and elementary" but always part of hegemonic projects and their contestation.

### *The Indigenist Challenge to the Ethnographic Tribe*

Though within mainstream anthropology in Kerala the tradition of writing isolated and static tribal ethnographies continues, under the influence of the rise of the AGMS it has become undeniable that many of the people considered tribal are not isolated or stuck in the past and are in fact setting an agenda that addresses modern Kerala society. In the course of the 1990s, as the AGMS was mobilizing, and more so from 2001 onward, when its large demonstration in Thiruvananthapuram for the first time gave it massive media coverage, disciplines other than anthropology started to pay attention to Adivasis.

In this last section of this chapter, I will give a brief overview of the most significant publications outside of anthropology that have been inspired by the rise of the AGMS. The overview, starting with activist publications and moving to literary and cinematography studies, biographical works, and political economy and development studies, is certainly not exhaustive but is merely meant to give an impression of some of the ways in which in fields other than anthropology, the AGMS has inspired deviance from the ethnographic state.

Activist studies of the Adivasi movement in Kerala, though theoretically sometimes eclectic, set the tone for a different approach. Particularly active in this is C. R. Bijoy, a Malayalee activist-intellectual who has written a string of pamphlets and papers on the Adivasi movement in South India from his close cooperation in it. *A Search for Justice: A Citizen's Report on the Adivasi Experience in South India,* published in 1997 and written by Anita Cheria, C. R. Bijoy, K. Narayanan, and Edwin was a break-through in that it presented the experiences of Adivasi communities as part of the general directions that Kerala society was moving in and posed the challenges thrown up by Adivasi leaders as concerning Kerala society in general. In the course of the 2000s, an increasing number of activist publications by Dalit intellectuals started adding to this collection. A notable contribution is the work of T. G. Jacob and P. Bandhu (2002) on Dalit-Adivasi movements in South India and later on the crisis in Wayanad, the state with the highest concentration of Adivasis (see also Jacob 2006). There has also been increasing attention to Adivasis from documentary filmmakers. C. Saratchandan, for instance, powerfully documented the story of the Muthanga Struggle in *Evicted from Justice.*

Besides activists, some academics also started paying attention to the political challenge posed by the AGMS. The most decisive break with the tradition of ethnographic knowledge on tribes in Kerala comes from the discipline of literary studies in a thesis for the University of Hyderabad by K. C. Bindu, titled "Constructing the Adivasi Identity: Reading the Dominant, Reading the Adivasi." It is, to my knowledge, the first explicitly self-reflexive and critical study from Kerala that, though based on fieldwork, does not seek to document Adivasi lives or reflect an "authentic Adivasi voice" but rather studies, in the author's words, the "various cultures which have constructed the Adivasi identity, including the Malayalee, upper-caste, Hindu culture of which I am part … [and] the academic culture which draws its life breath from the Western notions of the 'primitive' … [to which] I can claim a membership … too" (2003: 1f). In her work, Bindu directly addresses "the sharp division that emerged with the tribe as outside caste" that "appears as a shadow" to "the imagination of India as a conglomeration of castes" (6f). Her work is path-breaking in Kerala as it critically examines the way that the tribe is constructed in contemporary as well as historical debates in Kerala (and India) as "a site to critique modernity" (22).[23]

From the early 2000s onward, within the disciplines of literary and cinematographic studies there has also been a move to deploy the genre of the biography to describe Adivasi (and Dalit) lives. This is a novel development in that earlier, with few exceptions, only upper-caste lives were deemed worthy of such detailed attention. By giving a view into lived reality, these life stories help break the stale and romanticized imaginary surrounding tribals. The most elaborate biography to appear so far of an Adivasi activist is C. K. Janu's biography, *Mother Forest,* written by Bhaskaran (2004). As the title signals, the author does to some extent work within the tradition of depicting tribal people as natural remnants of a beautiful but vanishing past. He even does his best to emphasize the "innocence" of Janu by writing the first part of the biography in a literary style that avoids capitals, punctuation, and complicated sentences, meant to thereby remain close to Janu's own words, though running the danger of having readers mistake the sarcasm and wit that characterizes Janu's speech[24] for a wondering, naive attitude. Yet despite these romantic literary interventions, already simply by being a biography, *Mother Forest* inevitably breaks with the paradigm of tribal ethnography. Also noteworthy in the biographical genre is the work by Brigitte Schulze (2004), who made an extensive internet archive of transcribed interviews with Adivasi and Dalit activists, forming one of the first English-language sources with literal transcriptions of interviews with Adivasi activists on the stories of their lives and political aspirations. Even more noteworthy is the film *Guda,* which she helped to produce in 2003 together with K. J. Baby and which centers on the coming-of-age of an Adivasi girl in Wayanad. For the first time in Malayalee cinema, Paniya and Kuttunaikan children act the lead roles in the movie and even helped produce it.

Publications in other disciplines than literature and cinematography make less of a break with colonial constructions of Adivasiness and usually continue to treat tribes and castes as absolutely dichotomous entities. What we do see, however, is that following the rise of the AGMS, economics, political science, and development studies have given increasing attention to tribes, which in itself is a novelty as other disciplines than anthropology usually took little notice of these groups.[25] Together with C. R. Bijoy, Ravi Raman helped bring attention to the Muthanga struggle in an article in the *Economic and Political Weekly* and was among the first to bring the Adivasi struggle in Kerala to an international academic audience with his sympathetic description of the struggle in *Social Analysis* (Raman 2004). More theoretical but equally engaged contributions followed from political science, among which the article by K. K. Sreekumar and Govindan Parayil, "Interrogating Development: New Social Movements, Democracy, and Indigenous People's Struggles in Kerala" (2006), for the first time explicitly discussed the AGMS within the "new social movements" paradigm rather than as an instance of age-old "tribal rebellion."

In reaction to the government's renewed commitment to "tribal development" after the AGMS's 2001 demonstration, an increasing number of articles and books in development studies have also focused on Adivasi livelihoods. Darley Kjosavik (2004) was one of the first from within international development studies to focus on Adivasi livelihoods and the challenge posed by the AGMS while remaining sympathetic to the achievements of the Kerala model of development. In 2006, J. Chathukulam and M. S. John awoke scholars outside of Kerala who engaged in the study of tribal development to recent developments within Kerala—a state usually ignored in the larger Indian debate. That same year *The Wayanad Initiative* appeared, a large-scale study commissioned by the government of Kerala to the Indian Institute of Management in Kozhikode on Adivasi livelihoods in Wayanad. In fact, this government-commissioned study went further than most independent studies in deconstructing romantic culturalist notions of tribal life. For instance, it explicitly stated that "being a 'tribe' in Wayanad does not have much to do with traditional customs and practices, but has much to do with the extent of their marginalization in social, economic and political domain" (2006: 41). The political realist tone of the study—confronting cultural stereotypes—quite significantly challenges the reigning paradigm.

Hence we see that though within the discipline of anthropology, where Adivasis used to be confined, the genre of the tribal ethnography and its concomitant theoretical presumptions often still continues, with the rise of the AGMS other disciplines have taken an interest in Adivasi livelihoods and movements and started producing knowledge that transcends the confines of traditional tribal ethnography. What remains to be done is anthropological work that helps to deconstruct the notion of the tribe and its associated prejudices in Kerala by showing the concrete contradictions that Adivasiness poses for

Adivasi movements themselves in the way that, for instance, Amita Baviskar (2005a), Nandini Sundar (2008), and Alpa Shah (2007) have done for other parts of India. This is one of the challenges this book takes up.

## Conclusion

This chapter has not revealed the secret of where the people figuring in the rest of this book really come from. It did not intend to do so. The question of the ethnogenesis of particular social groups in Kerala is certainly interesting, for instance in revealing just to what extent and how social inequalities reproduce themselves over time. Yet the aim of this chapter was to trace the broader history of how and to what effect these groups came to be labeled as tribals. The two processes—of ethnogenesis and categorization—are interrelated, but they are not the same. Describing how and to what effect people become known as tribal is precisely intended to demonstrate the nonsense of debating whether these people are genuinely tribal as well as to emphasize that the essential difference that the notion signals is a (govern)mental construct and not a useful tool to study historical relations. "Tribality" is a category born of Western fantasy and colonial imperatives backed up by certain currents of anthropology willing to lend it substantive analytical value. It was carried over into independent India and shaped the terms under which different social interests could be contested. Government anthropologists in India continue to have to venture out on fieldwork trips, usually a few days at most, in order to watch people perform their tribality and accordingly make decisions on whether or not they should be registered as Scheduled Tribes in the Ethnographic Survey of India and receive the entitlements that come with that status.[26] What I have done in this chapter is to help create more space for alternatives to this state gaze by deconstructing the taken-for-granted notion of the tribe and exposing the colonial and bourgeois baggage it carries with it, relying on the critical work done by scholars who have engaged in a similar agenda of historically deconstructing the tribe.

There are limits, however, to historical deconstruction. Mere deconstruction seems to leave a vacuum that in the absence of the reconstruction of an alternative research agenda continues to be filled by the ethnographic state. That is why my book does not stop at the deconstruction of the essentialist differences between tribes and nontribes, peoples inside and peoples outside global capitalism, those fighting against the state versus those fighting to capture it, but continues to enquire into the reasons for the rise of indigenism as a form of politics mobilizing around the notion of the tribe. In the next chapter, however, I first follow up the historical deconstruction of the tribe in colonial and academic practice with a description of the trajectory of contemporary political mobilization around the notion in Kerala. My aim is to trace the various interpretations of Adivasiness in Kerala and the recent history of how certain social conflicts and desires came to be framed as concerning Adivasiness.

## Notes

1. The 1857 Great Revolt or Sepoy Mutiny also confirmed officials' ideas about its source in the caste system since "ideologies of pollution and exclusion" had formed the spark of the mutiny when a new cartridge greased with pig and cow fat was introduced to the soldiers (Dirks 2003: 130).
2. Archana Prasad (2003) describes these ideas as "ecological romanticism" and indeed traces their origin to the English opposition to the industrial revolution.
3. The 1871 Criminal Tribes Act criminalized many itinerant *jatis* and—with help of the Salvation Army—forcefully settled them to make them available as labor in factories (see Radhakrishna 2001).
4. Scheduled Castes, in contrast, cannot legally be Muslim or Christian (i.e., Muslims or Christians cannot claim SC status) since the experience of "untouchability"—a key defining characteristic of Scheduled Castes—is argued to exist only in Hindu religion (despite the many evidences that caste discrimination continues after conversion, even within the Church itself—see Mosse 2012: 209ff.). Excluding Muslims and Christians from SC status has long been a strategy of Hindu nationalism to discourage Dalits from converting to Christianity or Islam.
5. According to the much-debated Article 46, declaring "The State shall promote with special care the educational and economic interests of the weaker sections of the people and, in particular, of the Scheduled Castes and the Scheduled Tribes, and shall protect them from social injustice and all forms of exploitation."
6. This is, of course, known from the trajectory of many other national independence movements as well. Frederik Cooper (2008), for instance, has powerfully recorded how the demand for equal citizenship rights that animated the early liberation movements in French Africa lost out as "national independence" became the dominant agenda promoted by indigenous elites.
7. One such update was, for instance, Rostow's "stages of growth" theory, propagated around the world in the 1960s.
8. I take this basic distinction between modernist, romantic, and radical currents of socialism from Priestland (2009).
9. According to Sinha (2004: 74), however, Ghurye never did any fieldwork for his PhD.
10. The term was used by Gandhi to emphasize the fact that (former) untouchables were part of Hindu society. The term is strongly rejected by the Dalit movement today for its paternalism, its attempt to keep (former) untouchables in the "Hindu fold," and for the way it has been used to ridicule the actual paternity of Dalit individuals.

11. In addition to the randomness of SC/ST categorization, there is also the fact that many communities bearing the same name—and considering themselves a unity—but living in different administrative districts today have different legal statuses; and the fact that legal ST status in most cases evaporates when so-called tribes travel outside of the region where they are registered as such.
12. A tribe whose members manage to become successful farmers, for instance, can be reclassified as a Scheduled Caste or an Other Backward Caste.
13. Ambedkar's struggle against the Hindu legitimation of caste ended in a similar dilemma. Having long announced he would not die a Hindu, Ambedkar for years managed to resist the urge to fix himself in any other category, but near the end of his life made the decision that, within the hegemonic frame of fixed, religious categories, he should make his point by converting to another religion, that of Buddhism.
14. As Paul Erik Baak describes, the British had varying degrees of success in mobilizing tribal labor. Some communities labelled "tribal" seem to have been particularly reluctant to serve as plantation labor, and the total number of people in some of the hilly areas where plantations were started was often not enough for the required number of laborers. Mobilizing labor from the coastal areas, however, also proved difficult since in the nineteenth century many ex-slaves were still tied to landlords, through obligations but also for a level of security in times of need. They moreover were not enticed to face the confinement and bad living conditions of plantations surrounded by forest (Baak 1997: 94 ff.).
15. There are even "scientific" formats for this kind of documentation and one of the "great achievements" of Krishna Iyer (whom we will meet later on in this section) was, according to Kumar Suresh Singh (2002: xxi), to simplify the British official H. H. Risley's twenty-seven-point format for the ethnographic survey of India into a fourteen-point one.
16. Still, however, I have heard some anthropologists and Indologists, inside as well as outside India, tell me about their fascination for the different skull types of the tribes.
17. William Logan was the special commissioner appointed in 1881 to enquire into land tenure and tenant rights in Malabar (the Northern region of what is now Kerala, then ruled directly from Chennai/Madras), following the revolts by predominantly Muslim (Mapilla) tenant farmers in the area. Interestingly, Logan was inclined to argue *against* culturalist arguments—in his report on the Mapilla uprising he refused to go along with culturalist arguments depicting the Mapilla riots as communal (Muslim vs Hindu) riots and instead pointed to the large-scale dispossession of Mapilla tenants' rights that had preceded the riots.
18. *Vikasanam* literally means "expansion" but has been adopted in Kerala as the Malayalam referent for "development."
19. Aiyappan's monograph on the Paniya was written in 1973 but published only in 1992, four years after his death.
20. Marriama Kalathil's (2004) study of unwed mothers among the Irular in Attappady echoes the exact same concerns. Typically, it mentions only extreme cases, such as a nine-year-old "charming, beautiful and innocent" girl who "who fell prey to the lust of a settler" (58) and never suggests that something other than deception might drive the women to relate to wealthier neighbors.
21. Mathur had apparently not been following what the AGMS had actually been doing as Janu had addressed the issue of unwed mothers several times explicitly in public speeches. It is true, however, that she did not—as she explained to me during an interview—give it the prominence that "civil society" expected her to give to the issue considering the fact that she was unsure publicizing the issue would do the unwed mothers much good. She moreover argued that the phenomenon was part of the overall oppression of Adivasis that the AGMS was addressing.

22. As a paternalist protective measure, tribals cannot legally sell their land to nontribals.
23. A later such critical contribution to the study of Adivasi issues in Kerala is Susamma Isac's (2012) "Perceptions and Experiences of Development: A Study of Two Tribal Communities in Wayanad district, Kerala," which stands out as a critical, fieldwork-based thesis with sensitivity to the different voices of Adivasi interlocutors.
24. Having interviewed Janu various times, this is certainly the impression I and my research assistants got from her, and, indeed, most people close to her describe her as witty and ironic rather than innocent.
25. A notable exception is the work by professor of economics M. Kunhaman at Kerala University, who wrote about "the tribal economy of Kerala" already in the 1980s.
26. Townsend Middleton (2010) has done research on these contemporary ethnographic practices of government anthropologists, demonstrating how field visits are politically negotiated between power brokers of the supposed tribe and the politicians commissioning the government anthropologists, who invariably are frustrated by what they then see as a staged rather than genuine performance of tribality.

– Chapter 2 –

# THE IMPORTANCE OF BEING ADIVASI

The colonial baggage that has attached to the notion of the Adivasi continues to pose dilemmas for the Adivasi Gothra Maha Sabha. Mobilizing effectively as "Adivasi" requires lots of activist labor. This is not only because Scheduled Tribes constitute only about 1.5 percent of the population of Kerala. It is also because what it means to be Adivasi is neither something that movement participants necessarily agree on, nor something that is easily kept out of the realm of oppressive "common-sense" interpretations. Activists generally see "Adivasi" as similar to "Dalit," both intended as explicitly political, autonomous references beyond established caste and tribe frames. Yet even the word "Adivasi" is a literal translation of the Latin term "aborigine" (Bates 1995: 103f.) taking it back to the colonial imaginary that often becomes a latent part of activists' own ideas of what it is to be Adivasi. Some scholars worry in reaction that in shaping their political program around Adivasiness, activists have inevitably entered a realm that will merely "reinforce rather than contradict the prejudices directed against them" (ibid.). They worry that it will bring about a reactionary "return of the native" (Kuper 2003). This chapter focuses on the dilemmas that emerge as activists negotiate the contradictions of using an overdetermined notion of Adivasiness for the purpose of emancipatory praxis.

It will become clearer in this chapter why I use the notion of indigenism, rather than tribal politics or Adivasi resistance, to capture the kind of intervention the AGMS is engaged in. I have done so precisely to emphasize activists' efforts to try to escape the ethnographic state and challenge political boundaries in two major ways. The first is the AGMS's effort to destabilize taken-for-granted notions of identity. Indigenism signals a politics that goes beyond the concern with categorization and exclusive identity—beyond the particular. It does exactly what Dipesh Chakrabarty on a cautionary note observes about global indigenous politics: that it operates at a "rhetorical" rather than strictly "referential" register, increasing in "use-value ... in proportion to the decrease in ... referential content" (2005: 240). When the AGMS refers to "ancestral land," a "tribal way of life," or "indigenous belonging," these phrases should be interpreted in a rhetorical register, as references not to concrete local facts but to social relations and ideals. The dynamism and ambiguity of the AGMS's interpretations are precisely why the movement has contributed to the emergence of a new political block in Kerala as it allows for local specificities to become part of wider frames of reference and for political vision to override the short-term preoccupation with claiming exclusive benefits. Indigenist initiatives hence stand in contrast to "tribal solidarity movements ... asserting political solidarity of a tribe or of a group of tribes vis-à-vis ... non-tribals" (Sinha 2002: 252), and "centered upon the deployment of a proven membership of specific and reified identities" (Cederlof and Sutton 2005: 161).[1] I call the AGMS "indigenist" precisely for its transformative political agenda and capacity to upset the usual language in which political debate is conducted.

A second way in which the AGMS should be considered indigenist is its critical attitude toward the given past. Cultural stereotypes and common sense are not simply strategically confirmed in the AGMS but are actively reworked. This is particularly important since the AGMS, in basing its visions of the future on a specific interpretation of the past, necessarily runs into the problem of having to negotiate the historical baggage of the "tribe." If used too instrumentally, the AGMS risks confirming the perilous, hegemonic meaning of what Adivasi politics is about. It moreover risks thereby ultimately disempowering itself since dominant readings of indigenous identity are often particularly awkward for the more proletarianized "indigenous people" who form the backbone of the AGMS (cf. Baviskar 2005b, Sylvain 2002, Robins 2003). The AGMS hence does not simply rely on tropes of tribal innocence but engages with more dialectical and therefore necessarily contradiction-ridden interpretations of Adivasi legacies. Its politics is indigenist as it goes to the heart of what Gerald Sider (2003: xiii) describes as the challenge of struggling "within, and also against, their own [indigenous] histories and their own cultures and simultaneously within and against the histories and cultures that others try so intensely to impose upon them."

I start this chapter with a discussion of the trajectory of the emergence of the AGMS as a chain of framing events through which poverty and landlessness became recognizable as part of the historical oppression of indigenous people. In the second section I then move on to discuss in more detail the various ways in which Adivasiness has come to be understood in Kerala and how the AGMS tries to give Adivasiness a more coherent and politically useful content through "conscientization" efforts. Concluding this chapter, I will reflect on the need to understand why despite—and perhaps *because of*—the ambiguous interpretations embedded in the notion of Adivasiness, it has nevertheless become a magnet for political action in Kerala.

## Becoming Adivasi: To Frame or to Be Framed

The AGMS relies on a variety of interpretations of what it is to be Adivasi, some of which contradict each other or even are internally contradictory. The balancing act of the AGMS is about how not to succumb to these contradictions, how to try to impose coherence without relying on the taken-for-grantedness of the notion of Adivasiness. A major tension in the AGMS, which both signals its core weaknesses and strengths, is that over time it has shown itself committed to an agenda determined predominantly by the interests of the landless agricultural laborers among Kerala's Scheduled Tribes, yet has often had to draw on the authority of the ethnographic state, whose notions of Adivasiness are much more amenable to other, less proletarianized Adivasi communities. We see this play—of trying to make tribal imagery work for the AGMS while at the same time attacking the hegemonic practices it perpetuates—throughout the trajectory of the rise of the AGMS in the course of the 1990s and into the mid-2000s.[2]

None of the conflicts the AGMS took up were necessarily or only related to Adivasi politics. The AGMS's trajectory can be seen as the fruition of a considerable amount of "framing work": the work of shaping particular grievances onto broader and more resonant claims and tying different social conflicts together as requiring the same kind of (indigenist) challenge (Tarrow 1998: 21). This kind of reading is a common one in social movements studies in the West but is less common in the study of non-Western societies (Bayat 2010: 4).[3] Often it is assumed that collective action in India does not involve much deliberate action or political choice and simply mobilizes traditional affiliations of kinship, caste, or ethnicity. Between the Dumontian interest in what makes India different from "Western democracies"—hierarchical values, a lack of (the myth of) individualism, ritualism, a lack of separation between public and private—and the insistence in social movement studies on a strict definition of social movements that builds on Western history, attention to Indian varieties of modern political contestation often gets lost. But whereas contemporary forms of claims-making in India indeed grow out of a different local history and thus will not look the same as they do in the West, indigenist activism in Kerala is not merely a ritualistic performance of taken-for-granted ethnic ties but relies precisely on the radical democratic challenging of inscribed and traditional ideas of what it is to be Adivasi.

Formal resemblance to traditional techniques of protest does not mean that the context and meaning of such protest remains unchanged. Many forms of protest in Western Europe today—the riot, the petition, or the demonstration—were equally part of traditional repertoires and have gained their modern meaning by their changing context, rather than form. The indigenist movement in Kerala has drawn extensively from the Indian protest repertoire: activists have organized *jathras* (marches,) *dharnas* (sit-down strikes), the occasional *hartal* (a shut-down strike whereby all economic activity comes to a halt), *gheraos* (encircling a public official), *bhook hartals* (hunger strikes), and even have resorted to the extreme of suicide through public immolation. Guha and Martinez-Alier (1997: 14) argue that many such Indian techniques are aimed—as they traditionally have been—towards "shaming the state." Yet this is not all they do. These techniques also include tactical and strategic considerations aimed at a modern liberal-democratic system. Take the *jail bharo andolan* or "jail fill movement," a demonstration whereby protesters deliberately seek arrest: in doing so they hope to embarrass the government about putting large numbers of its citizens in jail but also seek the tactical effect of filling up the jails, making future arrests more difficult, and thereby making ordinary people more willing to risk joining a demonstration (hence it is often undertaken the day before a large demonstration). Its symbolic effect is, moreover, undertaken not just with an eye to the Chief Minister or authorities but rather with public opinion, mass media, and voters foremost in mind. Despite the traditional techniques, symbols, and discourses through which the AGMS is often represented, there is, as we will see, deliberate political work involved in the making of the democratic indigenist challenge in Kerala.

## *Adivasi Mobilization in the Shadow of the ST Land Act*

From the early years of what became the Adivasi Gothra Maha Sabha, the movement encountered the dilemma of framing an Adivasi movement that would hold a balance between ensuring the realization of legal rights available to Adivasis while at the same time rejecting state definitions and limitations on what Adivasiness ought to be—as Nandini Sundar (2009: 1) observes of Adivasi politics more generally, "people yearn for the state to observe its own laws, even as they protest against the content of the laws." In exploring the trajectory of the Adivasi struggle in the shadow of the ST Land Act in Kerala, I follow Nandini Sundar's (2009) sensitivity to understanding how laws structure social identities and access to resources, and vice versa. We will see the complexity of poor people's relationship to the law, which, as Sundar argues, is often a crucial part of their politics, even if at the same time it confirms that they "fight on a terrain not of their own choosing" (ibid.: 3). The trajectory of Adivasi mobilization in Kerala also, however, shows the liberating potential of poor people challenging the confines of legally determined politics, especially where they retain the solidarity of more powerful "civil society" allies.

In the 1980s in Kerala, Adivasi politics was rather overdetermined by the law: public debate was centered almost exclusively on the revision and implementation of the "Kerala Scheduled Tribes (Restriction of Transfer and Restoration of Alienated Land) Act" of 1975 meant to restore "alienated land" to "tribals," who themselves were hardly involved in the debate. It was, as Sreekumar and Parayil (2006: 232) put it, a "juridico-legal battle against political society[4]" by (non-Adivasi) "civil society" actors, convinced that all over India "the root cause of all human rights violations perpetuated on [tribals] can be traced to land alienation, since the tribals depend on land for their identity, existence, security and livelihood" (in Puthucherril and Vijayabalan 2001: 1). In Wayanad, the district where there is the highest concentration of Scheduled Tribes in Kerala and where the AGMS emerged, land relations are historically far more complex than the notion of tribal land alienation suggests.

Land alienation, as put forward in the juridico-legal battles preceding the rise of the AGMS, is assumed to have happened recently, as a consequence of settler migration, and to all tribal (ST) communities in Wayanad. In fact, however, already in the late fourteenth and fifteenth century, regional *rajas* placed most of the agricultural and forest land in Wayanad under the control of Nair *janmis* (landlords) and temple authorities (Kjosavik and Shanmugaratnam 2007: 1208f).

This turned community ownership of land by for instance the Kurumas (now an ST) into tenancy under the Nair landlords (ibid.: 1209), though other communities, such as the Kurichiyas and the Mullu Kurumas (also both STs now), could continue paddy cultivation on communally held land. At the same time, the Paniya were reduced to becoming the agrestic slaves of landlords (ibid.: 1210).

With the 1792 conquest of Malabar (of which Wayanad is part) by the British and the 1805 defeat of Pazhassi Raja, the insurgent overlord of Wayanad, the area became part of the British Madras Presidency. During the subsequent British revenue settlement that was completed in 1816, the overlordship of the landed aristocracy was acknowledged—and strengthened—in order to create an agrarian class loyal to the British and to facilitate the establishment of British tea and cardamom plantations. Full proprietary rights were given to the *janmi,* effectively establishing this class of big landlords as the sole legal proprietor of land in Malabar (Panikkar 1978: 880). In so doing, the rights to communally held land that the "high-caste" Mullu Kurumas and Kurichiyas had earlier held onto were legally ignored (Joseph 1986: 43), though informally many of these use rights agreements continued.

Since under the British revenue settlement uncultivated land was exempted from taxation, *janmis,* many of whom used to own slaves, had less incentive to continue organizing production on their land. Hence a number of erstwhile slaves—mostly Paniyas and Adiyas—started to work on the plantations instead (Kunhaman 1985).[5] Meanwhile, uncultivated forest land, which formed the livelihood basis of a small minority of Adivasis such as the Kattunaikans, was divided by the British into "private forest land"—mostly *Devaswam* land, historically given as royal endowments to temple authorities—and "revenue land"—mostly the former lands of the insurgent Pazhassi Raja. The first Communist government of Kerala in 1957 made an attempt to pass the Kerala Private Forest Act, which would have provided for the redistribution of *Devaswam* lands to landless people, but the act never passed the Legislative Assembly (Kjosavik and Shanmugaratnam 2005: 1247).

Many local communities in Wayanad were thus already landless or dispossessed of traditional land usage claims when the first wave of settler migration from Travancore came in the 1930s, led by relatively prosperous Syrian Christian farmers in search of new commercial opportunities in rubber and tea production (Baak 1997: 162ff.). This was followed by the main "colonization" thrust from 1940 to 1970—a time when also poor subsistence farmers from Travancore joined the migration wave (Joseph 1986: 124). An oft-repeated refrain today is that the Communist-led Kerala Land Reform Act of 1963, which gave tenant farmers ownership over land, worked out perversely for tribals because, through it, the settlers who had taken over their land in this period were able to claim the status of tenant vis-à-vis the tribal landowner and acquire title to the land of the tribals (e.g., see Cheria et al. 1997). The story is however even more complex as the status of land customarily used by certain Adivasi households in Kerala had until the land tribunals of the 1970s never been established as one of full ownership. It was not the land reforms as such but the local organizational strength of settlers, combined with bureaucratic indifference and casteism, that turned certain informal lease agreements between such Adivasis and settlers in favor of the latter. In other cases, Adivasis even got evicted from the land they had been using, as local landowners feared the Act would have provided these Adivasis with the ownership titles (*pattayam*) for the land under their occupancy.

The legal struggles that came in the wake of the Kerala Land Reform Act did not mean much to the largest and most proletarianized tribe in Kerala, the Paniya, who—with a few exceptions—never held land to be alienated from in the first place. The Paniya and similar proletarian groups such as the Adiya, the tribe to which C. K. Janu (the AGMS's leader) belongs, in principle have less symbolic appeal for legal activists concerned with indigenous rights than do the more recognizably tribal, landed groups such as the Kurichiyas, reputed to be experts in wielding the bow and arrow.[6] While the more proletarianized groups later came to form the forefront of the AGMS, the landed (or in some cases ex-landed) Adivasi groups stood to benefit most from the juridico-legal battle over alienated land. In 1986 the necessary regulatory framework to implement the Tribal Land (Restriction of Transfer and Restoration of Alienated Land) Act had been finalized, but implementation was not forthcoming. At this, Dr. Nalla Thampy Thera, a social activist and public interest litigator, famously petitioned the Kerala High Court demanding a speedy implementation of the act. In reaction, the court eventually, in 1993, ordered precisely such implementation. Yet this in turn provoked a scuttling of the act as opponents of the law tried to pass an ordinance that would legalize all transactions of Adivasi land up to 1986. When the "Adivasi struggle" is retold, these legal battles are often included in its trajectory (e.g., Krishnakumar 2001). Enthusiasm for such legal struggles became all the more pronounced around 2006, when the "Scheduled Tribes and Other Traditional Forest Dwellers (Recognition of Forest Rights) Bill" was passed, again seen as crucial to Adivasis' existence in Kerala even though proletarian groups like the Paniya have little connection to the forest and little to gain from the bill. Inevitably, the juridico-legal agenda and the indigenist movement often clashed, notably in 2001 when Thera (and others) publicly criticized Janu for what Thera called her "diverting public attention from the main issue concerning tribals, that is, restoration of their alienated land" (*The Hindu,* 20 October 2001).

The indigenist break with the preceding tribal politics that was led by nontribal activists and symbolically favored the less proletarianized tribal communities came with the increasing militancy, in the course of the 1990s, of people who themselves claimed an Adivasi identity. They were supported by local NGOs, such as Solidarity and Hilda, but also by national level activists such as B. D. Sharma (former National Commissioner for Scheduled Castes and Scheduled Tribes), Ram Dayal Munda (former vice-chancellor of Ranchi University in Jharkhand), and Krishna Iyer (a well-known progressive Malayalee High Court Judge in Delhi), who all offered different views on the "Adivasi question." Initially it was not clear to what extent activists would be able to put to political use these supporters' heavily scripted language, often harking back to ethnographic tribal stereotypes. The 1992 Coming Together, or *Sangamam,* organized by what came to be known as the South Zone Adivasi Forum, was however a key transitional moment. The initiative still lay primarily with non-Adivasi social workers and NGOs,[7] yet in the course of organizing the Sangamam, Adivasi activists started to take an active role.

The idea for this particular Sangamam seems to have arisen during a state-level convention in January 1992 (Cheria et al. 1997: 66). Early that year, C. K. Janu and several other activists had visited Adivasi organizations in Jharkhand and attended a national Adivasi conference in Pune (Maharashtra). Back in Wayanad, after local consultations, Janu and others then decided to take 12 October 1992 as the day to organize the first large meeting of Adivasis from different states and tribes (or *jatis*) of southern India. The day was highly symbolic as indigenous people all over the world were preparing protests to mark the 500th anniversary of Columbus's "discovery" of the Americas and the oppression of its indigenous peoples. To claim part of this "500 years of indigenous resistance," Adivasi activists in Northern India had already decided to join in these protests. By June 1992, activists in southern India had decided to organize their own celebration as well. Columbus day was integrated into local Adivasi history by tying it to the heroic struggle by "the Adivasis of Wayanad led by Thalakkal Chandu" (a Kurichiya warrior) who "on this very day 190 years ago … beat back the British imperialist force destroying Panamaram Fort, 16 km from Mananthavady" (Bijoy 1993: 1357). The international discourse of indigenous people's leading role in the anti-imperialist struggle was hence made to resonate with the history of South India. A link was made to the international indigenist struggle, though to do so activists still needed to rely on imagery of the upper-caste Kurichiya Adivasi community. At the Sangamam itself, however, Kurichiyas no longer formed a majority. Instead, most of whom were gathered there were the more proletarian Adivasis—the communities that NGOs focusing on "the poorest of the poor" had been working with.

According to non-Adivasi intellectuals who supported the Sangamam and reported on it, the Adivasis gathering at Mananthavady aimed to find a "renewed vigor to strengthen their struggles against decimation as a distinct people" (Cheria et. al. 1997: 1). The meeting is thus represented as concerning "the reclamation of their [Adivasi] identity, land, history and culture," "pride as a people," and refusal "to be subsumed and decultured" (Ibid.: 66). It is described as "the confluence of aspirations and articulations of the Adivasis of this land to survive as a distinct people with an ecological worldview and culture" (ibid.: 69). Paniya and Adiya activists who later carried the struggle on, however, spoke to me of the Sangamam as marking the beginning of their struggle for land—not for ancestral land, but for land to own and cultivate. Mananthavady, they told me, was the place to receive trainings in preparation of the land occupations that followed. With NGO support, the Sangamam also included other events, such as presentations by scholars from the region on "Adivasi life," photo exhibitions, an exhibition-cum-sale of "Adivasi art," "cultural performances," including of K. J. Baby's famous play *Nadugadhika,* and finally a "cultural procession" from the venue of the meeting through the town of Mananthavady, thought to be "an expression to assert the cultural identity of Adivasis" (Cheria et al. 1997: 79). Whereas the Paniya and Adiya activists I spoke to mentioned the Sangamam as a time when they were only just starting to find their voice, the NGO workers involved were eager to emphasize that the event was organized "exclusively by Adivasis" (ibid.)—a notion that was widely circulated in the media.

In most Paniya and Adiya activists' retelling, the Sangamam functioned mostly as a "meeting place" from which only later the political program of land occupations grew. The NGOs supporting the event, however, claimed that it was an expression of Adivasi "self-assertion" and this claim became the target of a storm of criticism from political opponents. The *Mathrubhumi,* the second largest newspaper in Kerala, gave a lot of attention to the subsequent Bharatiya Janata Party (BJP)–led protest meetings and marches. According to the BJP, the "real intentions" of the meeting ought to be investigated by the government because in fact its aims were to promote "antinationalism." The BJP moreover alleged the event did not enjoy the participation of the major Adivasi organizations since it had been organized by "Christian missionaries" intent on "converting" Adivasis. On the other hand, the *Deshabhimani,* the official daily of the CPI(M), largely repeated—without reference—the allegations of one of the CPI(ML) factions that the Sangamam was not organized by Adivasis but by "foreign money" to serve the interests of feudalism and imperialism and subvert the growing people's struggle against the World Bank and the IMF.[8] From the beginning, it seems, political rivals were eager to reframe the movement as precisely *not* representing an Adivasi voice but rather a foreign one. The attack on the authenticity of the Adivasi mobilization would increasingly pose a problem for the movement, certainly as the more subaltern and political interpretations of indigenism started to develop and bring the movement further away from stereotypical (supposedly authentic) images of Adivasiness.

### *Attempts at "Autonomous" Organizing*

The Sangamam of 1992 was followed by a number of actions publicly proclaiming the emergence of a new, autonomous "Adivasi consciousness" under the leadership of the South Zone Adivasi Forum (SZAF). According to the NGO workers who had been active in its emergence, the SZAF resolved to focus on the issues of "Land, Forest and Culture" (Cheria et. al. 1997: 95). The year 1993 had been internationally proclaimed the "Year of the Indigenous Peoples," and SZAF leaders visited many places in India—from the Narmada Valley to Jharkhand—to build stronger national links and partake in the preparations for the celebration of the Indigenous People's Year in Delhi under a reorganized Indian Council of Indigenous and Tribal Peoples. Another South Indian Sangamam was also held, this time at Kodagu in Karnataka. Though attended by prominent national organizations and activists, such as the Asia Indigenous People's Pact, the UN International Working Group on Indigenous Affairs, and Medha Patkar of the Narmada Bachao Andolan, there seems to have been less participation of Adivasis from Kerala. Interpreted as a failure by the organizers, it could well have signaled how the more militant Adivasi activists in Kerala were not interested anymore in symbolic gatherings and rather were getting ready to confront the Kerala government, particularly over the issue of land distribution. Though the second Sangamam was framed primarily as part of an ongoing "unification" of tribes—a discourse that the SZAF would continue proclaiming in the media—under the surface a differentiation of political interests was taking place whereby landless Adivasi communities increasingly refused to accept that more educated and landed Adivasi—and non-Adivasi—activists would set the agenda (Cheria et al. 1997: 105ff).

With the renewed attention to tribal issues, the Kerala government started to do its best to appear actively engaged with Adivasis, if on its own terms. It started launching one after another "welfare scheme" for tribal communities and in July 1993, declared Kerala a "total tribal literate State" (*The Hindu,* 4 July 1993). In terms of media coverage, an interesting shift happened around this time. Earlier media coverage was mainly about the "misery" and "deprivation" facing tribals: "Most Chippankuzhy tribals are anemic" (*The Hindu,* 4 August 1991) "Misery of Suganthagiri Adivasis is unparalleled" (*Indian Express,* 19 October 1991), "School [attended by tribal children] sans teacher for 21 years" (*The Hindu,* 19 March 1992), "Tribals ... hounded by fear" (*Indian Express,* 2 September 1992). By 1994, however, media headlines of misery and fear among tribals in Kerala became remarkably less numerous, replaced by reports of tribals "seething with anger" or engaging in a "stir for rights," "encroachment," "fast," "vote," or "take-over of forest land." Indicative of this turn was the launching on 26 January 1994 of the Adivasi Samyuktha Samara Samithi, a new front organization in Wayanad intent to secure land for landless Adivasis. The lack of implementation of the ST Land Restoration Act was again publicized as the context of the Samithi's emergence, though journalists I spoke to were actually upset that from the beginning C. K. Janu was not giving much importance to the Act. In the visions of the NGOs and civil society activists—among them many journalists—the so-called autonomous Adivasi movement would "reclaim the Adivasi lands legally due to Adivasis." As the initiative of the movement moved towards Paniya and Adiya activists, however, the movement started leaving the confines of the existing legal frameworks and started focusing directly on simply acquiring land.

Though led now by Paniya and Adiya activists to whom the ST Land Act as it stood was of little use because it focused more on "alienated land" than on the needs of those who had for generations been landless, the media representation of the movement's demands continued to focus on the Act. In Cheria et. al (1997), who claim that the various agitations by Adivasi activists at the collectorate at Kalpetta (the capital of Wayanad) were about "the demand to implement the Scheduled Tribe Land Act," we can also read that these agitations were in fact dominated by landless Adivasi workers. Moreover, we can read that these Adivasi workers were particularly angry about the fact that the government apparently could easily find land for commercial enterprises and systematically closed its eyes to the encroachment by settler families on government or forest land, yet could find no land to offer landless Adivasis.

At the beginning of April 1994, out of the SZAF, the Adivasi Vikasana Pravarthaka Samithi (Organization for Tribal Development Workers) emerged, again led by C. K. Janu. The move to form a union of tribal development workers seemed modeled on the history of the Dalit struggle in India where organizations of Scheduled Caste civil servants (such as Kanchi Ram's BAMCEF) played a key role. Tribal development workers, among them Janu herself, were the only significant group of (low-ranking) civil servants among the Paniya and Adiya. In the same month, this Samithi led a group of two hundred Adivasi families in a march to Ambukuthy, in the vicinity of Mananthavady, to claim a piece of about sixty acres of vested forest land—the other sixty acres of which had already been encroached by about 120 migrant families. Forest officials and police soon intervened and launched a violent attack on the attempted settlement. In protest, Janu started a hunger strike, which she only quit after the Assistant Collector came to her hospital bedside to persuade her. Knowing well that promises by the Collector were not enough to ensure them land, the mobilization continued until the land titles were given.

In August 1994 Janu visited Geneva to take part in a meeting of the United Nations Working Group on Indigenous Populations. In November that same year, she went on to make headlines in Kerala by rejecting a ten thousand rupee Kerala State Award for "best Adivasi social worker." Rather than obey the label and thank the government for acknowledging her support to bring about "Adivasi development," Janu, whom newspapers now claimed to be representing the "Adivasi Development Action Council" (*The Hindu*, 16 November 1994), announced she would only accept the award if the Minister for Scheduled Castes and Scheduled Tribes would respond to a number of issues of concern to Adivasis, first and foremost the need for landless Adivasis to be given land as well as the implementation of the Land Restoration Act, the enforcement of the SC/ST Prevention of Atrocities Act, and DNA tests to determine the paternity of out-of-wedlock children of Adivasi mothers (ibid.). At the award ceremony, the organizers tried to skip over Janu's demands, to which she reacted promptly, returning the money and stating that if the government really wanted to pretend to honor her, it ought to honor her work.

The act of returning the award was immediately taken up by the media and became a crucial moment in the emergence of the indigenist movement. It signaled the growing militancy and confidence of the movement's leadership and the state's failure to coopt it. Janu's gesture went against any stereotype of Adivasis as innocent and not daring to—or even capable of—politicizing media attention. Janu confronted the Kerala public with the claim that it was the state's own discrimination of Adivasis and the lack of respect for their demands that was the problem. And this in turn caught the attention of Dalit groups. Janu's antipaternalist, proud gesture fit well with their political attitude and she immediately received the support of various Dalit organizations at colleges in Thiruvanathapuram. The Dalit Panthers in Wayanad came forward to offer her an alternative award and from then on actively supported the land occupations Janu organized. Many Dalit groups, such as the Dravida United Front and the Kerala Harijan Samajam, also supported the "Panavalli struggle," another land occupation that commenced in March 1995 and through which Janu herself, for the first time in her life, managed to acquire a plot of land.

By the time of the UN's proclamation of the "Decade of Indigenous People" in 1995, the beginnings were in place of a program that attracted support through claims to Adivasi history yet in many ways departed from traditional tribal politics. The subsequent first half of the Indigenous Decade in Kerala was filled mostly with a combination of land occupations, still usually framed around—though not always actually in line with—the Scheduled Tribe Restoration of Alienated Land Act. National and international networking occurred less, and there was instead an increase in local direct action. Further allegations by opponents of the movement that it was "foreign-funded"—and thus not "truly Adivasi"—came to a climax when Janu dared Revenue Minister K. E. Ismail to prove his allegations that she and her fellow activists were foreign funded or face legal action ("Janu dares Minister to prove allegations," *India Express*, 23 October 1996). The minister, apparently, had received a fax summing up the demands of what was now the Adivasi Ekopanan Samithi and had from this, according to Janu, concluded that she must be funded by "outsiders" since "no true tribal can afford fax expenses" (ibid.).[9]

Still under attack and scrutinized on the question of "authenticity," Adivasi activists often temporarily returned to an explicit embrace of the legal discourse of "ancestral land." In October 1996, agitations against pro-settler amendments that were made by the CPI(M)-led government to the ST Land Act came to a head with a hunger strike by the leader of the Dalit Liberation Front and a march on the secretariat by a group called the Adivasi Samrakshana Vedi. What animated these strikes was not so much the defense of the Act but the desire to make a point of the perceived bias within the CPI(M) against Adivasis and Dalits. That same year, an outfit calling itself the Ayyankali Pada—after Kerala's most important Dalit leader—encircled the collector of Palakkad district, W. R. Reddy, for nine hours in order to demand the withdrawal of the amendment. Uproar followed the "hostage-taking" and Janu felt pressured to publicly condemn the incident and paint the activists as clearly not Adivasi considering their "violent" behavior ("'Hostage drama didn't help tribal cause,'" *Indian Express,* 13 October 1996). Early August 1997, the Adivasi Ekopana Samithi, in the words of one of its chairmen K. M. Salimkumar, decided to observe 15 August not as Independence Day but as "Betrayal Day," again primarily—it was reported—in protest against the amendment (*Indian Express,* 4 August 1997). In 1998, finally, after many doubts had been voiced by the central government as well as by national Scheduled Tribes and human rights institutions, the president of India, who at the time was K. R. Narayanan (the first, and so far only, president of India from a Dalit community—and a Malayalee too), decided not to give the amendment bill its necessary assent ("Tribals jubilant over President's decision," *The Hindu,* 19 March 1998).

### *From Kurichy to Kundala: Visions of a Dalit–Adivasi Struggle*

By 2000, halfway through the UN Decade of the World's Indigenous Peoples, the movement led by Janu could be seen to depart more resolutely from the dominant script of the ST Land Act, articulating an agenda that was more broad-based and transformative than the legal confines of the Act would allow. The year 2000 was a decisive moment as Janu joined a struggle at the Dalit colony of Sachivothamapuram near the village of Kurichy in Kottayam district. The colony was one of the first so-called Harijan Colonies, set up in 1939, in the context of the caste reform movements, to provide erstwhile bonded laborers with a place for themselves, independent of their landlords (den Uyl 1994: 124). The colony was a place of vibrant Dalit activism, particularly through the Dalit Women's Society (which also included men) that was founded there in 1992. The struggle at Kurichy is often left out of the retelling of the trajectory of the indigenist movement but has been claimed by activists themselves as a key moment. At a commemoration of the Kurichy struggle four years later, activists also invoked the AGMS strike in Thiruvanathapuram and the Muthanga struggle that followed the Kurichy struggle, vowing to "rededicate themselves to the struggle that Sreedharan started" (*The Hindu*, 9 February 2004). Sreedharan was the person who committed suicide during the Kurichy struggle, and whose memorial altar as a "Dalit martyr" was unveiled by Janu that day.

From interviews with people at Kurichy, I learned that the main issue of the struggle had been a high-voltage electricity line that a private developer had been planning to erect over the colony, with permission of panchayat members who had allowed themselves to be bribed. The developer had planned the shortcut in order to save money on material so that more of the allotted money could end up in his own pockets. For this purpose, however, a dangerous high-voltage electricity line would be drawn over the colony (which itself, ironically, had only a very unreliable power supply) and trees would have to be cut. Even some houses would have to be partly demolished. As Krishnamma, the daughter-in-law of Sreedharan, told me, "It was obvious to us that this kind of trick would only be pulled on a Dalit colony."

People understood that those scheming to erect the electricity line were assuming Dalits lacked the awareness to stop it. As Krishnamma said, "Those planning the scheme could not get it into their mind of course that one of our relatives was an engineer working at the Kerala Electricity Board and was able to inform us of all the technical details." One of the first things people at the colony did was send a memorandum to the Minister calling on him to intervene, followed by a petition to the court. Meanwhile, however, the developer was continuing his efforts to draw the line over the colony and so the inhabitants decided direct action was necessary. One day, when most men were out, electricity workers came to erect the electricity poles. Krishnamma described the scene: "We went to the junction and each of us put ourselves in the pits that were made to erect the electric posts. In fact it is women who took the initiative to get things done here." Emphasizing their awareness, Krishnamma continued: "We stood united as we were convinced about the pros and cons and the consequences."

After several attempts, however, the electricity workers eventually did succeed in erecting the posts. At this, one of the Dalit engineers from the colony, in front of a crowd of police, climbed into one of the poles and cut the line, proudly proclaiming "I am doing democracy." Again, however, the line was reconnected. At that point, inhabitants decided to start a hunger strike. Krishnamma told me, "My husband was the first person who took the initiative for the hunger strike. He had been striking for five days. … His health was getting worse: we wanted the police to arrest him and take him to the hospital." This, she explained, was usual practice, yet when it came to Dalits, the police was apparently not concerned with the risk of a hunger striker dying. Therefore, she said, "Around five o'clock we planned to besiege the panchayat [municipal] office. Soon all of us assembled there and rushed to surround the office. We took the panchayat officials hostage. All of a sudden, the district collector and superintendent of police came to the spot and called us for discussion in a nearby house. After the discussion they agreed to arrest my husband and moved him to the hospital." As her husband was taken to the hospital, another person took over and continued the hunger strike until the electricity board had assured them they would drop the plan.

A few days later, however, inhabitants of the colony were told the Supreme Court had ordered that the electricity line plan was to continue. Again a group of police and officials came to charge the line and again most men of the colony were at work. Krishnamma said her reaction was to grab a can of kerosene and rush out: "Without a moment of thought, I snatched one of the kids and carrying a can of kerosene I stood still in front of them. And I shouted at them, 'Only stepping over my dead body will you be able to get the line charged.' Then for that day they stopped working and dispersed." The climax of the struggle, however, came the next day:

> When the officials turned up, my husband went up to the terrace holding one of Ayyankali's [Kerala's historical Dalit leader] photographs. He had dipped himself in kerosene and with a light in his hand he was standing on the terrace while we were quarreling with the police. The Superintendent of Police Vinod Kumar saw Jayan [Krishnamma's husband] standing there and ordered the policemen to snatch him. By the time they were close to Jayan they tried to beat him with a *latti* [bamboo stick]. Then somebody pushed me and I raised myself up and snatched the latti. With that latti, I remember beating somebody. Then a crowd of women police rushed toward me. The atmosphere worsened and seven of us women were dragged into the police jeep. Then someone shouted "Brothers, our sisters are being arrested!"

The added gender dimension to the humiliation the protesters were experiencing escalated the scenario. As Krishnamma went on to tell, "Our father [Krishnamma's father-in-law] heard this [that the women were being arrested] and came running and shouting. All the colony people were there.… Dad was collecting stones and made a circle with them and filled it with dry leaves. Then he poured kerosene onto it.… He was demanding our release and was asking them to stop the work. The SP [Superintendent of Police] shouted 'We are not going to stop the work. Go to hell.' Then he [father-in-law] screamed, 'I will die.'"

Emphasizing her knowledge of constitutional rights, their neglect when it comes to Dalits, and the culpability of the police, Krishnamma continued: "The police had to get him arrested in order to rescue him. Either they had to arrest him or had to seek the help of the fire brigade—as per the law. But nobody cared about father's voice. Everyone was trying to force Jayan down from the terrace. With a ladder some policemen tried to catch him. But he threatened to commit suicide if the police touched him. Meanwhile dad poured kerosene all over his body, then fired the pile of dry leaves and jumped into the fire."

Many activists emphasized that these events at Kurichy were crucial to the Dalit-Adivasi struggle in Kerala. Sunny Kapicadu, one of the leading Dalit activists in the area, came to the colony as soon as he heard of the struggle going on. He told me, "It was a turning point. As a person I felt one thing at the time: if this action is a failure, if it ends in a big *latti* charge [police beating] … what can I do then … I will commit suicide … I was the working committee chairman … and that was my decision … we have no other option, we will commit suicide … not just me, Geethanandan [leader-to-be of the AGMS] also—as a person I felt it and I'd do it. Otherwise we cannot live in Kerala. I felt it, I have no other option then, not only I but all leaders. … so many persons would commit suicide. We cannot go anywhere else in Kerala, if this action failed."

Afraid the struggle might produce more martyrs and worried it would affect their electoral chances, the CPI(M) government eventually intervened to ensure the high-powered line did not cross the colony. This victory thereby became a significant turning point. As Sunny Kapicadu told me, "It was a breakthrough in the movement. After that we started the Adivasi actions—up to Muthanga. This same team went to Wayanad with Janu, destroyed that engineering college in Kundala."

Indeed, the "Kundala struggle" was the next major moment in the building up of the indigenist movement. According to newspapers that ignored the Kurichy colony episode as part of the struggle, Kundala was "the first direct action after the 'Pallakad collector hostage drama'" (*The Hindu,* 3 September 2001). The struggle emerged in the context of the stagnation of the pace and scope of success in claiming land for landless Adivasis in the early 2000s and the reluctance of the government and existing political parties to acknowledge the emerging indigenist movement. Therefore, when Janu and Geethanandan, who had also been active at Kurichy, heard about a conflict developing between a local Adivasi community and the government at Kundala, they decided to lend their support and signal the emergence of a state-wide indigenist platform. They interpreted the conflict at Kundala—a rather peripheral town in Idukki district, near the border with Tamil Nadu—as a typical case of "development" taking place at the cost of Adivasi livelihood. The issue, as indigenist leaders framed it, was that the government had decided to erect a government engineering college on land of Kundala's Muduvan community—a relatively isolated ST community. This was forcing the Muduvan community to be evicted from the land—a classic case of Adivasi dispossession. I was told that, initially, the engineering college had been planned on land taken from the large Tata Tea plantation in the area (see also Mukundan 2001). But the government backed off at the last moment from claiming a piece of land from Tata and instead preferred to dispossess Adivasis for a college they themselves would probably never be able to attend. The government, meanwhile, was defending the project for following an affirmative action policy of erecting prestigious government colleges in areas of relative under-development. Interestingly, when I visited the Kundala Muduvan community and talked to Martin, the leading activist from the community itself, I realized that there were different possible ways—besides "Adivasi dispossession" and the "Adivasi struggle for land"—in which the struggle could have been framed.

I was surprised that the first, second, and last thing Martin and others from the community told me about was the practice at this Muduvan community that menstruating women would retreat into a special hut in the forest for the duration of their period. I did not quite understand at first how this was of relevance to the political struggle and was almost assuming they must be telling me this so emphatically because they were assuming that as an anthropologist this was the kind of information I would be interested in. Martin showed me around the area where people (who turned out to be from an SC community in Tamil Nadu) were working the community's considerable land holdings and where the landscape was dotted with huts attached to empty concrete houses (sometimes with a cow inside). The empty concrete houses were the outcome of a Swiss-funded (and obviously not entirely successful) development project. The community had—

somewhat more successfully—also been the target of Indira Gandhi's twenty-point program, which from 1979 had invested seven million rupees in setting up a cattle farm there. I was told the farm had run until 1996, when government funding was stopped. People were still tending the cows and having them graze on the mountain but the farm building itself lay abandoned. And so it was precisely this structure that was to be turned into a government college.

Despite having heard of the trend of land grabbing through the setting up of large educational institutions in South India, I could not quite, at first, figure out how the relatively small building and compound on the large area of land would entail the eviction of the Muduvan community off the land. This is when it was made clear to me why Martin and others had been so emphatic about the traditional rites of Muduvan women: a major problem for the local community was that with the engineering college, young men would come to the area, which was something the community leaders wanted to avoid at all cost. As Martin exclaimed, "If some outsiders come here is it possible for us to live like this? Would it be possible for us to mingle with them? *It would not be possible.* If it's settlers, it is easy for them to adapt. If there were some educated people … it would be easy for them … but here the Adivasi way of living and practices are entirely different. We are to do certain things all alone."

In other words, the college in question would not physically push inhabitants off the land but would form a threat because of the outsiders it would attract to the area and their potential disruption of the gender traditions and honor of the community. Once interpreted as an issue of "Adivasi land dispossession," however, the struggle itself further confirmed this frame. Seeing that the construction of the college was continuing, the activists, as at Kurichy, decided to take matters into their own hands. On 24 March, they organized a big Adivasi "cultural event" and that same evening they demolished the part of the college that had already been erected, clashing with outsiders—including CPI(M)-affiliated *goondas* (thugs)—who had been mobilized to defend the structure and attack the activists. Many activists got badly injured and there were again many arrests. Three days later, opponents came back to attack the Muduvan community itself and the Muduvans had to flee from their land into the forest. An old man who was unable to walk and therefore had to be left behind in the flight subsequently died from neglect. This, in turn lead to headlines of a "Tribal death due to starvation" (Mukundan 2001), further suggesting the land-starved condition of Adivasis (even though the Muduvans in question were relatively well-off).

After several further actions at Kundala and *hartals* in different parts of Idukki and Kottayam districts, Janu started a public hunger strike on 28 April. She made a number of demands, first and foremost that the government "restore tribal lands to its tribal owners and rehabilitate all the landless tribals" (Mukundan 2001). Inaugurating the hunger strike, the chairman of the Confederation of Human Rights Organizations of Kerala fiercely condemned the "anti-tribal attacks" at Kundala. A former Member of the Legislative Assembly, ignoring the fact that Muduvans had not just struggled "against development" but had in fact also criticized how development funds for their cattle farm had been withdrawn, claimed that "the education Minister Joseph has tried to impose development upon the chest of Adivasis, which they do not want" (ibid.). Another speaker then urged the government to take the hunger strike more seriously since Janu was "not only a known Dalit leader of Kerala, but also a woman" (ibid.). Under pressure, the government eventually decided to set up a commission to investigate the issue, which indeed put an end to the plans to erect a government college near the Kundala Munduvan colony. According to Martin, the commission had respected Adivasis' "isolated way of life." The indigenist activists spearheading the struggle meanwhile claimed it publicly as another key victory both in terms of the Adivasi land struggle and their struggle for dignity and respect.

### *The Muthanga Struggle: Within and Against the "Adivasi" Frame*

Whereas Kurichy had helped strengthen the movement internally by allowing for a broader ideological interpretation of the indigenist struggle and confirming Adivasi ties to Dalit networks, Kundala had been a success particularly in allowing for local conflicts to be interpreted as part of a wider social pattern that Janu's movement was confronting. The movement now seemed able to successfully play the "Adivasi" card without being played by it. This set the stage for the next phase that started when, in 2001, indigenist activists in Wayanad reported on a number of starvation deaths occurring in Adivasi colonies. The authorities tried to argue that in fact drinking, neglect, or disease (especially TB and dysentery) had caused the various deaths. Yet activists rejected these arguments and claimed it was obvious that structural solutions were necessary. Some announcements of "free rice for tribals" and medical camps (*The Hindu*, 12 July 2001) were not going to make the desired impact. According to activists, the root problem was Adivasi landlessness and in the name of the Adivasi-Dalit Samara Samithi (Adivasi-Dalit Action Council) they announced a "restoration of rights march." Dalit activists who had participated in Kurichy and Kundala thus traveled to Wayanad to help mobilize Adivasis for what became the Avakasa Sthapana Yatra (Rights Assertion March). As the struggle gained more attention, it also however started to become publicly framed again as a classical tribal struggle.

Early September newspapers still mentioned the Adivasi-Dalit Action Council (e.g., *The Hindu,* 9 September 2001), but two weeks later on 18 September, when the "Adivasi Solidarity Day" was announced, many were leaving out the "Dalit" part of the organization's name and were reporting instead on "The Adivasi Action Council." They did so even when reporting on the death of Kallara Biju, a Dalit from Vaikom[10] who is remembered as a martyr since he died from a heart attack while traveling with Adivasi activists to Thiruvanathapuram, the end point of the rights march (*Indian Express,* 19 September 2001). On 3 October 2001 the Adivasi Gothra Maha Sabha was formed at the capital to take the struggle forward. From 29 October onwards, activists organized what came to be known as the *kudil ketti samaram,* a relief camp strike, erecting refugee huts in front of the Chief Minister's official residence. The strikers demanded that poverty be alleviated, jobs provided, and the government Adivasi Welfare Fund be put to its proper use. Most media attention, however, went to "the Adivasi land issue," pushing poverty alleviation and employment demands to the background. Newspapers commented that the relief camp strategy, a novel one according to them, was tolerated by the Chief Minister because he did not consider the "agitation of tribals as a 'political' one" (*Indian Express,* 3 September 2001).

Despite the chief minister's attempts at depoliticization, the aspirations of the organizers to form a new political block started to materialize at a state-wide level. With this, however, the tensions in the indigenist discourse also increased. The most difficult issue to handle in the indigenist frame was again that of "alienated" land as envisioned under the 1975 ST Land Act: on the one hand, activists were pushed to claim back "ancestral" land for landless Adivasis and to do so in light of the continuing legal battle around the Act, but, on the other hand, those most active in the struggle had neither potential claims to land under that act, nor sentimental historical attachment to such land and preferred to simply receive any nearby land without settler claims on it. After the protesters had been camping in front of the State Secretariat building forty-eight days, the chief minister finally reached out to the movement and agreed on a settlement with Janu that promised that all landless Adivasis in Kerala would receive one to five acres of cultivable land and that distribution of such land would start on the first of January 2002. Many commentators saw the fact that Janu dropped the emphasis on "ancestral land" a "climb down" (Sreekumar and Parayil 2006: 244; K. S. Singh 2001), though AGMS activists considered this agreement signed on the 16th of October 2001 a clear victory.

Activists in the AGMS did, however, remain doubtful as to the implementation of the agreement and pledged to undertake direct action if the promises turned out to be empty. In the meanwhile, in April 2002 another major struggle was inaugurated—again by Janu, who by now had become *the* Adivasi leader of Kerala. The action was against the pollution by a Coca-Cola plant at Plachimada in Palakkad District (see Aiyer 2007). Since a significant part of the affected population was Adivasi and Dalit, some activists saw the potential of it becoming another episode in the "Adivasi struggle" (see Bijoy 2006: 1). In a demonstrative march through the affected area on 4 August, many of the activists who had earlier been part of the refugee hut strike participated. The overwhelming popularity in Kerala of a struggle targeting such a clear symbol of American and corporate imperialism as Coca-Cola, however, won out over the framing of the struggle as one more specifically on behalf of Adivasi-Dalit land rights. It did remain a secondary theme, emphasized, for instance, in alliances between the anti–Coca-Cola struggle and Adivasi organizations in India's mining belt. But since in the rest of Kerala the main problem that the AGMS was confronting was not so much dispossession by multinational companies but rather a negligent government reluctant to distribute land to landless Adivasis, engagement of other than locally resident Adivasis in the Plachimada struggle petered out.

Even with the pressure building up on the Kerala government to implement the promises of the 2001 agreement, the pace of government action was frustrating. It was trying to delay redistribution by claiming it either could not find enough land or did not know the number of landless Adivasi families. Bureaucrats sympathetic to the indigenist movement within the Tribal Resettlement and Development Mission (TRDM), the institution set up to honor the 2001 agreement, were hoping the AGMS would organize agitations in order to strengthen the mission's bargaining power vis-a-vis the government to push through its plans for land redistribution. And indeed, by the end of 2002 a momentum was building up of landless Adivasis invading government plantations and other lands the government had tentatively earmarked for redistribution. On 27 October 2002, the AGMS organized a surprise action to claim parts of Aralam farm in

Kannur district—a huge, seven-thousand-acre cooperative farm, of which half had been bought by the state government from the central government in order to be redistributed to Adivasis. Through direct action, activists hoped to break through the legal battles over the actual implementation of this plan that had produced continuous delay in the handing over of the land. When even this, however, did not seem to move the government, the AGMS leadership decided that the problem could only be confronted through action that would attract "higher-level," nation-wide attention and thereby help to increase the pressure on the Kerala government from the outside. They decided to claim land at the Muthanga Wildlife Sanctuary, a depleted nature area[11] falling under the central government legislature and therefore likely to attract national attention.

The AGMS leadership also chose the Muthanga area because they could claim it as an Adivasi homeland: shrines were found in the area that were believed to have belonged to Adivasi ancestors. To the media, AGMS leaders described their journey to Muthanga as "a line of thousands of refugees going to their ancestral lands" (Janu and Geethanandan 2003). They claimed that "those who returned to Muthanga conversed with the spirits of the mountains with ease, as though they got back their freedom that they lost centuries ago. They, the Paniya, the Adiya, the Bettakuruma, the Kaattunayaka, the Kurichiya, etc., belonging to all the tribes of Wayanad, woke up their gods in unison" (ibid.).

What the activists left out of this discourse was that few of the Adivasis gathering at Muthanga had any roots there and that they were claiming the land to build houses and cultivate their own plots. Some of the participants in the Muthanga occupation were in fact surprised to find out the targeted land was a wildlife sanctuary and worried about the wild animals that roamed the area. Yet, the image of Adivasis returning to their homeland to live in harmony with nature inspired many civil society organizations and helped the AGMS gain support, which was desperately needed as, soon after the AGMS settled at Muthanga, all political parties started mobilizing against the occupation.

The AGMS's public representation of the struggle however started to backfire as "facts" were circulated about the "real" nature of the occupation. The Wayanad Environmental Protection Organization, an environmental group led by local landowners in the area—some of whom used to graze their cattle on the land and were enraged by what they considered a manipulation of "innocent Adivasis" by "outside" activists—came out with a "Spot Investigation Report."

It was entitled "Invasion of Wayanad Wildlife Sanctuary: Some Disturbing Truths" and "revealed" that "[m]ost of those who occupy the makeshift tents inside the Sanctuary are from far away places … and most of them are having ration cards and houses in those areas." The report also complained that "the Agreement [of 2001] was a real selling of the Adivasi cause when compared to Adivasi struggles around the world … because nowhere in the world there is a demand for alternative land for alienated land. … Instead of the robbed land, the victim agrees to accept land 'somewhere'!"

As I learned from Adivasi elders in the area, it had long been a practice by landlords to periodically ally with Adivasis against perceived threats of landless migrants from other parts of Kerala settling in the area. This explains all the more why this organization of landlords was enraged by the idea that Adivasis would stop defending "their" land—often the land in fact under control of the landlord, where the Adivasis were merely permitted to live—against settlers. They resented that Adivasis would follow in these settlers' footsteps and demand land "anywhere" for themselves.

The Wayanad Environmental Protection Organization thus also twisted the fears of police repression that Adivasi communities living near the site of the land occupation had voiced into proof that "Ms C. K. Janu is not representing the real Adivasi cause now because she and her gang men threatened the local tribal people living in the periphery of the Sanctuary." These arguments were soon taken up more widely by political opponents of the AGMS and provided the government with an excuse to intervene. On 19 February 2003, about 500 armed police officials were sent to evict the occupation, escalating into brutal violence. One Adivasi activist and one policeman died during the eviction, and massive arrests and custodial torture followed. There were many incidents those days, too, of locals identifying random Adivasis and hauling them to the police station for their supposed complicity in the Muthanga struggle. At that point, in reaction to the violence, most political parties and other opinion-makers turned to condemning the "atrocities on Adivasis." *The Hindu* (16–17 June 2003) published a long two-part article by Supreme Court Judge V. R. Krishna Iyer lamenting the plight of "the artless, powerless Adivasis, native to this habitat, … terrorized by law out of their forest dwellings."[12]

To reconcile the organized resistance shown by AGMS activists during the eviction with the image of the innocent Adivasi and to shift the blame for the escalation away from the police, stories started to circulate that the violence of the Muthanga eviction had been instigated by non-Adivasi outsiders: either the People's War Group (a Naxal contingent active in Andhra Pradesh) or the LTTE (the then Tamil Tigers in Sri Lanka) must have mingled with the "innocent tribals." This sympathy for the "real" Adivasis, however, did not prevent the government from filing court cases against the movement's participants that dragged on—and continued their intimidating and paralyzing effects—for years after.[13]

The Muthanga struggle clearly brought to the fore the "dark side" of the indigenist frame (Shah 2007) when applied to Adivasi workers. Yet Muthanga cannot be simply regarded as a failure for the indigenist movement as it did push the established political parties to take the indigenist challenge seriously. Not able to simply repress the movement, political parties mobilized against it by in fact taking on board much of its program. The newly created Adivasi wing of the CPI(M), for instance, became particularly active in Wayanad after 2003—something Janu and others see as a sign of the victory of the AGMS rather than of its defeat. Moreover, the AGMS—for better or worse—developed a political-party wing, the Rashtriya Maha Sabha (Political Grand Council) in order to try to get at least some direct representation in the state parliament and sustain the pressure on existing political parties to either cater to Adivasi needs or see these "vote banks" shift toward the Rashtriya Maha Sabha. Despite the experiences at Muthanga, in which hegemonic indigenist interpretations became obviously oppressive, many Adivasis and Dalits continued to believe in some form of indigenist "identity politics" and would not revert to framing their issues in the old language of "class." Having sketched the historical trajectory of the emergence of the AGMS and its indigenist framing, I now look into instances of how Adivasiness is interpreted in Kerala in more detail.

## Traveling Models, Common Sense, and Conscientization

The AGMS became recognizable as a new political force in Kerala thanks to the way it reframed a series of conflicts, which otherwise may have been reduced to concerning "a lack of development" or "the plight of agricultural laborers," as questions of Adivasi discrimination and oppression. "Adivasiness" itself however remains a complicated notion. The questions I address now, therefore, are how AGMS activists navigate between internationally circulating models of indigenism and local "common-sense" understandings, and, especially, how activists "conscientize" sympathizers towards a politically more useful understanding of what it is to be Adivasi, meanwhile encountering the many tensions and dilemmas embedded in the concept.

### *"Traveling Models" of Indigenism and Their Tensions*

The main cause of the rise of indigenism around the world is often assumed, somewhat tautologically, to be the growing strength of the international indigenous people's movement (e.g., see Niezen 2003). International influences on Adivasi politics in Kerala are, however, largely indirect and reproduce the tensions and contradictions inhabiting Adivasi politics in general. AGMS activists call upon discourses with clearly identifiable international origins mostly when there is a need to draw the attention of actors beyond Kerala, to appeal to a global civil society audience, or to introduce new ideas for which no established local discourse is available. Examples of direct international references include how excerpts from Chief Seattle's famous speech were read to celebrate World Indigene Day (*The Hindu*, 11 August 2006)[14] or the proclaimed pride of indigenist activists in Kerala when Cathy Freeman (an aboriginal Australian) won a gold medal at the Olympics in 2000. Often these references remain similar to Communist references in Kerala to "the land of Soviets where all are equal" or "the heroic strikes of red Chicago":[15] they invoke an imaginary connection but remain abstract, floating on top of local realities. Sometimes, however, ideas that originate in national and international exchange do become part of local indigenism, so much so that without an awareness of the international scene, one could easily mistake them for unique local expressions. The frequent usage of environmental metaphors and insistence on the leading role of Adivasi women, for instance, I first took for unique qualities of Janu's leadership, until I discovered their strong resonance with international indigenist discourses.

The actual participation of AGMS leaders in international fora has been limited. In the mid-1990s, Janu traveled to Geneva and Thailand on the invitation of the UN Working Group for Indigenous Rights. She moreover took part in the Intercontinental Caravan for Solidarity and Resistance that toured Europe (see Madsen 2001) on the invitation of Global People's Action, a direct-action-centered alter-globalization network. Regional-level activists such as C. R. Bijoy put AGMS activists in contact with national networks, such as the National Front for Tribal Self-Rule and the Indian Confederation of Indigenous and Tribal Peoples. Yet despite these initiatives, direct networking beyond Kerala remains limited. The Indian government continues to refuse to acknowledge exclusive claims by any social group to "indigeneity," thereby hindering international indigenous cooperation. International exchange is moreover further obstructed by the intense suspicion harbored in Kerala towards most "foreign" cooperation. Growing out of a combination of postcolonial and Cold War suspicion of foreign intervention,[16] it is difficult for any political grouping in Kerala to receive international support, let alone money,[17] and not be buried under hostile suspicions. For me it was initially even quite difficult to meet C. K. Janu since she was worried that being seen with a white woman would reopen the storm of such criticism that had confronted her after her foreign trips in the 1990s.

Despite the relative weakness of international influences, some themes circulating in the international political landscape of indigenism do make a complex appearance in Kerala. The three international "traveling models" of indigenism that Anna Tsing (2007) distinguishes—the "sovereignty" model originating along a Canada–New Zealand axis, the "pluri-ethnic autonomy" model traveling through Latin America and the United States, and the "environmental stewardship" model coming out of the Amazonian struggles—find their echoes in Kerala and evoke what Anna Tsing calls "nodes of tension." The environmental take on indigenism is, for instance, reproduced by AGMS activists when they claim that Adivasis are less alienated from nature and can lead the way for "modern" citizens to regain a healthier, more sustainable way of life. In the context of the erosion of Kerala's food sovereignty and the pollution of its natural environment, this take on indigenism helps the AGMS acquire allies. Tensions appear, however, when Adivasis are cast as inherently more respectful of nature not because their livelihoods are closely related to it or because they want to resist commercial agriculture but simply for "being Adivasi." Janu played into the environmental discourse when in a piece in *Indigenous Affairs,* the influential publication of the International Working Group on Indigenous Affairs, she described the relationship of Adivasis to their environment in terms of the earth being their "mother" and the forest their "father." In fact, such a discourse sits rather uncomfortably with the mortal fear that Adivasi workers usually have of forest animals and especially of wild elephants (see also Shah 2010: 99ff.).[18] As we saw in the first part of this chapter, when AGMS leaders adjusted their language to the dominant eco-indigenist imaginary, this gained them a large audience but also backfired terribly.[19]

Likewise, the indigenist theme of "sovereignty" serves AGMS activists in modeling their search for pride in Adivasi "culture" and their efforts to unite Adivasis into a political block. The revaluation of the historical roots of various Adivasi *gothras* (clans) to demonstrate Adivasis' sophisticated civilizational achievements before their subjugation by the Aryans is quite popular among AGMS activists. The internationally dominant reading of indigenous sovereignty also, however, invokes many tensions. One is the fact that the interpretation given to sovereignty by organizations in the United States or even in the northeast of India (e.g., the National Front for Tribal Self-Rule) hardly fits the situation in Kerala where Adivasis historically live much more intermingled with other communities. Importing a notion of autonomy that stresses territorial sovereignty moreover raises the specter of secessionism, which in turn tends to invoke particularly brutal state suppression. A more internal problem is that by organizing explicitly on a "clan" basis, the fault lines of community divides also tend to deepen even though the aim is to valorize one's community. There is the danger that the process leads to a Sanskritizing competition for status. As Dr. Ambedkar warned in his *Annihilation of Caste,* "The literature of Hindus is full of caste genealogies in which an attempt is made to give a noble origin to one['s own] caste and an ignoble origin to other castes," which according to him contributed to the general "anti-social spirit" of the caste system (Ambedkar in Rodriguez 2002: 269). In principle, sovereignty does not imply cultural purity, but claims to sovereignty tend to be tolerated by society at large only if communities can demonstrate a degree of cultural "authenticity" (see Sonntag 2005), which in turn places pressure on Adivasi communities to start policing each other for signs of authenticity.

The "pluri-ethnic autonomy" model of deepening democracy that Tsing identifies as dominant in many parts of Latin America is perhaps the most relevant for Adivasi activists in Kerala. Unlike in Latin America, in India the issue for Adivasis is not so much to reform the constitution. With Dr. Ambedkar having been responsible for drafting it, India's constitution is already one of the most progressive in the world. The fight by Adivasis in India is therefore instead against the casteism that prevents the constitution from being implemented in practice. The form that this legal democratic struggle takes is not, however, always unproblematic. As happens in Latin America in debates over the legal definition of who is to be considered indigenous, also in India legal categorizations sometimes come to overshadow commitments to a more democratic reading of indigenous identity. In India this can be seen in the strict legal and mental separation of Scheduled Castes and Scheduled Tribes. The fact that Dr. Ambedkar drafted these constitutional constructs tends to make them all the more unquestionable among activists. Against Dr. Ambedkar's intentions, the category of the Scheduled Tribe thus usually remains taken for granted as the "other" of caste society, a category to which the critique of caste is only indirectly relevant. Dr. Ambedkar sometimes did use hegemonic evolutionary language, for instance in writing that it was Dalits who were made into "savages" (i.e., into uneducated paupers), in contrast to Adivasis, who always were savages; as he argues, it was the "indifferentism" of the caste system that made "the aborigines … *remain* savages because they [the caste Hindus] had made no effort to civilize them, to give them medical aid, to reform them" (Ambedkar in Rodriguez 2002: 279, italics added).

What we see is thus that the few themes that do resonate with international "traveling models" of indigenism are ambiguous. As we will see next, however, also everyday, locally engrained interpretations of indigeneity—the "common sense" notions of what it means to be Adivasi in Kerala—are full of ambiguity.

### *"Something the Government Calls Us"*

The common-sense discourse among most educated Malayalees is that there are thirty-five tribes in Kerala, all with distinct customs and traditions, that they live in the forest, and are innocent and hapless. The fact that this discourse is repeated even by many educated Adivasis shows just how immune the discourse is to empirical scrutiny. The fact that the number thirty-five refers to the number of Scheduled Tribes in the government census and has changed over time as so-called corrections are made and certain groups are removed from or added to the list somehow never upsets the idea that it is their "distinct customs and traditions" rather than the government that determines the tribality of these groups. The idea that they "live in the forest" is also stubborn enough to withstand any empirical test. Once I overheard an educated Malayalee acquaintance telling one of his friends how I was doing research on Adivasis and was thus spending a lot of time "in the forest." I turned to him saying I was not going to the forest, simply to the edge of the village where many Christian farmers also lived. All I got in return, however, was a blank stare and then an outright negation: "yes, to the forest." Likewise, "innocent" and "hapless" (and another chain of synonyms including "artless," "naïve," "destitute," "poor" [*pavam*], and "child-like") seem eternally valid markers of Adivasiness, for if ever an Adivasi would instead show herself cunning, this would surely have been under the influence of forces external to herself—if not Naxals, or Tamil Tigers, then some even more foreign outsider, or, alternatively, alcohol. The qualification that the person in question was actually not a "real Adivasi" would usually follow.

When educated Malayalees other than my research assistants were around when I talked to Adivasi workers, it was usually almost impossible for me to quiz the latter on what they saw as what it is to be "Adivasi." Whenever they started telling me something that did not fit the "thirty-five forest-dwelling, innocent distinct communities" scheme, the more educated bystanders would usually feel the need to intervene and warn me that I was talking to the wrong people on this issue, that these uneducated Adivasis did not know what it meant to be "Adivasi"—instead, I should talk to P. R. G. Mathur or some other anthropologist or, if anything, consult these bystanders as they, at least, were educated. The Adivasi worker in question would often keep silent and would sometimes later emphatically underline her supposed "ignorance," telling me things like "It's true *chechi* [elder sister], we don't know anything about these things," or "We were unaware of all that in our mind, words, and deeds (*manasa vacha karman*)." As the seemingly apologetic ending of many Paniya songs goes: "I have no learning; I have no intelligence (*budhi*). I do not know the regulations. I do not know the authority. Let not my words go wrong" (Aiyappan 1992: 98).

Sometimes, however, I got an uneducated Adivasi worker to reveal a bit of the "hidden transcript" below the public disguise of ignorance and talk to me about her interpretation of what it meant to be "Adivasi." A particularly interesting exchange I had was with Velli, a woman whom I often met in the Paniya colony where I did most of my fieldwork. Velli participated in the Muthanga struggle but not in a leadership role. She had not attended school, though she could read and write a little because of literacy campaigns in the area. She said she used to go for day labor in the paddy fields whenever she got the chance but for most of the time I knew her she did not work since she had a badly infected wound on her hand. The wound had started as a little accident while harvesting ginger but had become a major infection, even affecting her baby who was struggling with a bad skin rash. I often spoke with Velli about her ordeals—she knew well, she told me, that the ointment the doctor prescribed her during his regular public hours was probably not as potent as what he might offer her if she managed to see him during his after-hours when he charged high sums of money as a private doctor: "for us private treatment is very difficult to get." Everyday necessities, in combination with not being able to work properly, made it almost impossible for her to get the right treatment for her and her baby, and so she was usually necessarily compromising either on her diet or her medicines. When I tried to assist her financially, the money usually went to lightening the burden of harassment by creditors. Though everyone in the colony was poor, Velli was stuck in a particularly difficult situation. Against this background, the interpretation of what it was to be "Adivasi" that I got from Velli revealed quite a different "common sense" on Adivasiness among ordinary Adivasi workers themselves:

I: So what does it mean when you say "Adivasi"?

Velli: Nothing. The government [*sarkar*]. … When we say Adivasi, we mean the Paniya.

I: But what does the word mean?

Velli: It's not about the meaning of the word. That's only when we say Paniya—then we mean Paniya. It is the government who calls us Adivasis. We are just Paniyas.

I: Janu [the AGMS leader] also uses this word though, she always talks of Adivasis. … Why is that so?

Velli: She is an Adiya. She is also an Adivasi.

I: But I never hear you talk about yourself as Adivasi.

Velli: That's because she [C. K. Janu] has a job [*joli*], that's why she calls us Adivasis. She is a professional, so she calls us Adivasis. … You see, we all have different songs. Their speech is different. Ours is different. The [Kattu]naikans, Urali, Adiya, and us, all these have different languages.

I: I see—but what about the Kurichiyas and Kurumas [officially ST and included in the AGMS]. Are they also Adivasis? Which all groups are included in this group of Adivasis?

Velli: Paniyas, [Kattu]naikans, Urali, and Adiya. These four … they are all not rich. They are also like us.

I: And these other two, the Kurichiyas and Kurumas?

Velli: They are different.

I: Are they not Adivasis?

Velli: No, their caste (*jati*) is different.

I: Why so?

Velli: Why … because they have a lot of money of course! Anyway, it is not we who give ourselves such names as "Adivasis." It's the government who gives such names. We are just Paniyas.

Velli's answer exposes different meanings of Adivasiness. She starts by saying what should perhaps be obvious but nevertheless seems hardly reflected on by educated Malayalees: that "Adivasi" is used as a synonym of "Scheduled Tribe," which is simply a legal category—"something the government calls us." Velli emphasizes throughout that the only category that she feels naturally defines her is that of being "Paniya," the name of her *jati* (caste) that at the same time literally means "worker," someone who does *pani* (labor—not *joli,* salaried work). When I confront her with the fact that it is not just the government but also the leader of the very movement she had joined to occupy land who speaks of "Adivasis," she explains that this is the case because Janu is educated and has a salaried job: all such people have an understanding of Adivasiness that coincides with that of the state. Yet then, as if remembering the mainstream, "proper" understanding of Adivasiness herself, Velli also starts giving me the riddle of how many Adivasi communities there are and how they all have their particular "songs" and other cultural characteristics, until I interrupt her to push her some more on whether then all groups that the state has listed as Scheduled Tribes are Adivasi. To newspaper-reading Kerala, it is obvious that Kurumas and Kurichiyas are Adivasi, and Velli no doubt knows of the heroic deeds and legendary "tribal resistance" by the Kurichiyas against the British. Yet at this point, she decides to give her own reading of what it really means to be Adivasi: to be of a caste that is poor, which according to her excludes the Kurichiyas.

Velli's final interpretation of what really defines Adivasiness—namely poverty—is a notion I often encountered among ordinary Adivasi workers who had not been in leadership positions in the AGMS. For instance, a group of Adiya workers I was interviewing got into a discussion that concluded that it would be great if one of them would become rich, "though we would then not be Adivasi anymore." If anything, poverty and a lack of education were what many of them themselves saw as definitive Adivasi characteristics. Despite the fact that, rhetorically, "cultural distinctiveness" is a key point for the state to decide on Scheduled Caste status, Velli's interpretation is not altogether different from the way the state *in practice* applies its criteria for Scheduled Tribe status since "forward" ST communities can become reclassified as Scheduled Castes or Other Backward Communities. It is in this context, where Adivasiness is common-sensically associated with negative social markers such as poverty and lack of education, that the AGMS has had to struggle to "conscientize" people into a more "proud" and politically assertive interpretation of what it is to be Adivasi.

### *"I Am an Adivasi; Who Dare Play with Me Now!"*

"Conscientization," often described in Kerala as "making people politically aware," involves changing people's existing idea of their social world—changing what has become taken as common sense. As Gramsci argued, common sense is a powerful basis on which to build a political block, but it is also problematic since its robustness indicates the political hegemony of the status quo and the extent to which consciousness is shaped by existing relations of power. Yet, as Roseberry (1994) emphasizes, the hegemony that is crystallized in common sense is never a total achievement and needs to be constantly reworked in order to sustain itself against its internal contradictions and external challenges. This is where the potential for political intervention by "organic intellectuals" such as C. K. Janu lies to give a new, emancipatory meaning to taken-for-granted ideas. Hence "Adivasi identity" can also be turned into a tool to demonstrate the contradictions and the violence—rather than the consensus—underlying common sense (cf. Smith 2004). Having been at the receiving end of "conscientization" efforts by liberation-theology inspired social workers in the 1980s herself, Janu had first-hand experience with Freirian methods of upturning common sense and awakening a more politicized understanding of social reality.[20]

During one of the interviews I held with Janu in 2006 at her home, she spoke about how the AGMS had changed the idea of what it meant to be Adivasi:

> Before the [Adivasi] Gothra [Maha] Sabha was formed, there were many incidents in which Adivasis lost their identity and came in line with the mainstream. Those who are educated did not admit to being Adivasi, they preferred not to come to colonies like this. But with the active work of the Sabha, there came a mentality among them that made them say "I am an Adivasi" without any reluctance. Earlier when I used to go to places, Adivasis would not speak to me. I always tell everywhere that I am an Adivasi. So they didn't come and talk to me; maybe they felt that if they talked to me, others would also view them as Adivasis. … Now that the Gothra Sabha has become active and made them realize that Adivasis all over the world have a distinct identity, people became interested in saying "I am an Adivasi." These days when officers come to me they introduce themselves as Adivasi. They say it because when we do it there is some kind of closeness between us. They never used to say that before. Now what happens is that the Gothra Sabha attempts to preserve the identity which the Adivasis lost in earlier times. We give classes to children and form small groups to make them understand our tradition and our identity. This is an approach taken by the Gothra Sabha. So now officials, when they come to meet me, they introduce themselves as Adivasis. If they belong to SC [Scheduled Caste], they say that "I am an SC." They are not unwilling to say that they are Pulaya [one of the largest Scheduled Castes in Kerala]. This feeling came in people after the formation of the Gothra Sabha. Our people never used to look boldly into the face of others and do things. But now when I go for work and stand in the city waiting for

> the bus, I have seen our people say things like "I am an Adivasi; who dare play with me now!" ... Okay, the guy was drunk, and maybe he was talking from his unconscious mind ... but still ... it was not there before.

In the context of Janu's description of the AGMS's efforts to disrupt a common sense that depicts Adivasis as ignorant and destitute, an identity to be ashamed of rather than take pride in, it is relevant to remember Roseberry's (1994: 360) emphasis on hegemony as a concept to understand not consent but struggle. Roseberry moreover argued, with Gramsci, that even though subordinate populations are never simply the deluded and passive captives of the state, their political organizations are also not autonomous expressions of subaltern politics and culture (ibid.). Janu is trying to articulate a politically useful Adivasi identity, yet she is not doing so under conditions of her own choosing. Recovering an Adivasi identity, Janu implicitly argues, is something that cannot be done solely by proletarian, impoverished Adivasis but needs the alliance of educated and government-employed Scheduled Tribes. It also is not something that can be left entirely to the common sense of Adivasi workers—rather, it requires classes for Adivasi children where they can learn about their "own identity." Whereas Janu describes the process as one of self-awakening and internal reform, her use of the Scheduled Caste category for Dalits also plays on state-centric definitions. Janu sees the changes the AGMS has brought as the regaining of pride in one's true identity, but she also tells how the process whereby people came to "admit" this identity is inextricably tied to the activism of the Adivasi Gothra Maha Sabha—that it was through the intervention of the notion of a shared Adivasi identity that people came to feel "some kind of closeness" (rather than the other way around).

There are many contradictions involved in the process of creating an Adivasi identity to take pride in—for instance, the fact that the process inevitably also invites humiliation. Moreover, while using the notion of Adivasiness to launch a radical challenge to the status quo, common sense interpretations of Adivasiness receive a new lease on life. I once asked Janu about the fact that while talking about the identity of Adivasis so much and claiming she proudly presented her Adivasi identity, she would usually go to press meetings wearing a sari rather than dressed in the particular style characteristic of Adiyas. She laughed and explained:

> Then people will stare as if looking at a wild animal, if a person from us goes to a press meeting wearing our traditional dress. We can't even think of what that person will feel at that time. It would be a problem. But if we go wearing

> sari, nobody will stare since it is a common dress. So we can feel free. We have to accept certain things according to the situation, though we don't like it. We accept this not as a part of anything else, but as a part of finding solutions to our problems. Then it is okay. It becomes a danger when we do this to be a part of and to be accepted by the public and society. If I wear this dress to be a part of the common society, it is a danger. But it will not be a danger if I wear this as a part of solving the problems of our community.

It is thus quite literally in order to be heard—rather than stared at—that Janu adjusts the language and symbols of contention she uses. Her capacity, from her own Adivasi working-class background, to negotiate the contradictions she encounters and effectively confront the status quo is no doubt a reason for Janu's leadership position in the movement.

The project of "conscientizing" gets a different expression among upper-caste and/or middle-class sympathizers of the movement. A prominent sympathizer is K. J. Baby, a famous playwright and the founder of Kanavu (Dreaming), an alternative, participatory school for Adivasi children. He was one of the first to believe in the need for a proud Adivasi identity, and it is interesting to see how he describes the process he started with his pupils in the making of his famous play *Nadugadhika,* in which the history of Paniya slavery and emancipation is dramatized. He claims that "thinking was a strange and difficult process" for his students (1993: 31). According to him, "the refuge of the forests, the harmony with nature, the solace of one's identity with the tribe" had sunken into "depths of total restlessness" due to "poverty, ignorance and ruthless exploitation" (29). Baby writes that this "ancient genus," "the only positive element in their drab lives" had been "completely lost" (29). As he saw it, the challenge was to recover this genus to "re-commence their long stunted cultural growth" and provoke "thinking" in a "people who had completely forgotten their past" (29). In songs describing their slavery, Baby sees only the "false consciousness" of seeing themselves through their masters' eyes: "centuries of slavedom have now made them identify themselves as mere slaves" (10), he claims, reading this, for instance, in the refrain of Adiya songs: "We are the slaves of the lords of the hill, we are the slaves of the lords of the fields." Baby thus leans strongly toward interpreting the ignorance and timidity he observes among Adivasis as fully internalized adaptations to oppression rather than as tactical adjustments to cope with—and at times confront—existing relations of power.

The discourse that seeks to liberate Adivasis from thinking of themselves as "mere slaves" and from being "ignorant," "having forgotten their past," and having a "stunted cultural growth" comes to function as another element in hegemonic notions of Adivasiness, likewise provoking resistance and strategic adaption by Adivasi workers themselves. Akkathi, a Paniya woman I frequently interacted with during my fieldwork, at some point told me she thought K. J. Baby was merely training Adivasi children to perform songs and dances for others—that he was "exploiting" them. At other times, however, during earlier encounters, she had often praised Baby's work in "uplifting our community." This ambiguity and contradiction was in fact characteristic of ordinary Adivasi workers' responses to conscientizing efforts.

Ambiguity and contradiction clearly accompanied the encounters I observed of Thankachen *mashe* (teacher), a Pulaya man from Central Kerala who had come to the AGMS land occupation at Aralam to run a *gothra padasala,* an alternative evening school, "to generate and mobilize a tribal consciousness" among children of the various Adivasi "clans" (*gothras*). He also said he wanted to help revive the cultural unity of the original people of the area (including Dalits). As I spent several mornings with Thankachen following his daily routines, I often sat by as he talked to Adivasi elders—*moopans*—from whom he collected and recorded traditional songs and stories as well as other traditional knowledge, particularly of medicinal herbs. This knowledge he would transfer to his students during evening classes, in a wooden shelter that doubled as a temple. Talking to me, Thankachen often expressed his admiration for the kind of knowledge he was gaining from the Adivasi elders. As he told me, "They may be wearing shabby clothes but they have beliefs that are far superior." His project, he claimed, was also helping him regain the "harmonious lifestyle" he had lost as a Dalit.

One day I was sitting by as Thankachen, clad in the kind of white dhoti befitting a *mashe,* was teaching one of the songs, "My Homeland," that he had collected in the morning from a Paniya moopan whom he considered one of the most authentic sources of Adivasi knowledge at the land occupation. The children repeated the lines after Thankachan, and after a while the moopan herself came and sat on the side to watch the class proceeding. Somewhere halfway through the song, Thankachen turned to her to ask whether he was singing it correctly. She smiled ironically and said, "Aren't you the one who should know best?" At this the class became a bit restless and another Paniya moopan sitting on the other side of the space used the opportunity to start telling a drunken story, half falling off his bench as he did so. In reaction, one of the younger men standing

**My Homeland**

My homeland of eternal glory
My homeland that flourished into glory
Is stamping me down

I am the one who laid the foundation of ancient civilizations
I am the one who brought prosperity to this land
With the power of my labor

The serf was left with nothing
I became an out caste in my land
The world I have built is mine no more

One with wilderness, I gained the essence of culture
I turned sacred river shores
Into salubrious fields

The land that flourished with my sweat
The land in which River Bhageeradhi
Flows with the power of my prayers

My homeland, my homeland

That trampled me down
My homeland, which chained me
Into the cages of starvation

**Figure 2.1** My Homeland

around with a *thudi* (traditional Paniya drum) to accompany Thankachen's singing started making fun of the drunken moopan, parodying his gestures, making the disturbance of the class complete. And as Thankachen tried to restore order to the class, the drunken moopan spit his tobacco on the floor of the *padasala*—an act that Thankachen, well aware that the place was used at night as a temple too, could not but show his disapproval of. He stopped the lesson and looked distressed at the moopan, at which the two young men standing around eventually picked the moopan up and escorted him away, joking, "His royalty retreats."

The contradictions involved in the scene are palpable. On the one hand, Adivasi workers themselves—the parents of the children at the *padasala*—built the shelter and were paying Thankachen *mashe* their tributes for educating their children into a purportedly Adivasi consciousness that framed the struggle for land they were involved in. Participating in Thankachen's efforts to collect "Adivasi culture," they had become aware of what was expected of them in this regard. On the other hand, the irony of a white-clad non-Adivasi *mashe* teaching the children about "Adivasi culture" while Adivasi elders sat around to watch was not lost on those present, certainly as the elders implicitly started commenting on it. Caught between the need to put existing relations of power to their advantage as much as possible, while at the same time needing to confront them, ordinary Adivasi workers' reactions to efforts at their so-called conscientization are as ambiguous as the efforts of AGMS leaders to negotiate the Malayalee common sense of what Adivasiness is about. With all its contradictions, Adivasi consciousness nevertheless remains crucial to the AGMS's efforts to forge an alternative indigenist political block.

## Conclusion

> "And just when they seem engaged in revolutionizing themselves and things, in creating something that has never yet existed, precisely in such periods of revolutionary crisis, they anxiously conjure up the spirits of the past to their service and borrow from them names, battle cries and costumes, in order to present the new scene of world history in this time-honored disguise and this borrowed language" (Marx [1952] 2008: 15).

At the same time that a indigenist movement was taking shape—a movement that did not operate simply according to the scenario set by ethnographic state definitions of "tribality"—the various nodes of dissension within the indigenist frame also started to be mobilized by opponents. Hence just as a political movement was developing that posed a real political challenge to the status quo, counterefforts of measuring the movement according to an imagined schema of real Adivasiness intensified, as did efforts on the part of indigenist activists, for instance at Muthanga, to fit their political challenge into time-honored tribal disguise and speech borrowed from state ethnographers.

The political dilemma of indigenism is reflected intellectually in indigenous studies scholarship, caught between a deconstructionist and a strategic essentialist approach. The deconstructionist approach to indigeneity considers Adivasi identity a colonial and/or bourgeois-nationalist construction (e.g., see Bates 1995; Bindu 2009) that mixes notions of supposed indigeneity, a purportedly tribal way of life, and an official legal category (the Scheduled Tribe) into an essentialist, romantic myth. The deconstructionist approach warns against the danger of the exclusionary shadows of indigeneity: nativism, "communalism," and "oppressive authenticity" (Sissons 2005) through which proletarian Adivasis who fail to fit romantic images of Adivasiness become marginalized even further (see Baviskar 2007; Shah 2007; Whitehead 2007).

This chapter and the preceding one have drawn strongly from the deconstructionist approach as I have criticized the essentialized and essentializing meanings that have historically attached to the notion of the tribe and have paid attention to the political framing (rather than spontaneous fit) of social conflicts as indigenist ones. Ideally, such deconstructivist scholarship counters the reification of Adivasi identity and creates space for more radical political interpretations. Had the influence of this scholarship been stronger on the media in Kerala at the time of Muthanga, perhaps arguments about whether or not the activists there were "real Adivasis" could have been exposed as nonsensical from the start. Instead, merely a vulgar version of deconstructionism reached the mainstream media, where it worked to undermine the legitimacy of the AGMS precisely by showing that it was not led by "real Adivasis."

This is a danger that the strategic essentialist approach warns against as it prefers to see Adivasi identity as a social fact and a generally accepted reference to a shared (though not uniform) history of marginalization and resistance and a different way of life, embodied in those people asserting themselves as Adivasis (e.g., see Routledge 2003; Xaxa 1999). Scholars working according to this approach are particularly sensitive to the fact that deconstruction can undermine the legitimacy of Adivasi identity as a political discourse and thereby disempower the many democratic initiatives based on it (Karlsson 2003). Such scholars are more inclined to place themselves in the position of Adivasi activists and represent their concerns to a wider audience rather than see their role as analyzing the contradictions within the movement.

The dilemma between deconstruction and strategic essentialism is real and I have no solution to it, though I do propose a way in which to at least go beyond the deadlock of the two approaches against each other. For one, deconstructionist scholarship has exposed all the complexities and problems of "Adivasi identity." But it too seldom takes the next logical step to then ask why, despite all the problematic baggage it carries, Adivasiness has nevertheless started to attract so much political energy. Why, despite the seeming inevitability of indigenism's nodes of tension, is it such a popular discourse today? The present chapter underlines the pertinence of the question of why activists undertook the effort of building an indigenist movement in contradistinction to the Communist movement. I have shown that not only historically and theoretically but also in practice, the attraction of indigeneity cannot be assumed to lie in the ready availability or simple, natural fit of indigenism to particular communities' historical experiences but is in need of a complex political and structural explanation. By asking under what conditions activists tend to reinforce rather than reject the stereotypical images directed at them I do not discredit contemporary Adivasi leaders. Rather, I try to understand the limitations on political mobilization in a neoliberal age, as well as formulate a critique of the romanticized imaginary that global civil society demands of subaltern representation.

Strategic essentialist scholarship, on the other hand, has shown itself particularly aware of its potential impact on ongoing indigenist movements and the need to accommodate to global civil society. Yet even such scholarship can strengthen the movements in question all the more by focusing more attention on the political and economic grievances they emerge from rather than on the claims they make to a unique identity to overcome these problems. Attention to the structural causes for the rise of a movement also avoids the problem of a strategically essentialist reproduction of indigenist discourses contributing to a self-reinforcing mechanism of further essentialism. In the following chapters, I hence turn precisely to the question of the underlying causes of the rise of indigenism in Kerala.

## Notes

1. Cederlof and Sutton (2005) observe this exclusivist dynamic in Tamil Nadu's Adivasi politics.
2. Apart from my fieldwork notes and interviews, this section also draws on a collection of clippings from local and national newspapers from 1990 to 2010. For the period 1990–2005, these include all clippings from *The Hindu* and the *Indian Express* that referred to Adivasi or tribal issues—a collection of which I received part from the librarian of *Solidarity*, an NGO working to promote literacy and political consciousness in Wayanad, and which for the other part I complemented by systematically combing through newspapers that journalists and the CPI(M)'s archive in Thiruvanathapuram gave me access to.
3. Asef Bayat (2010) has made interesting innovations in social movement theory in the study of non-Western societies but particularly in terms of the social change produced by *nonorganized* forms of action, through large numbers of ordinary people's everyday collective (if fragmented) practices that he calls "social nonmovements."
4. By "political society" they do not mean a reference to Chatterjee (2004) but rather simply to political parties.

5. The British planters' lobby, together with Christian missionaries, encouraged this shift by legally abolishing slavery in 1833 (Kooiman 1989).
6. Not surprisingly, the first tribal minster in Kerala, P. K. Jayalakshmi, elected in 2011, is a Kurichiya (and an "archery star," as the *Deccan Herald* of 21 May 2011 reported).
7. In the late 1980s, big international donors that were active in South India, such as Oxfam, embraced the *sangamam* model, hoping that the funding of small community-based organizations would foster a people's movement to claim rights from the government, which might ultimately dissolve the dependence of these organizations on outside funding. The 1992 Sangamam was envisioned as a coming together of many such small community organizations.
8. A small extreme Left organization calling itself Yuvajana Vedi even staged something I was to experience personally a decade later: they *gherao-ed* (encircled) a German tourist who happened to be in the area and hung a placard around his neck with the words "Imperialist spy" (Cheria et. al. 1997: 82).
9. Quoted in the *Indian Express* of 6 October 1996, Ismail said, "Who is this Janu to claim to speak for tribals? Do you know she has even been faxing representations to me almost every other day? How many real tribals can afford to fax letters? So is it not clear that she is supported by well-funded outsiders?" He then went on to allege that the Palakkad hostage drama had nothing to do with tribal activism: "The four people involved were not tribals but cheap criminals."
10. Vaikom is a town in Kottayam district which is of national fame because of the Vaikom Satyagraha (1924–25), sometimes claimed as the first anti-untouchability civil rights struggle in Indian modern history.
11. The area had formerly been occupied by a eucalyptus plantation supplying a paper factory owned by the Birlas, one of India's wealthiest business houses (Raman 2004: 129).
12. The article went on to lament—entirely out of context—how Adivasis' "unlettered ways [and] their naiveté make them easy prey to exploitation by cunning settlers" and to argue that "the tribal is part of bio-diversity and is its sentinel rather than its hostile," therefore requiring "a compassionate forest legislation restoring the traditional forest resources to the tribals."
13. The first verdict by the Chief Judicial Magistrate Court, acquitting seventy of the accused (including Janu and Geethanandan), was only held in 2011. Many adivasi workers have spent more than a decade having to forsake a daily wage and pay busfare to present themselves to court twice a month—a number of them have died before receiving a verdict.
14. The newspaper article reporting on the reading also noted that Chief Seattle's speech had been taken from a Hollywood movie, whose script was rather far removed from the original words of the chief.
15. Referring to the 1886 general strike in Chicago for the eight-hour workday and its brutal police suppression—a day commemorated on International Workers' Day (the first of May).
16. Such suspicion should not be considered mere paranoia. Note, for instance, that the American ambassador in India at the time of the first Communist government in Kerala explicitly tells in his memoirs of how American money was indeed involved in supporting the dismissal by the central government of the first democratically elected Communist government in Kerala in 1959 (Moynihan 1975: 41).
17. In order to receive money from foreign donors, an organization needs official FCRA (Foreign Contributions Registration Act) status. Obtaining an FCRA is a difficult and costly bureaucratic process—so much so that a distinct market value has become attached to NGOs with FCRA status. Being a social movement, the AGMS does not have FCRA status, though an NGO such as Solidarity, which used to be closely associated with the movement in its earliest phase, does.

18. Many Adivasis I spoke to who had participated in the Muthanga struggle even considered elephants almost as direct messengers of the state: the story of how an elephant had stormed their settlement as if sent by the forest guards to destroy it was repeated to me many times. Janu eventually clarified that the elephant had actually been possessed by alcohol—and ensuing diarrhea—since it had stumbled upon a vat of illegal liquor brewed in the area and had drunk it whole.
19. A more logical ally might have been the international Via Campesina movement (e.g., see Borras, Edelman, and Kay 2008) yet, for reasons that would deserve in-depth research, this international movement's allies in India have not been peasants or agricultural workers—as in Latin America—but rather the higher-caste farmers who are often their most direct oppressors.
20. *Bodhavalkaranam,* the raising of one's consciousness or awareness (*bhodam*), is in fact part of a long philosophical tradition in South India (see Halliburton 2001: 1126). The early Communist movement gave it the interpretation of "overcoming false consciousness." However, in the late 1970s—the heydays of the CPI(M)-affiliated but "nonpolitical" popular literacy movement in Kerala, the KSSP—consciousness raising gained a more explicitly Gramscian meaning, and in Wayanad it became part of the spread of liberation theology and Paulo Freire's "pedagogy of the oppressed" (Zachariah and Sooryamoorthy 1994: 80ff.). During this phase, the beginnings of an emphasis on Adivasi identity also started to appear.

# PART III

## Contention and Conflict at the End of a Reformist Cycle

– Chapter 3 –

# Electoral Communism and Its Critics

Part 3 of this book studies the political dynamics through which social inequalities in Kerala in the course of the 1990s became contested in indigenist terms. The level of analysis here is that of "tactical" relations of power (Wolf 1990: 586): those operating within a given political-economic setting as opposed to the structural relations of power shaping the setting itself (which I consider in part 4). I look, more specifically, at how indigenism arose from the interaction among the political parties and social movements most eager to confront poverty and inequality in Kerala. In doing so, I go beyond the most common political explanation offered for the rise of indigenism, namely the democratization argument. The latter can be summed up as the idea that indigenism emerged in the past decades as states were forced by newly emerging "international norms" on the recognition of indigenous people (Jung 2008) to become more tolerant of "difference" and give up their attachment to "ethno-national homogeneity" (Yashar 2005). In this chapter and the next, I critically rethink this argument and question whether indeed the move towards greater recognition in liberal democracy necessarily signals a process of democratization.

Many scholars have been critical of aspects of the supposed democratization underlying the rise of indigenism. They have made similar observations on the complicated and even problematic relationship between indigenous difference and the state as I have in part 2 of this book. The legal determinations of indigeneity and their distance from the everyday lives of many Adivasis that I noted find echoes in Elisabeth Povinelli's (2002) critical description of how "recognition" of aboriginal communities by the Australian state happens on the latter's terms—she argues that the "cunning of recognition" lies in inviting new, sometimes even more all-pervasive forms of oppression.

The importance of local interpretations of indigeneity, which I also discussed, is likewise stressed by Anna Tsing (2007), who argues that the particular history of the nation-state is still more important in defining political trajectories of indigenism than are the new technologies through which indigenous movements become part of a transnational scene. Beth Conklin (2002) has provided some of the most explicit analyses of how indigenous activists try to strategically deploy dominant images of indigeneity yet thereby also tend to invite difficult contradictions and liabilities. Thus there have certainly been scholars who have given a critical interpretation of the kind of democratization that may have produced the rise of indigenism. Yet when analyzing the historical trajectory producing new indigenous movements, both those more optimistic about the possibilities offered by liberal democracy as well as those who have raised critical sidenotes, tend to remain within the liberal paradigm. They have ignored the possibility that the rise of indigenism may have been caused not so much by the democratizing pressure put on states by the international indigenous movement but, on the contrary, by how a previous global cycle of democratization became locked in the state and thereby started obstructing earlier avenues of popular protest that indigenous people had been using—the possibility, in other words, that indigenism may be a symptom of states becoming in fact *less* sensitive to democratic pressure.

In Kerala, many reasons combine to raise critical questions on interpreting the rise of indigenism according to the liberal framework as a process of democratization: the prominence of a state-determined common sense about indigeneity, the weakness of transnational social movement influences, the perils that the strategic use of indigeneity discourses invite. Here we may then all the more place the causal emphasis for the rise of indigenism elsewhere than in democratization. I seek to do so by addressing more explicitly the question of why indigenous people did not mobilize along existing political platforms. For if, despite all pitfalls and limits, indigenism were the only possible program around with which to rally for land rights and to challenge poverty and marginalization, its emergence would have to be a sign of democratization. Yet if most contemporary indigenist activists in Kerala started their political biography in Communist groups that claimed land reform and the emancipation of the "toiling masses" as their priorities, and if the Communist Party historically—and still—receives the majority of Scheduled Tribe and Scheduled Caste votes for this very reason (Thachil 2008), then the question we should be asking is why people in Kerala became attracted to indigenism rather than Communism. By asking this question and focusing on the political interactions of indigenous movements with the state, particularly in relationship to their main political rivals, a different perspective emerges—one that sees the rise of indigenism as caused more likely by the crisis of liberal democracy than by its forwards march toward a "completion of the process of decolonization" (Niezen 2003: 194).

Whereas the next chapter looks in more specific detail at the political dynamics between indigenist and Communist activists that further contributed to the distinct political form that indigenism took, in this chapter I set out to analyze the rise of indigenism through different activist biographies.[1] These demonstrate the lived process of how contention against electoral Communism gradually, out of combined practical and ideological disillusion, turned away from class and towards a critique articulated more in terms of culture and caste. The historical trajectory of the rise of indigenism against the background of the declining appeal of the original Communist movement is hence traced through the biographies of five exemplary Malayalee activists: P. K. Kalan (life-long Adivasi Communist Party member), Ayinoor Vasu (lower-caste Naxalite turned indigenist supporter), M. Geethanandan (ex-Nalite Dalit turned indigenist), C. K. Janu (practical Adivasi Communist turned indigenist), and Soman (committed Dalit Communist turned indigenist).

## The Naxal Challenge: Mobilizing the Margins

To be able to situate each biographical story, it is useful to consider the general three-fold periodization that most scholars agree on regarding the recent history of Kerala according to the vicissitudes of the Communist movement. The first period in this scheme starts in the 1930s and ends in 1957 with the coming to power of the Communist Party in Kerala. This period is characterized by the convergence of three types of social movements under the leadership of the Communist Party: the community reform movements that were particularly active in the southern Princely States of Travancore and Cochin, where they were mobilizing to compete for modern social status and demand greater participation in public administration (Mathew 1989); the (Muslim-majority) peasant movements against the squeeze on their livelihoods by the colonial state and (upper-caste Hindu) landlords that dominated the northern Malabar region under direct British rule (Herring 2008; Menon 1994; Panikkar 1992); and the movement for Indian independence and Malayalee nationhood, initially under Congress leadership, which created an overarching framework bridging these regional movements. The coming together of all these struggles into one coherent Communist movement led this period to be characterized by what Dilip Menon (2005: 308ff.) describes as "euphoric visions of a new order and a rampant rejection of past hierarchies." This found expression in the "participatory organizing" (Williams 2008: 36) of the proletariat and the peasantry into militant entities and in utopian popular songs, literature, and films.

The second phase, from 1957 to about the mid-1970s, was characterized according to Menon (2005) by the move to "electoral communism"—what the radical Left called the degeneration into "parliamentary cretinism"[2]—and the disciplining of cadres. It was a period of "organized class struggle" (Heller 1999: 13) or "protest politics" (Williams 2008: 36), which, as we will see in the second part of this chapter, is characterized alternatively as leading to the successful implementation of redistributive policies such as land reform and social welfare (as the Communist Party claims) or, as many indigenists now claim, as causing issues of caste inequality to be brushed aside "as a largely upper-caste leadership assumed power and defined regional culture in its own terms" (Menon 2005: 310). The third phase, then, started in the mid-1970s. Just as the United Nations published its 1975 report praising Kerala as a model development state, the state also started to see declining class militancy. This decline was optimistically dubbed a "class compromise" by Patrick Heller (1999: 117), who saw it as the outcome of the "institutionalization of conflict" through which the CPI(M) had secured labor's claim to the social surplus. Michelle Williams (2008), likewise reinforcing the optimistic efforts of the CPI(M), describes this phase, in which the CPI(M) tried to counter economic stagnation through decentralized politics anchored in civil society, as a shift "from hegemonic to counter-hegemonic generative politics" (35). As we will see, however, activists in Kerala have a less optimistic reading of political trends in this period and instead notice a growing complicity of Communism with existing relations of power. Whereas the biographies in the first part of this chapter throw light particularly on the transition from the first to the second phase, those in the second part of this chapter better describe the shift from the second to the third.

Regarding the first transition, from "euphoric" Communism to electoral Communism—and the Naxal challenge that emerged in the process—the most well-informed, sympathetic, yet critical insider's account is probably K. Damodaran's as told to Tariq Ali (1985). Damodaran was one of the early leaders of the Communist Party and remained a Communist (with the CPI) till his death in 1977. In the interview with Tariq Ali, he talks critically about the Stalinist line that Malayalee Communists defended in the 1930s and 1940s and about how they identified themselves completely with the Soviet Union.[3] He also describes how by following the dictates from Moscow, the party in its early phase stumbled from one blunder to the next. He argues that the strength of the Communist movement clearly lay in its grassroots, union-based organizing since despite the many tactical mistakes of the Communist leadership, the party kept a significant following. In 1948, the party leadership even adopted the notorious "ultra-left" Ranadive theses, which stated that the newly independent, Nehru government of India was to be overthrown since it represented "fake independence"—a highly unpopular opinion at the time and one that even many of the ultra-left Naxal leaders two decades later had difficulty in adopting (Banerjee 1984). Ironically, Damodaran (1985) points out, in practice the party was making an opposite turn: its decision in 1951 to participate in the General Election in order to replace the "anti-democratic and anti-popular Nehru government" by a "People's Democracy of Democratic Unity" in fact put it on "a course which can only be categorized as parliamentary cretinism" (355): "the word 'class' was replaced by the word 'party' and the word 'state' was replaced by the word 'government.'" According to Damodaran, it was already then that the party started to become more interested in acquiring parliamentary majorities and in collecting allies to form governments than in class struggle.

Yet immediately after the first Kerala election, the turn to parliamentary politics still boosted the party. As Damodaran describes,

> Immediately after the victory the workers and poor peasants, in the main, were jubilant. They felt very deeply that the new government would satisfy their demands. There was a tremendous feeling of pride and strength in the working class. I remember hearing poor, illiterate workers telling policemen on the streets: 'Now you daren't attack us because our government is in power. Namboodiripad is our leader. We are ruling' (1985: 357).

Their joy, Damodaran says, increased as they saw how uncomfortable the victory was for landlords and capitalists and as the Communists made radical speeches in the weeks after the election, constantly emphasizing their support for the struggle of the workers. What the Communists in power soon discovered, however, was the limits of effecting changes within India's federal setup, where civil servants receive their orders from the central government rather than from Kerala's chief minister. Workers in turn started to discover that many of the promises of the Communists were restricted to speeches. As Damodaran (1985: 359) says, "Nothing radically new happened and after a while the novelty of having a communist government began to wear off. In some cases jubilation turned to passivity and in others to open and bitter disillusionment."

Damodaran's own disgust with the reality of electoral Communism came soon after the election victory, when the police shot three workers participating in a trade union struggle against the owner of a factory in Quilon (now Kollam), led by the Revolutionary Socialist Party. Afraid to alienate the police and strengthen the anti-Communist campaign (the so-called Liberation Struggle) that was gaining momentum, instead of condemning the action, the Communist government decided to justify it and even made Damodaran travel to the spot to make a speech to that effect. As he recalls in conversation with Tariq Ali, "That night when I returned home I really felt sick inside" (1985: 361).

The 1964 split of the party into the smaller CPI and the more influential CPI(M), was another blow to the morale of many ordinary followers of the Communist Party. It was generally understood as the result of a disagreement over whether to, in line with the Soviet Union's agreement with Nehru, adopt the strategy of allying with progressive elements within the national bourgeoisie in a so-called National Democratic Front, or to instead wage an uninhibited campaign against Congress and in favor of a People's Democratic Front. The disagreement became intensified with the Sino-Soviet split in the early 1960s (Nossiter 1982: 179ff.). However, many Communist Party members I interviewed still looked back on the split of the party with pain and did not believe it was justified by any reason. Damodaran, who was intimately involved in debates within the party at the time argues that "the major reason for the split was internal differences related to the question of electoral alliances" (1985: 368). The leadership of the two camps, he argues, basically had a consensus on "parliamentary cretinism." The differences developed over the best tactic to win more seats: whether to break Congress by allying with other parties such as the Jan Sangh and the Muslim League—the strategy adopted by what became the CPI(M)—or whether to do so by aligning with progressive sections of Congress against its Right wing—the option advocated by what remained the CPI. According to Damodaran, who stayed with the CPI, the consequent popularity of the CPI(M) was due to the fact that it claimed it had split off from a "revisionist," "Rightist" CPI that was struggling not for revolution but electoral victories. In reality, however, Damodaran observes that the CPI(M) leadership was equally engaged in simply "trying to win elections" (1985: 369).

Under the influence of Chinese Communism, the early 1960s was also a period in which Communist Party members reached out farther into the rural areas, which later led to the rise of Naxalite factions splitting off from the party. It was hence during this period that the party first appeared in the lives of many Adivasi workers in the more remote rural areas. In the famous play on Paniya slavery and liberation by K. J. Baby—*Nadugadhika* (1993)—the advent of Communism in the region is parodied in a manner that has become increasingly common among non- or ex-party members. The landlord of the Paniya workers in question makes several appearances on stage, every time dressed in whatever happens to be the most convenient political outfit at the time: Congress flags at the time of Independence, then red flags and empty Communist slogans as soon as the party appears as the more influential political patron that may help him maintain his dominance over the workers. Not all Adivasi workers, however, agree with this perspective. As we will see in the following sketch of the life of P. K. Kalan, C. K. Janu's uncle and a follower of the Communist Party all his life, there were Adivasi workers like him who genuinely appreciated the party as a progressive force. The following biographical portrayal of his engagement with Communism is based on an interview I had with him in the spring of 2006 at his home in Thrissileri, in the late afternoon and evening of a day I spent at a CPI(M) rally organized in honor of Kalan's artistic achievements as president of the Kerala State Folklore Academy. My interview is supplemented with transcribed excerpts of an interview by anthropologists D. D. Namboothiri and Vinod Krishnan with Kalan in May 2005. About a year after I interviewed Kalan, on 17 November 2007, he passed away, having reached over 70 years of age.

### *Kalan: "People Became Human Beings with Communism"*

P. K. Kalan was born around 1930[4] in Thrissileri in Wayanad as the eleventh child of an Adiya family. His parents worked the fields of whatever local landlord they were attached to that year: there was still the practice then of workers being exchanged among landlords, as if they were their property, at the annual festival of Valliyoorkavu.[5] During his youth, Kalan moved to Coorg[6] in Karnataka several times. He told me, "Probably some landlord in Coorg bought my parents. That was how things were then. We were sold and bought!"

Kalan remembers his parents working from early morning to late evening, only for his father to often return to the fields again at night to guard the crops against wild animals. The children meanwhile would be sent into the forest to graze the landlord's cattle. Just how hard this enslaved life was can be glimpsed from the fact that of Kalan's ten siblings, only one, his elder sister, survived childhood. Kalan also fell gravely ill once when he was still very young. The fact that he recovered was interpreted by the elders as a miraculous omen.

When Kalan reached his teens, the Tamil landlord his parents were working for at the time assigned him to look after the family's children. This allowed him to learn Tamil on top of his already existing command of Adiya, Malayalam, Coorgi, and Kannada. Because of a Malayalam textbook one of the landlords gave him, he was able to gradually teach himself to read, practicing his skills on any scrap of paper or poster he could find. His ambitions soon extended to becoming *moopan* (headman), though initially his critical attitude towards some of the traditional practices of his community brought him in confrontation with the elders. As Kalan explained to me, there used to exist all kinds of "untouchability practices" between Adiyas, Paniyas, Kurumas, and others in the area—intermarriage used to be frowned upon. Kalan was against such practices "separating human beings" and over time the elders started accepting his ideas and seeing him as a reformer. He was made assistant to the moopan and eventually, after a lot of training, became the moopan of his community.

When the Communist Party started making inroads into the area in the course of the 1960s, Kalan had already achieved a position of leadership in his community. It was thus under his leadership that the community started becoming involved in the party. Kalan explained his attraction to Communism to Namboothiri and Vinodkrishnan (2005):

> We never knew before what communism meant for us. We only knew that they were working for a society in which there would be no rich and poor. We were told about a country called Russia where there were no poor and rich, where everybody is well fed and where every child attended school. The Communists told us that soon it is going to be a similar system in Wayanad too. Impressed by the stories I heard about Russia I was turning a Communist. I attended party classes regularly and soon I was becoming an active worker of the peasant movement led by the Communist Party. Through me the idea of a possible classless society was reaching my community members too. Every member of my community was becoming a communist.

Indeed, as Kalan told me, "People here became human beings with the advent of communism. Communism turned man into a human being."

To my initial surprise, in contrast to younger Adivasi workers such as C. K. Janu, who never consciously experienced the system of slavery that existed in Wayanad until the 1960s, Kalan, who in his younger years did experience the system himself, was much more inclined to be forgiving or even affectionate about his former landlords. Unlike generations after him, he considers landlords' involvement in the Communist Party not a sign of hypocrisy but rather a sign of their good intentions. He appreciated the fact that the Communist Party included both workers like himself and their landlords, as it was precisely this that allowed the party to achieve a stunning accomplishment: "to end the system of bonded labor without any atrocities committed on us [in retaliation]!"

An excerpt from Namboothiri and Vinodkrishnan's (2005) interview with Kalan emphasizes this point:

> Under the banner of the KSKTU [the CPI(M)'s Kerala State Agricultural Workers Union] we led victorious struggles against the local landlords, including my own. It was our struggle that led to better wages for the Adivasi agricultural workers in Wayanad. I was in the forefront. The struggle led by us against the local landlords never turned violent. Both sides—the landlords as well as the agricultural workers—were refraining from any possible violent turn to the struggles. Probably due to this, even after the long struggles, the agricultural workers and the landlords were having a friendly disposition. Often the landlords sought our help when new settlers occupied the land. Many years later when I was elected as the representative of the District Council as a Communist Party member, the same landlord against whom we led a series of struggles in the sixties congratulated me by hugging me tight! It was one of the most touching moments I experienced in my life. Former landlords and we have changed a lot!

Compared to other activists, Kalan was also remarkably disinclined to emphasize the differences between movements on the Left—between the Communist parties, between parliamentary Communists and the Naxals, and even between Communists and the AGMS. The red line through his actions was a flexible combination of loyalty to the Communist Party and to what he called "my people" together with a practical strategy of avoiding violence. He even admitted to having compromised with Congress during the Emergency period (1975–77). During this period the government combined a policy of suspending civil rights and harassing (and often disappearing) Leftist activists, including Communists, with a grand twenty-point *Garibi Hatao* (Eradicate Poverty) campaign, including the promise of effectively abolishing bonded labor, implementing land reform laws, and providing housing for the "economically weaker sections." Kalan narrated his decision to Namboothiri and Vinodkrishnan (2005):

> Without the consent of the Party, I shared platforms with local pro-government[7] sympathizers. It was not very comfortable for me … but I had reasons to cooperate with them. It had much to do with a historic decision, the decision to abolish bonded labor, made by the Congress Party with regard to Adivasi communities in India. The decision had deep personal overtones to me. My community were slaves to local landlords for centuries. Almost all of my community members had tormenting memories of the things they had actually experienced. I too had similar memories. I moved from household to household telling my people about the consequence of the decision of the government to abolish slavery. I even shared the stage with state leaders of the Congress party glorifying the government decision. I never bothered how the Communist Party reacted to my association with the ruling party. My conscience was clear. Perhaps because of this, the party never took any disciplinary action against me. The party might have thought that I was practicing a clandestine political activity. Perhaps I was. Sharing platforms with people preaching views inimical to mine was a painful experience. But it provided some support for my community. An urgent decision was made by the then state government to allot 32 houses for my people in my village. I should add this too. These [housing] benefits however had no way altered the political priorities of my people or me. We all remained strong supporters of the Communist Party (Marxist).

Throughout my interviews with Kalan, he showed sympathy towards Naxal and indigenist movements, yet stressed that in his view—and because of his personal circumstances—the Communist Party's approach of avoiding violence was preferable over the Naxal attacks and the confrontational approach of the AGMS, both of which have invited police repression. Kalan recounted his early experience with the Naxals:

> The conflict we had with the landlords was moving in a new direction in the late sixties. Dissent was emerging in the local leadership of the KSKTU [the Communist agricultural workers' union] but we knew little of the rise of a more revolutionary group within the union. For us the young party cadres working with us were just party comrades who wanted to lead a more militant struggle. They insisted on us joining them. Some of my community members joined the radicals. I was not aware at the time that these young radicals were sympathizers of the "Naxalites." For me they were just comrades of the KSKTU.

It was only when he realized that they were in favor of a violent struggle against the state that Kalan became apprehensive:

> I had reservations about the means they [the Naxals] opted for, but still I was sympathetic to them. Their leader, Varghese, who later was killed by the po-

> lice in a fake encounter, came to my house a number of times, requesting me to take an active role in the "Naxalite" movement in Wayanad. I had genuine sympathy for the leader and for the group of young cadres he was leading. I would definitely have joined them, but for my mother. She was seriously ill and she was insisting on my presence near her always. I had to keep my commitments. (Namboothiri and Vinodkrishnan 2005)

Others in Kalan's community, however, did join the Naxals and even targeted the local landlord at some point. In connection to this, the police took Kalan in for questioning but let him go when they became convinced of his innocence. As Kalan told me, "Many who had sympathy for them [the Naxals] remained with the parent organization [the CPI(M)]. I did too. I became fully involved in the party. After all, it was this party that gave me my political awareness."

Kalan says his reasoning in this also drew on the lessons provided—in CPI(M) networks—by the experience of the Communist Party in Andhra Pradesh. There Communist militants led the Telengana uprising between 1948 and 1951 only to provoke brutal suppression by the Indian army and eventual political annihilation of the party in the state. Kalan repeated a conspiracy theory I had heard from many CPI(M) members, that the violence promoted by the Naxals, which was used by the state as an excuse to repress Communist parties in general, may well have been "fostered by the imperialist powers to destroy Communism in India."

When it came to Janu, Kalan never condemned her in my interview with him and instead proudly told me, "It was for the first time a woman from our community rose up like that. It was the Communist Party who brought her up. She grew with us. Her father participated in our struggles for wages. She was still small then. When she grew up she came with us to the party and started working in it. She was talented. Had no formal education but still, when she participated in struggles, she grew aware of things. She grew with the party."

About the AGMS and the Muthanga struggle, Kalan stressed it was "foreign" infiltrations in combination with a "betrayal" by Congress that caused the violence at Muthanga. He downplayed the differences existing at the time between the Communist Party and the AGMS, and instead emphasized how the former came to the rescue of the AGMS activists when they were in jail:

> I discussed this [the formation of a separate movement] early on with Janu. I told her, "We will not be able to control the organization; others will come in between. We need to build it up gradually, locally, with help of the party—involving foreign countries is dangerous." They didn't listen and formed an organization. The struggle happened. I'm not saying it was wrong. Struggle is

> needed. But there were some mistakes. Though it was not wrong. But it ended up hurting human beings and finally it was we [the Communist Party] who protested it. When they were arrested we went to Trivandrum, conducted a strike at the secretariat.

Kalan, unlike the activists whose story I present next, remained a loyal party member all his life, which seems at least partly related to the practical and tactical flexibility with which he managed to connect his Communism with the needs and aspirations of his Adiya community and his leadership position in it. The most explicit way in which he managed this was perhaps in his role as a Gadhika performer ("tribal folk artist," as newspapers call it) and president of the Kerala State Folklore Academy. Kalan used his Gadhika performances, expressive recitals that as a moopan he had become expert in, to introduce his community to Communist ideas while at the same time celebrating a typical Adiya art form. Kalan also never got into any personal conflict with the Communist Party. He was highly successful in terms of becoming the first Adiya president of an entire block *panchayat* when in 1990 the party fielded him as a candidate in the local elections in Mananthavady. Yet, while gaining a lot of recognition from the party and beyond in his role as *panchayat* president, Kalan, unlike some of the other activists I will discuss shortly, never got involved in fights over how *panchayat* money would be spent. Having grown up owning absolutely nothing and having come to appreciate this as a supposedly Communist ideal, Kalan's material ambitions were minimal—his home, where we conducted the interview, was no more than an ordinary *kutcha* house with mud walls. When other *panchayat* members reasoned that Kalan was to have a proper cement (*pukka*) house as *panchayat* president and decided to award him fifty thousand rupees to that effect, Kalan rejected it: "I was comfortable with my humble dwelling that had no proper wall or roof. Communists cannot afford luxuries. I prefer dying as a Communist in this hut without the burden of any luxuries over me."

* * *

Kalan's story is typical of those Adivasi and Dalit workers in Kerala's more peripheral regions who became actively involved in the Communist movement when it arrived on the scene there in the course of the 1960s. For such communities in the coastal, semi-urban areas of Kerala, where the Communist movement had been actively organizing already since the 1940s, increasing disillusion marked the late 1950s and 1960s instead. Many continued with the party because they hoped to be able to push it in a different direction, because their livelihood and status had come to depend on it, or because they held too dearly to the image of it as it used to be and the sacrifices people had made in the party's name. Yet there were also those who became inspired by the Naxalbari rising to reject "working within the system" and to part with the parliamentary-oriented Communist parties altogether. This early (late 1960s, early 1970s) Naxalite movement took its inspiration from the uprising of May 1967 in Naxalbari (in West Bengal), which grew out of the local organizing of "tribal" and other workers by the CPI(M). It was only during this struggle that the revolutionaries broke with the CPI(M) to form the CPI(ML), which eventually came under the leadership of Charu Mazumdar. According to the CPI(ML)'s most important chronicler and critical sympathizer, Sumanta Banerjee (1984: iii), the CPI(ML) was an outgrowth of a tradition of Indian peasant revolts and, in its rediscovery of the revolutionary potentialities of the peasantry, "posed a challenge to the ideological sclerosis of the parliamentary Left in India, which had settled down to the efficient management of the status quo by participating in a few provincial governments."

By autumn 1967, the Naxalbari revolt had encouraged many erstwhile Communist Party members to condemn the party for its "illusory" practice of capturing state power rather than "smashing the state machine." The so-called Indian Revolutionaries, guided by the thought of Mao Tsetung, set out to create "liberated zones" and confront the state, rather than capitalism, as their primary enemy (Banerjee 1984: 98)—a tendency that would continue with the later New Left movements. Although the CPI(ML) grew out of the parliamentary Communist parties, the violent repression of the Naxalbari revolt by the CPI(M) government in West Bengal—partly out of fear on the part of the CPI(M) that Naxalbari would otherwise provoke the Center to intervene—hardened the split into one of outright hostility.[8]

Kerala was to be the first place outside of West Bengal where Naxalism, the revolt against "establishment Marxism" (Ajitha 2008) gained a following, even though a relatively small one of only about a hundred or so men—and the odd woman, most famously Ajitha, the daughter of the main ideologue of the movement (see Ajitha 1990, 2008). According to T. J. Nossiter (1982: 359f.), the small number of Naxalites in Kerala was related to the relatively small number of "tribals" in the state, the success of Communist reforms in creating at least some minimal securities for the rural poor, the "provincial" character even of college campuses in Kerala, but also the "rurban" settlement pattern (the blurring of the distinction between urban and rural areas) and traditional social controls of Kerala that make it virtually a "policemen's paradise" (ibid.: 361). Yet a small group did emerge in the late 1960s around Kunnikkal Narayanan, formerly a secondary leader of the CPI(M) who got into contact with Communist radicals in West Bengal and later, back in Kerala, started translating Mao's works into Malayalam and organizing reading groups. Of this group, Areekkal Varghese, a young man from a poor Christian family that had migrated from Idukki to Wayanad in the post–World War II migration waves, was to become the most revered revolutionary. He was shot in February 1970 in what later[9] was confirmed to be a staged "encounter." Before Achutha Menon, senior CPI leader and chief minister (in coalition with Congress) at the time, gave the order to round up the Naxalite movement—leading within months to its demise—the group had organized a number of successful attacks on police stations and notorious landlords. Ayinoor Vasu, the activist whose life I turn to here, participated in one of these attacks. As we will see, his life, having joined the Communist Party in the 1940s when it was already strong in his native town of Kozhikode, exemplifies a rather different experience with the party than that of Kalan. Together with fellow anthropologist K. C. Bindu, I interviewed him on a long rainy afternoon in his home in Kozhikode in August 2009.

### *Vasu: "Even the CPI(ML) Became Saturated with Upper-Caste Tendencies!"*

Ayinoor Vasu grew up in the northern coastal city of Kozhikode (Calicut under the British), born in 1930 to the ancestral home of an Izhava (lower-caste) working-class family. At the age of fifteen he had completed his fifth standard in school and started working at a factory near his home town: the Commonwealth Trust Weaving Factory, one of the first textile factories in Kerala, set up by the famous Basel Evangelical Mission in 1874. Though Vasu only ever attained the first year of upper primary school, his informal education is vast as he made extensive use of the system of public village libraries, public lectures, and political theatre plays that were part of the early Communist movement. "My university was this local library," he recalls; "This whole area owes so much to that library." Already at the age of twelve, he was introduced to the "scientific socialism" of Krishna Pillai, an early Communist leader (who never lived to experience the electoral turn of his party since he died in 1948 of a snake bite; see Krishnan 1971). Though Vasu's father used to be with Congress, Vasu grew up in a time when all radical activists once in Congress had now joined the Communist Party. In 1947, Vasu became a for-

**Figure 3.1** Vasu at his home

mal member of the (then still undivided) Communist Party, active in organizing the weaving workers of his area. With a certain nostalgia Vasu remembers the early days of the Communist movement:

> Comrade Krishna Pillai, the father of the Communist movement in Kerala, he was forming unions in our factory in Calicut. It was the proletariat, organized in unions, who actually formed the Communist movement then. Petty bourgeois intellectuals and white-collar workers used to consider them *chetta* [lower-caste ruffians]. They were the people who had been formed by the library movement. The factory unions were the bases of the Communist movement and Krishna Pillai himself was a coir worker in Alleppey. It was a Communist Party by the proletariat itself—sure with some upper-caste elements—but with workers at the base. These days they [the CPI(M)] claim the credit for this party but it's a totally different party.

When the party split in 1964, Vasu identified with the CPI(M) but soon became more inspired by Mao's thought, made clandestinely available by Kunnikkal Narayanan. Heeding Mao's call to move to organize the countryside, Vasu went to Wayanad in the late 1960s to help fight against bonded labor and mobilize the tribal workers of the area. At first, they fought to increase the amount of paddy (rice) paid to the workers; later, under a lot of resistance from landlords fearing the end of the bonded labor system, they went further and pushed for wages to be paid in cash. Vasu recalls what he experienced in Wayanad at the time: "Adivasis were really living under the torture of the landlord's *goondas* [henchmen] at the time. If they resisted at all, they were murdered. There were many such incidents. Comrade Varghese told me how in Thrissileri there was this Brahmin who had murdered one of his workers and then tied up the body, pretending it was suicide ... the police would do nothing."

In 1967, there was the first ever *gherao*-ing (encircling) of a landlord in Wayanad as part of Varghese's work, then still under the CPI(M)'s banner: the landlord's family was trapped in their house as workers stood outside demanding a greater measure of rice to be paid to them. By the end of 1967, the CPI(ML) was formed, and by 1969 Vasu finally got to meet comrade Varghese, who was ten years younger than him and was already working underground at the time. As Vasu recalls, it was mostly the bonded laborers living around Varghese's base in Thirunelli who were part of the Naxal movement then, and most of them were Adiya (C. K. Janu's "tribe") though there was also at least one Kurichiya (more "forward" ST community) among them.

To Vasu, the CPI(ML) made sense since the CPI(M) seemed entirely unaware of whom the most oppressed in society were:

> They were always concentrating on urban workers, working directly with Marx's interpretation without adapting it to the conditions in Asia. The Chinese Communist Party had some idea, because Mao himself had been working in rural areas in the 1920s. He wrote that you had to concentrate on the rural areas and capture the cities by surrounding them from the countryside. But the Indian Communist Party really lacked any such insights. They always had in mind that the factory workers in places like Bombay were the ones to be organized. Even in Kerala, it was cities like Allepey, Calicut, Kannur, where coir workers and all were being organized—never the rural areas. It was a mistake.

What was an ideological mistake however took on a vicious turn as CPI(M) members became involved in attacks on Naxalites. Vasu recalls an incident in Nilambur where CPI(M) members were seen with the landlord's *goondas* killing a CPI(ML) comrade, Chandy, while one of the party members held a red flag. Even Vasu himself was the target of CPI(M) attempts on his life and had to flee back to Calicut from Wayanad several times.

Unlike the CPI(ML) faction led by Kunnikkal Narayanan, Vasu did not, however, agree with the tactic of attacking police stations:

> Narayanan believed the main enemy was imperialism whereas the Naxalbari leaders believed it was feudalism. I believe Narayanan made a mistake there.

> Of course both are enemies but when we need to concentrate strategically on whom to attack? I still believe Narayanan was wrong then. He was not clear about it in his mind that what we experience here directly is a feudal system. And that caste is the main issue in India—class difference is expressed through caste here. It's the ideological basis of Indian feudalism and what makes it so oppressive and enduring. The Indian Communists never really discussed this issue of caste and its ideology, the Brahminical ideology.

To explain the relationship between class and caste, Vasu recalled the metaphor of ice and water: "Both are the same substance, ice is solid and frozen whereas water is fluid, it can move—caste is like ice, class is like water. This should be clearly understood by any Communist, but unfortunately few have understood it. Or even if they understood it, many leaders were upper-caste and so they would not act on it."

According to Vasu, land was the primary issue—and always had been in Kerala: "Even I remember making way for Brahmins on the road … the only way you existed earlier was through land and since the Brahmin owned the land, he was everything. It is this feudalism that is the main enemy we need to fight."

From this understanding, Vasu argued that the main strategy ought to be to organize people to claim land in defiance of the landlords—only then, when the police comes in, should they be prepared to counter that attack. Narayanan, in Vasu's view, had it all wrong in wanting to attack the police directly. Ironically, the first time Vasu was captured by the police, in 1969, was when he had traveled to Narayanan's faction to dissuade them from attacking the Kuttiyadi police station.

Vasu was acquitted from the Kuttiyadi attack but captured by the police again in 1970, this time for his participation in the Thirunelli action—the attack, led by Varghese, on several of the cruelest landlords in the area, two of whom were killed. Vasu was badly tortured by the police and spent seven and a half years in jail, mostly in solitary confinement. It was only he and Francis, the son of the Naxalite who had been murdered with CPI(M) compliance, who were put in solitary confinement for so long. Francis went mad and eventually died. Vasu only just avoided losing his mind entirely: "It was the books my brother brought me, when he was still alive, that prevented me from becoming insane. Still, my relatives remember how when I came out of jail I would be talking aloud to the moon … many comrades in jail went mad."

When finally released in 1977, Vasu settled down in Calicut again and made a living by running an umbrella and wood shop by day, helping to rebuild the CPI(ML) in the evening hours. Vasu, however, became disillusioned with the new CPI(ML) he encountered, which to his astonishment, had again become led by upper castes. "The CPI(ML) was supposed to be a proletarian party but while we were in jail, it had been filled with university graduates, upper castes. … I have nothing against upper castes but I do oppose Savarna [upper-caste] ideology and especially feudal ideology … and this is what happened, as with the CPI(M), even the CPI(ML) became saturated with these upper-caste tendencies!"

Seeing the new leadership reminded Vasu of what one of the police officers at the time had claimed: that he had personally planted his children among the Naxal leadership to destroy it. According to Vasu, two essential attributes of a real Communist Party had faded entirely from the CPI(ML): "Firstly, the question of leadership: it was no longer the proletariat. But secondly, there was the ideology. A good ideology should be sharp, as sharp as that of the enemy and good for practical usage. Ideology should not be just an ornament that is not being used; it should be a strong weapon. Ideology should not just be correct; it should be used!"

Looking back, he regrets not having read Ambedkar while in jail:

> That was a mistake. If I would have, I would have gotten a clear perspective and could have resisted the stealing of the leadership by the Savarnas that happened again with the CPI(ML). It is because at one point I was completely brainwashed by the CPI(M), portraying Ambedkar as a British agent. In fact Ambedkar did the class analysis, the work the CPI(M) should have done. What Mao did in China, Ambedkar had already done in India. Mao and Ambedkar diverge totally on solutions—Ambedkar imagines a bourgeois democratic government in the end—but in terms of their analysis they are very similar.

Having lost faith in the CPI(ML) as it was, Vasu left it in 1981 and became closer to a number of Ambedkarites. He also started reading Ambedkar, though his interpretations usually differed from those of Ambedkarites: "We talked often about the first volume of Ambedkar, *On the Annihilation of Caste*. … only a Marxist will understand that this is actually a class analysis of India."

Looking back, Vasu does think the original CPI(ML) was important in several respects: enforcing the implementation of the, until then, merely *proclaimed* end of slavery, ensuring Adivasi children started attending school rather than herding the cattle of upper castes, and making sure Adivasi workers were paid in money and that Adivasi women working in upper-caste households got paid as well. Vasu also pointed to the land reforms implemented:

> There was a time, in the late fifties when the Communists were not yet paper tigers. When they were raising precisely the issue of land reforms and landlords saw to it that the government fell. Until the 1970s, there was no way of implementing the land reforms in many places. Only when the Naxals came was land reform implemented, when the landlords were too afraid to open their mouths, when they were given the choice: your head or your land. They beat us with one hand, certainly, but with the other they gave in to at least 10 percent of our demands. It was like a stone against a mountain, it was always clear the Naxalite movement would fail … yet some things it achieved.

Still committed to class struggle, after leaving the CPI(ML) Vasu became particularly involved with the ongoing struggles of workers for better wages and more secure employment at a notoriously exploitative and environmentally polluting rayon fiber factory, owned by one of India's wealthiest capitalist families, the Birlas, at Mavoor (near Kozhikode). In reaction to the fact that all the major trade unions (the CPI[M]'s CITU, the CPI's AITUC, and Congress's INTUC) were colluding with management (see Mohan and Raman 1988), in 1983 Vasu became one of the chief initiators of a new, independent workers' union, the Gwalior Rayons Organization of Workers (GROW). In 1987, after the management had shut down the factory in reaction to workers' demands, Vasu once more found himself in direct collision with the CPI(M). For during GROW's earlier struggles, under a Congress-led government, the CPI(M) had sworn to have the factory reopened as soon as it won the elections. In 1987, when the CPI(M) did win, it however backtracked, first denying such promises at all and then arguing that the party was legally "helpless" to take action. In protest, Vasu and the other GROW leaders held many hunger strikes, accompanied by workers' demonstrations, hoping to at least secure retrenchment payment for the workers. Yet in an environment where capital was only happy to find an excuse to leave Kerala, the struggle could not come to a real success.

Thus, when Janu started organizing Adivasis in the 1990s, Vasu found a much-needed new source of inspiration: "I noticed Janu for the first time when she came to Calicut with seventy Adivasi women to hold a demonstration. … I could not believe it!" Vasu explains his surprise at the militancy of the women, remembering the Adivasis who were his comrades in the late 1960s as much more timid:

> I remember how Adivasi men used to behave: in the Thirunelli-Thrissileri action, we were just getting ready to go … we took a kind of "last supper." … we didn't know who would live and who would die. … it was in one of these Adiya's houses, some ten or twelve people were sitting around to eat. Two young Adivasi men were sitting on both sides of me. Varghese had made them sit

> next to me—at first they did not want to sit next to me. They felt threatened by me. … they were sitting next to me but slowly, slowly they moved towards each other and then towards Varghese because they were so nervous about sitting next to me.

His comrades were timid also during the actions against the landlords: "We were with a group of Adiya men and at some point there was some shooting … there were four men, and the very moment there was firing, two of them straight away ran off. … Now imagine this is the very same community from which a woman leader emerges and comes to Calicut to lead seventy women!"

When, in 1993, Janu was brought to the district jail in Calicut because of her participation in a land struggle, Vasu went to talk to her. It was then that he realized Janu's movement was in fact the fruition of the earlier Naxal movement: "I asked her first where she came from. 'Thrissileri,' she said! I said, 'There were eight Adivasis with me in jail, do you know them?' She said, 'A person called Kalan [not P. K. Kalan], my uncle was in jail.' I knew him!"

According to Vasu, "Janu herself does not know she is the ideological daughter of the Naxalite movement. Even now she doesn't know—she is brainwashed in some way as to not give credit to the Naxal movement." Yet Vasu envisions Janu's movement becoming part of a bigger movement: "There will come a time that people understand that their emancipation comes from Mao, and that time Janu will be part of that movement also—she will see the iron shield of feudalism and see that caste can only be broken by guns."

To Vasu's regret, Janu never had the chance to become self-educated like he did with the library movement:

> She lacks more of an ideological base for the struggle—she thinks you can solve the question of land through peaceful means, but it is not possible. The problems of landlessness will not be solved if some Adivasis get land. Janu may be sure that some people will actually get land and lead middle-class lives without too much struggle but 70 percent of India lives in poverty. … there's millionaires now but most of the people are in deeper poverty than under the British … and Adivasis are the worst off. And they are all caught in the agricultural sector. This oppression has been institutionalized by the state, but the most important culprit is the ideology of Brahminism. I am not sure Janu has this clearly in her mind.

According to Vasu, Janu runs the risk of repeating the mistakes of the early caste reform movements: "These movements were going for material progress only—but you cannot have material progress in the same social setup … you need to see social reform as changes in the mode of production." From this insight, Vasu has taken it upon himself to support Janu's struggle and hopes to lift it to a stronger ideological level. Vasu turned up in many of the stories of the Paniya workers whom I interviewed in Wayanad, who had stayed at his home after the Muthanga attack and mostly remember him, ironically mistaken, as the "CPM [CPI(M)] person who really cared for us!"[10] Through his interactions with Janu's movement, Vasu meanwhile is ever more convinced of the need for an interpretation of Marxism that focuses squarely on caste and finds its inspiration not in imported dogmas but rather in the vestiges of egalitarianism found in lower caste communities and especially in Adivasi communities. As he observes of his Adivasi comrades, "Even now there is this idea of sharing among them that you don't see among other communities. If a few make a lot of money, the whole group will not go for work that week and enjoy themselves. … among non-Adivasis you can have a starving person and a feasting person as neighbors. Among these Adivasis, that will be impossible."

## Post-Communist Challenges: Towards Culture and Caste

For many Leftists, the post-Naxal period, after the first and most militant wave of Naxalism had been brutally suppressed in the 1970s, "began in a mood of despair with the prospect of social transformation deferred yet again" (Menon 2005: 312). In reaction, the beginnings of what may be called the New Left in India started to appear: heterodox groupings that were still often influenced by Marxism yet were also critical of it and combined it with a variety of ideas from other ideological currents. The early 1970s, for instance, saw the rise of the influential Dalit Panthers in Mumbai, inspired by Marxism/Maoism on the one hand but also by the American Black Panthers movement and Ambedkarism (Menon and Nigam 2007: 114). In the late 1970s, again in Maharashtra (Ambedkar's home region), there also arose the Satyashodhak Communist Party, which fruitfully mixed Marxism with theories of early Dalit leaders such as Phule and Ambedkar (Omvedt 1993: 67), and whose leader, Sharad Patil, explicitly propagated Ambedkar's warning that no true socialist reform would be possible "unless you kill this monster [that is caste]" (Patil 2009). To a lesser degree, Naxal activity also continued during the 1970s, though it faced increasing repression, which became draconian with the declaration of Emergency rule in June 1975. During the Emergency, much of the radical Left moved towards New Left movements in Kerala, and particularly to the People's Science Movement (or KSSP), which adopted the slogan "science for social revolution" as its motto in the late 1970s (Nigam and Menon 2007: 116). After the Emergency had passed, and when by 1979 many of those imprisoned as Naxalites had finally been released from prison, a new cycle of Naxal organizing began, one that was more peaceable, yet all the more factionalized, and ideologically deeply troubled. This new Naxal movement, rather than being an outgrowth of the Communist Party itself, was in opposition to it from the start.

It is this wave of Naxalism that Geethanandan, the activist whose story I turn to now, joined. Geethanandan became a Naxalite only to leave Communism behind altogether a decade later and eventually become the principal leader, besides C. K. Janu, of the AGMS. His life exemplifies the trajectory that many such "ex-Naxalites" took—away from class and towards "cultural" politics. I interviewed Geethanandan on numerous occasions in 2005 and 2006, and I spent many days as part of his entourage. Unfortunately, I never got the chance to visit his home, prevented always by urgent politics he had to take care of: the court cases following Muthanga, municipal elections, and conflicts with the CPI(M) at Aralam farm. Despite not being able to meet Geethanandan at home to sit down for long afternoons to discuss his personal biography, I nevertheless had all the more chance to see him in action as an activist and learn of his political dilemmas.

### *Geethanandan: "I Have Totally Rejected Such Statist Political Systems"*

Geethanandan was born to a relatively well-to-do Dalit family in 1954 in Thayyil in the northern district of Kannur, a stronghold of the Communist Party in Malabar (Northern Kerala). During his college days in the early 1970s, while he was studying marine biology, he became attracted to the CPI(ML) that was then of growing influence on campuses around India. In 1979, he joined a Naxal faction led by K. Venu,[11] the CPI(ML) ideologue who had been imprisoned during Emergency for his involvement in an attack on a police station in Kozhikode. After college, and while involved in the CPI(ML), Geethanandan worked for years at the accountant general's office in Thiruvanathapuram in a stable but dull job. Within the CPI(ML), fierce debates were going on at the time on the caste question, and, still inspired by Maoism, there was a deepening dissatisfaction with Western versions of Marxism that ignored non-Western forms of oppression, particularly those of caste.

Geethanandan became particularly interested in the work of Engels and his discussion of the work by ethnographers such as Morgan on premodern, more egalitarian forms of social organization: "Engels read many anthropologists who were there at the time … he analyses this primitive setup where exploitation was not possible, it was like an original commune. There are places where this still remains." Through his understanding of the traditional tribal societies described by Engels, in combination with a rising critique within the CPI(ML) of the continuing Stalinist praxis of the CPI(M), Geethanandan gradually became convinced that not class struggle but the struggle against the centralized state ought to be the primary revolutionary aim. These thoughts were reinforced by the calls for reform that emerged with Gorbachev as general secretary of the Soviet Union, which had strong reverberations in India, including on the CPI(ML). Developments within the Soviet Union confirmed to the Indian revolutionaries that the country had indeed become "social imperialist," hardly any better than its American imperialist counterpoint. These debates led to yet another factional split of the CPI(ML) in 1987 and eventually, by 1991, differences of opinion on how to proceed on the "caste question" and a general malaise with Marxist theory had become so prevalent that K. Venu decided to disband his CPI(ML) faction altogether.

In line with his political conviction on the need to break caste and patriarchy through intercaste marriage, Geethanandan by this time had married a Nair (upper-caste) woman and left his job at the accountant general to become a full-time activist. He moved to Thrissur where he concentrated on organizing workers in the informal sector—a strategy that had been a core program of the early Communists and was, under pressure of the CPI(ML), being revived as a key strategy to further the emancipation of workers. However, the lack of attention to the problem of caste due to the dominance of Communist ideologies started to bother Geethandan all the more in this work. Often it was caste taboos and the desire on the part of those higher up in the caste hierarchy to avoid begetting the same formal status as those considered lower in the hierarchy that prevented any united effort at unionization. In an interview in 2007 in *Tehelka,*[12] Geethanandan claims this was the time when he became a Dalit activist: "The trade union activities in Thrissur made me a Dalit activist. The people I worked with were extremely poor Dalits. Their problems required a caste-based approach rather than a class-based one because the discrimination against them was mainly caste-based. The Left never had any satisfactory answer to caste-based problems."

After Venu's CPI(ML) faction was disbanded, Geethanandan had decided not to follow any Marxist grouping anymore and instead increasingly turned to an ideology based on Dalit and Adivasi culture—even though some activists in the Dalit networks still eyed him with suspicion as to what extent he really appreciated Ambedkar over Marx (as one Dalit activist confided to me, "Geethanandan's head is always with Engels"). Despite his grounding in Marxism, Geethanandan however makes it clear that he has "totally rejected such Communist movements because they are all centralized political systems." In line with—though having left—the CPI(ML)'s view of the state as the main enemy, Geethanandan explained to me that statist political systems "like the Brahminical state, or the caste structure ... this same thing is there within the Communist Party. Just like the capitalist state, whether it's a capitalist state, a Brahminical state, or a Marxist state, they're all statist orders, they all have this graded hierarchy and power structure. I wanted to negate that structure, I wanted to go another way."

Geethanandan, indeed relying on Engels' study of primitive society, saw the negation of the recurrent problem of hierarchy within any state structure in earlier social forms, and particularly "in our culture, the traditional Dalit-Adivasi culture." He became inspired by what he calls "our culture, not by any ideology, not by anything from outside." Thinkers such as Ambedkar and Ayyankali were not so much ideologues for him but representatives of this culture, their ideas rising organically from the more egalitarian social forms that live on in Dalit and Adivasi communities. As Geethanandan says, "it is not about intellectual work but about our own cultural ideas and cultural background. We had our own way of life, that is the ideology—nothing more than that. We can use our life, our culture, our land ... to deconstruct and reject the higher systems. Of course Renaissance leaders are there, Ambedkar is there, Ayyankali, tribal leaders also ... so many people. But you cannot say exactly who is the spokesperson, who is the intellectual, who created the ideas; it emerges from our culture."

Hence, though emerging from a very ideological political grouping and while being widely considered the strategic brains of the AGMS, Geethanandan gradually placed his faith ever more in what he considered the opposite of ideology, namely the egalitarian "culture" of the original, primitive society living on in the world's indigenous people: "Our cultural traits and our cultural heritage is scattered in different areas and different countries and we would like to assimilate all these things. Who created this, is there a particular intellectual who created this culture? No."

As many radicals growing up as part of Kerala's ideologically conscious but increasingly impotent Communist movements, Geethanandan even came to see the situation facing Adivasis and Dalits in Kerala as more problematic than in other states: "It's because of so many factors, this Communism, this modern education … we are very scattered here because of it in our culture and ways of life—more scattered than in other states."

Travelling to other states, Geethanandan claims the original culture he is inspired by is usually stronger there, leading towards more spontaneous, rather than "strategic," politics: "They won't be thinking in this particular, rational, eh, way … they will be reacting immediately, spontaneously. But here [in Kerala] we will be thinking about this or that ideological question, having such debates and … nothing, nothing. When things happen to our people in Kerala, we think immediately about the ideology. The ideology question … we debate and do nothing. But outside, in Tamil Nadu for instance, they react immediately … then only some ideological question may come [laughs]. … it is totally different."

Geethanandan's frustration with endless ideological debates, especially in a context where they seemed increasingly distant from political praxis, makes him eager to represent the AGMS as a movement simply acting on the basics, without any ideology and grand strategy: "This movement, our movement, it's just people who are fighting for the right to live. That's our concern. To live. To have a political front for the right to live. That's the idea. That's the only idea behind our politics and our actions."

* * *

If, in the 1970s, Communist ideology was still a living force in the radical milieu of the urban college campuses in Kerala where the second wave of Naxalism was born, those encountering Communism for the first time in the 1980s could easily mistake it for an obscure and flexible discourse allowing those claiming to stand on the side of the poor to prioritize a policy agenda of attracting business investment over defending whatever social gains had been made through class struggle by workers and peasants. The CPI(M) in the 1980s was a party in the midst of a growing existential crisis and the escalating factionalism of a reformist leadership versus an orthodox old guard. Neither faction, however, was willing to be open to the New Left. Instead, the 1980s, with the rise of the Bharatiya Janata Party (BJP), were characterized by a "vigilance" among the parliamentary Left for "divisive, communal and separatist" forces (Surjeet 1998: 177). Identity-based mobilizations—whether Hindutva or not at all—were inevitably seen as representing such communalism. Not always, moreover, did the CPI(M) leadership manage to remember there were greater class enemies than the few fragmented Naxal groups that were gradually succumbing to their own ideological dilemmas. In states where the parliamentary Left had but a marginal presence, local Communist units continued to participate in popular struggles, yet in West Bengal and Kerala "realism" reigned among the parliamentary Left, used to justify its "necessary" compromises with neoliberal rule in the creation of Special Economic Zones and the acceptance of financial loans conditional on cutting public services (Menon and Nigam 2007: 107; Steur 2009).

The 1980s were also when liberation theology started to spread through Christian networks in Kerala, taken up by the more radical, Leftist-inclined clergy who took it upon themselves to organize welfare projects to empower and "conscientize" the poor. Liberation theology reached the peak of its performance in support of the agitation of Kerala's fisherfolk[13] (another historically oppressed community in the state) from 1984 to 1988 but was not confined to the coastal areas. Also in Wayanad, liberation theology had a definite influence on the clergy. Many of them, after coming into conflict with the defenders of the status quo within the church networks, left the church altogether and instead embraced the new opportunities opening up in the 1980s to continue their activities by founding NGOs. This was, for instance, the trajectory of Jacob Lukose,[14] who in 1987 founded Hilda, the Highland Development Agency, in Sultan Bathery (Wayanad). It is also that of the founders of Solidarity, an NGO based in Mananthavady (Wayanad). As Kaliyodath Narayanan told me in an interview, Solidarity from 1982 on aimed to "educate, conscientize, and motivate" the poor and "mobilize their own power" with the help of Freirian pedagogical methods. From an initial focus on so-called backward classes, the tribal population increasingly became the target of both Hilda's and Solidarity's projects.

In the words of her uncle P. K. Kalan, the late 1980s was the time when Solidarity "captured" C.K. Janu, who went on to become the leader of the new Adivasi movement emerging in Kerala in the 1990s. I turn to her story now, composed from two long interviews I had with her at her home in Thrissileri, combined with stories about her youth that I borrow from a biography of Janu, *Mother Forest,* published in 2004 by the Malayalee social activist Bhaskaran. The latter, the text of which is entirely transcribed from taped conversation, is an invaluable source. Yet the text is also frustrating because the translator, Ravi Shankar introduced a number of stylistic oddities, including using what he calls "the simplest language possible," in the hope of staying close to what he believes is Janu's "inner world" (Shankar in Bhaskaran 2004: xii). I should warn that this style, in the few quotes I use from the book, should not make the reader mistake the wit and irony that characterizes Janu's speech (as I experienced it during my own interviews) for naïveté.[15]

### *Janu: "They Were Just Using People to Get Votes and Lengthen Their Processions"*

C. K. Janu was born in Thrissileri, in Wayanad, in exactly the period when radical Communists were organizing there in 1967–68. As written in Bhaskaran (2004) she recounts her first impressions of Varghese, the Naxal leader:

> When I was very young, I had heard adults talk about Verghese [*sic*. (Varghese)]. They used to talk in hushed tones. I have heard that Verghese used to be active in the Thirunelli area. Though our people had great respect for him it was also mixed with some amount of fear. I heard that Verghese had led agitations against *vallipani* [the system of bonded labor at the time]. … I have heard that people like Verghese worked against this. Still, because of interference by the police and the [Communist] *Party*, our people were frightened into not speaking openly about Verghese. … I have heard that Verghese paid a visit to a *jenmi* [landlord] in Thrissileri and forced him to measure out the grain without chaff. Verghese was a man without fear. The new migrants who appeared among us are also not afraid of anything—the tree, the land, the forest, anything. I have heard that Verghese was very close to the people in our community and was keen to understand the problems of our people directly. I heard that Verghese took the trouble to live in our huts to understand us better. Apart from this, I have heard that he objected to the *jenmi* measuring out wages in bamboo measures and forced him to use a liter measure.[16] For all these reasons our people had great respect for Verghese. There were people in our community who had worked closely with him. But I have never seen him. (36ff.)

Janu's mother and father, a *moopan* (chieftain) of the community, both worked for one of the big landlords of Thrissileri, a formidable figure who only showed himself in person one or two times a year, leaving the supervision of the work to middlemen. As Janu told me, she had always associated the party with the landlords in the area since party members would often visit them—"I assumed they too were with the party—and most of them were." After having worked at age eight to nine as a maid looking after the baby of a female teacher in a nearby town, Janu returned to work in the fields with

**Figure 3.2** C. K. Janu at her home

her mother, who collected her wages at the time since her father had remarried and was no longer supporting the family. Hunger was an everyday experience during this period: even in seasons when there was enough work, all they got was *kanji-vellam*, rice soup with more water (*vellam*) than rice, which had to be supplemented by digging for tubers in the forest. The fear of starvation was constantly in the back of people's minds. At the age of fifteen, when she was spending her days working the fields, Janu for the first time had the chance to attend one of the Communist Party's rallies in Kalpetta, Wayanad's capital. In the text recorded by Bhaskaran (2004), she describes how nobody went to work that day, excited by the prospect of a day out. They were taken to Kalpetta in a lorry flying a red flag, with a party worker shouting slogans that they repeated. At the meeting itself, songs played about workers toiling in the fields, about sickles and hammers, and wages. Of those experiences, Janu says she liked them though she had no idea at the time what the slogans and songs were really about. Unlike for elderly Adivasis and Dalits, for Janu the early and radical spirit of the Communist Party itself is a distant past she never personally experienced. Varghese's ideals of transforming relations of power in the countryside were not something Janu associated with Communism. Instead, Janu came to know Communism for its purely economic promises—she considered the party a tool to get higher wages.

As part of the many projects for tribal literacy emerging in the early 1980s, Janu's sister was taken to attend school in a nearby town and live in a tribal hostel. Janu herself, however, never went to school. When she was around sixteen, KANFED,[17] the Kerala Association for Nonformal Education and Development, started to organize literacy campaigns in the area and a girl from the same caste as the landlord, a Warrier,[18] sometimes came to give classes after work. To Janu's frustration—as she wanted to learn to read and write—the girl seemed to be more interested in being able to claim her allowance from the organization than in actually teaching. Nobody in fact learned anything through the project, and in a way this was logical since "after toiling the whole day in the slushy fields it was very difficult to light the lamp of Literacy. one[19] would just feel like gulping down something and curling up to sleep" (in Bhaskaran 2004: 23).

Janu's experiences with activists of the KSKTU, the CPI(M)'s agricultural union, coming to visit them—usually to take people from the area for party processions—were better. She recalls liking them at the time and trying to use the pamphlets brought back from party processions to practice reading. What really helped her to learn reading and writing, however, was the arrival of Solidarity activists who were genuinely committed to teaching. Janu remembers how Sibi, the man who taught her, used to behave as if he was one of them, not bothered by caste taboos: "he would partake of the *kanji* and *chakka* curry made in our hut" (in Bhaskaran 2004: 24). He would "tell us about our own starvation and the meagerness of our wages" (ibid.).[20] Enticed by his enthusiasm, Janu says she would practice writing on a slate until deep in the night. After a while she was confident enough to start teaching others and become a literacy worker herself.

As Janu became increasingly active in the KSKTU, she also started to regularly attend party meetings and classes and promoting what she learned to others. Doing so, she regularly traveled to other Adivasi communities and in the process learned more and more about the general problems they faced—problems she, at the time, still believed were to be tackled through the party. Looking back, Janu says the party was indeed instrumental in forcing employers to honor wages, yet in a rather predetermined manner. When an employer failed to pay up, the party would support agitations but postpone the settlement in favor of the employer and in order to give more publicity to the party. Eventually, some party leaders would then orchestrate a behind-the-scenes settlement that would make sure the workers got at least part of the wages they asked for. Another variation was when Adivasi workers would want to demand higher wages and the party would organize a strike and forbid them to go to work while the landlord, whether he was a Communist Party member or not, brought in laborers from elsewhere to do the work. Only after they had sung enough songs and chanted enough slogans, usually just around election time, would the party then step up and come to an agreement with the landlords in question—often themselves party members—and make sure there was a compromise. Janu recalls, "Agitations for one rupee increase in wages would be settled with a fifty paise increase," so that people were at least left with the feeling the party stood with them (in Bhaskaran 2004: 30).

Janu, however, felt increasingly uneasy about party classes. It seemed to her that issues of importance to her community—such as agricultural land or better living conditions—hardly ever found their way onto the agenda of party meetings. It seemed party members were doing their best to not let Adivasi workers speak, and to talk to them in a dense, incomprehensible language full of discursive "tricks." Janu also noticed evasion tactics: "Somehow, whenever we raised issues relating to us in the Party the Party men would say that they had to consult their upper committee. The Party would just evade the issue. I have seen E. M. S. [Namboodiripad]. He came for a Party class. In our area, the Party, the *jenmi* [landlord] and the estate owners had grown to merge into a single giant tree" (in Bhaskaran 2004: 35). As Janu emphasized to me in this respect, "To the party, our people were just voters to win elections, it never really cared about us."

The trigger for Janu's break with the Communist Party, as she told me, was the struggle over a piece of land near Thrissileri that Adiyas used as a burial ground. They did not have the official ownership papers to the land but considered it traditionally theirs. When farmers from elsewhere started settling on the land around it, Janu and others feared that soon they would have no land left to bury their dead. On top of this came the fact that the Forest Department had increasingly been restricting people from entering the forest to collect food or fire wood, while even the land that people had been using to cultivate subsistence crops around their huts was increasingly taken over by settlers with better connections to the municipality and ways of legally appropriating the land. Anger over this, combined with the prospect of seeing the land where their ancestors lay buried also become encroached by others, enticed them to build a fence around the burial ground to prevent others from taking it, and to cut a path to be able to reach the burial ground. At this, the farmer whose land the path crossed called in the police, who arrested the Adivasi men involved in the action. Since the women involved were still free, however, they marched to the police station demanding the right to their burial ground. Sixty women squatted in front of the police station, insisting they would not leave until their right to the land was confirmed. At that point, rather than supporting their claim, the Communist Party stood up on the side of the farmer: it turned out there was an election of the local cooperative bank forthcoming in which the farmer's vote would be crucial, so the party tried to settle the issue in favor of the farmer. Janu found herself directly in opposition to the party and decided not to compromise. Instead, she decided to leave the party for good.

After leaving the party in 1991, what Janu had considered benevolent gestures of goodwill of the party in her youth she increasingly started to see as just hypocritical and malevolent strategies. Reflecting on the burial ground and other such incidents, she came to find the party always standing on the side of "money and power": "To the Communist Party, workers and landless people like us were just the ingredients of their rallying songs, the ornaments for their slogans. When we were starving, some leaders would announce another free kilo of rice; that's all."

Reflecting on how Adivasis would figure in the party's ideology Janu told me, "The party is great at creating folk arts academies, writing research papers on how poor we are, how we beat the *thudi* [drum], on how we dress, what plants we take as medicines, all 'under threat of extinction.' … It was in the interest of the party to keep us starving and poor, so they could use us to fill their processions." She further explained, "I knew that from within the party I could never do something for my people in an honest manner. … Yes, I was a member of the party. But I resigned from it. Why didn't they form this AKS [the CPI(M)'s Adivasi wing set up in 2001] and try to get land that time itself? When we formed the Adivasi Gothra Maha Sabha, conducted struggles by occupying land, made some agreement, started getting land, *then* they formed the AKS for fear that people would leave the party. A party that was in power and lost power so many times over the years. … Otherwise they would not have done this."

Janu is explicit about the reason for the rise of the AGMS, namely the demise of the Communist alternative. As she told me, "If they had formed this AKS while I was in the [Communist] party, I would not have formed the Gothra Maha Sabha. At the time when I was in the party, had the Left movement formed an AKS and conducted struggles for land, I would have come as a leader of that struggle. I would not have formed the Gothra Sabha. I had to form the Gothra Sabha out of the bitter experience that they, at that time, were just using people to get votes and lengthen their processions. Otherwise I would not have formed the Gothra Maha Sabha."

* * *

In the 1990s and 2000s, after Janu had parted with the Communist Party, there would be others who had been with the party for longer whose loyalty to the party finally broke off as the gap between the ideals with which they joined the party and the reality of how the party operated started to become grotesque and, moreover, started to turn against those unwilling to embrace the changes. Initially, in the early 1990s, it had seemed for a while that the CPI(M) would be able to reinvigorate itself due to the People's Planning Campaign, launched as a novel experiment in decentralized, village-level planning (see Isaac and Franke 2002). The plan was greeted with optimism by many New Left movements that were critical of centralization and keen to move away from grand narratives towards concrete local projects. Yet it also increased factional fights between the orthodox old guard and new reformist leadership within the party (see Menon and Nigam 2007: 108). The whole decentralization campaign came to be seen in a less optimistic light moreover when it emerged that the main ideologue of the campaign, Thomas Isaac, had as finance minister negotiated a loan from the Asian Development Bank that was conditional on a retreat of the state from social welfare, presumably orchestrated through "decentralization" (ibid.). The increased importance of *panchayat*-level decision making on the distribution of funding increased the likelihood of even ordinary party cadres becoming entangled in—or appalled by—shady schemes to appropriate public funding at the local level. Indeed, the 1990s were also marked by unprecedented degrees of corruption at all levels—including high-ranking leaders of the Communist Party (Menon and Nigam 2007: 108ff.). Most notorious became the "Lavalin scandal" in which as minister of electricity in the CPI(M)-led government, Pinarayi Vijayan, who later even became state secretary of the CPI(M), brokered a shady deal: at an exorbitant cost he had a number of hydroelectric generators replaced by the Canadian company SNC Lavalin, despite having been advised by a government committee to consider alternatives.

It was these kinds of corrupt practices that were the final straw for Soman, the last activist whose trajectory I consider here.[21] From Kottayam—which, with Alleppey, was one of the heartlands of the early Communist movement—Soman had joined the party in the mid-sixties when he was only fourteen years old. It was more or less the same time when P. K. Kalan in Wayanad joined the party, but Soman did so at a younger age and in a region where the party had already been heavily consolidated. His experience with the Communist Party is thus more similar to that of Vasu. Yet it took longer for Soman than for Vasu to translate his disillusion into a turn away from the Communist Party since there was less Naxal influence in the region of Kottayam, where the strength of the mainstream Communist Party kept it at bay. The revolutionary difference the Communist movement made for his Dalit parents also led Soman to remain loyal to the party longer. I interviewed him on two occasions, in 2005 and 2006, while visiting him at his home in the Sachivothamapuram colony, famous for the Kurichy struggle that took place there and which formed a landmark in the emergence of Kerala's indigenist movement (see chapter 2).

### *Soman: "If You Are Good at Corruption, You Can Get Along with the Party"*

Soman was born in 1951 to a Pulaya family of agricultural workers in the vicinity of Kottayam. His parents were landless, hardly making ends meet by working the fields of one of the large landlords in

**Figure 3.3** Soman at his home

the area. It was a hard life, and as a wave of mobilizations swept the region in the late 1950s, after the first Communist government had tried to enact laws granting landless workers the right to the land around their dwellings (the *kudikidappu* land), Soman's parents too joined the struggle. Eventually it yielded them a piece of land in the Sachivothamapuram colony. The family moved there in 1962, and Soman still lives in that very colony in a small two-room house, the front porch of which is now adorned by a large poster of Ayyankali, the early Pulaya anticaste reformer. It was at the time of the struggle by his parents to receive a piece of land, when Soman was still only a child, that he first came into contact with the Communist Party. He recalled, "When I was a kid, I saw the police beat up my father, in front of my mom. There were many policemen. In revenge I joined the Communist Party. I was not theoretically aware of things yet then. They took him to jail that day, and released him two days later. I had been sleeping close to my father the day when the police came to catch him. He did nothing wrong, just participated in the struggle for land."

The police brutality had been traumatizing for him as a young kid, Soman said. Not only had his father been badly beaten up, the police had also destroyed the family's few belongings, leaving them with not even a pot to cook in or anything to eat. In this context, he still vividly remembers the support his family got from Communist Party members when his father was jailed: "Those times no food was provided in the jail. So we were to take food to them. Ramachandran Pillai came here to carry the food for them. Those times nobody was ready to do that. That was the political situation that existed then. The Communist Party longed for a change. They visualized a nation like Russia, where nothing called inequality exists." The early Communist leader A. K. Gopalan also mentored Soman personally and made a strong impression: "If you worked with him you would understand, he never treated you as an inferior worker."

Looking back, Soman believes it was the way that Communist Party members had supported his family in their distress that made him loyal to the party for so long. On the other hand, he also believes that Marxism as a theory strengthened his commitment: "There are many political parties in India but none of them analyzes issues as closely as the Marxist party does, especially the CPM [CPI(M)]. They would analyze all the political developments, all over India. … Almost all of the big leaders taught me. There was one brilliant leader in the party, S. Ramachandran Pillai. He was an amazing teacher. And none can surpass P. Govinda Pillai in his knowledge. No other party has such brilliant leaders. A well-taught follower will never leave the party."

Theoretical clarity, Soman believes, is key to the survival of a political organization and its values. It is, moreover, something that, in the earlier days of the Communist Party, did not depend on formal education but on commitment and insight: "Even when there was a person like E. M. S. in the party, it was K. V. Pathrose who was the state secretary … and he only went to school up to fourth standard!"

In his early days in the Communist Party, Soman was an enthusiastic pupil of Marxist thought and enjoyed analyzing different social questions from a class perspective. This enthusiasm started to wane, however, when he saw other Communist leaders practicing something very different from their words:

> I used to see things in class terms. But around 1990 the middle class started to infiltrate into the party. And then we lost our voice. We held on to the party believing in the ideology. But in fact with such a proposition [of a class perspective] the party was working against the SC and the ST. Because we were not supposed to spread communalism, we could not mobilize the Paraya and the Pulaya. And we followed those beliefs blindly. But the Izhavas and the Nairs inside the party at the same time started getting organized on their own in terms of caste. But if we would try to do that, the party would punish us. A communist Izhava can participate in the SNDP [the Izhava reform organization] programs. But we, Communist SCs or STs, were not allowed to get involved in any other public meetings.

Other inconsistencies in Communist ideology and practice also started to bother Soman. Having always been taught that Congress was the party of capitalists and landlords and the main political enemy, responsible for the dissolution of the first Communist government of Kerala, he was stunned to see the Communist Party trying to form an alliance with Congress at the federal level in 1996: "They became the protectors of Congress! This is not something that can go unnoticed." With the demise of the Soviet Union, which Soman blames on the sustained campaign to this effect by the Americans, he had already noticed the Communist Party was deviating from its commitment to the working class more and more: "We can say that nothing called a Communist Party really exists now. The Communist Party has abandoned its slogan of the rule of the working class. Once it abandons that slogan, what is its relevance? I wonder what will be next … make some changes to the Manifesto?!" With his disillusionment with the party, Soman came to see no real difference anymore between Congress and the CPI(M): "The [Communist] party flag is redder. But politically they have no difference of opinion with other parties. They just take a pose against some issues to make the poor feel the Communist Party is still with its old values of uplifting the poor, the working class—but all they see when looking at us is a vote bank."

The main problem Soman identified was that "the rich"—and upper castes—took over the party: "Then its ruin started," he said. "There are many martyrs from our community, but nobody acknowledges them anymore. Their histories are excluded from the party's history." The last straw for Soman in terms of his loyalty to the party was his experience as a CPI(M) member in the *panchayat* when he got caught in the way of the self-enriching ambitions of some other party members. There had been plans for the renovation of the municipality's stadium—a large project—for which an open call for applications was to be organized. His colleagues, however, played foul and came up with three applications: one by the person they had set up to get the contract, the second by his servant, and the third by someone who turned out to not exist at all. When Soman found out about this and exposed the setup, all hell broke loose, and he himself was accused of corruption in retaliation. After the party, on his insistence, appointed a commission of enquiry and a report came from higher up, Soman was acquitted of the corruption allegations against him. After the whole experience, he had become so bitter with the party that he decided to leave it: "I said I came to the party not longing for a *panchayat* membership, but longing for a change in society. And I said I couldn't cooperate with the party like this. And they tried to kill me. And then I quit the party. Those who are behind the corruption are rich now. And I, who pointed all this out, am still living in poverty. … So my point is if and only if you are good at corruption, can you get along with the party. But I don't want to survive like that. The party is totally degenerating."

Thus after thirty-three years as member of the Communist Party, from age fourteen onward, in 1998 Soman decided to leave the party. Many of the people from his colony had preceded him; others followed him: "Here in this colony, almost all were with the party. Now few real supporters are there. Even Jayan's brother [the son of the man who committed suicide in protest during the Kurichy struggle under the then CPI(M)-led government; see chapter 2] used to be a party member. Now only seven families are left. Most are standing with the party only for benefits. Maybe they will get a piece of land, daughter needs a job … that way. It's not because of the party and its ideology [that they stand with it]." Bitterly, Soman notes that whereas he joined the party as it had stood with his father, nobody from the party came to offer their condolences when his father died a few years back.

Soman still emphasizes that he has nothing against the party ideology. Yet in leaving the party and becoming involved in Dalit-Adivasi activism instead, he has started becoming more concerned with the need for Dalits and Adivasis to organize on their own: "We have been voting for other parties for so long. Now, we thought, we should start voting for ourselves. So after many discussions, we formed the Rashtriya Maha Sabha [the political sister organization of the AGMS]." Even from a Marxist perspective, he now believes it is essential for Dalits and Adivasis—whom he calls "nations" rather than castes—to organize "themselves": "If we look at history, earlier there was much less of a gap between the SNDP [Izhavas] and our community. But now see how big the gap has become. They are much more forward. Why has this happened? Once you start to closely examine the situation, a theory will emerge. The means of production are the key issue for any nation. Only when we own those means, can we have decision power."

At every turn, Soman encounters the Communist Party proclaiming support for Dalit-Adivasi struggles, especially when these struggles have been defeated. Yet he is now no longer convinced about the genuineness of the support. After Muthanga, for instance, the then CPI(M) opposition leader Achutanandan condemned the violence, and a party congress decided on the need to grant land to landless Adivasis. Yet the CPI(M) never brought up the crucial issue that could have made a difference for the AGMS in the aftermath of Muthanga, namely the retraction of the large number of court cases against participants in the Muthanga struggle, which was financially and psychologically crippling the AGMS: "Why did they not pass the resolution to withdraw the cases? And when Muthanga happened, Achutanandan made a statement saying it was organized by the People's War Group [a Naxal faction]. Why was he doing that? The intention behind their deeds are clearly to shatter this community. Only when the Parayan and the Pulayan become aware of these hidden gimmicks can we say we are politically conscious. For that we need to organize ourselves theoretically. We need to understand the ruling class has only one agenda, that is to demolish this group."

As part of this vision, Soman emphasizes the commonality of Dalits and Adivasis and the need for them to stand together despite government attempts to isolate them by giving the one land, and not the other. "See, the imperial powers wanted to wipe out the SCs and STs [synonymous for Dalits and Adivasis] who were once the owners of this land. Subsequent governments in India, following the path of these imperial powers, have also marginalized them. It is not easy to organize these people but it is the only way forward."

* * *

There is a type of biographical trajectory that is relevant to understand the shift from Communism to indigenism that I have not yet discussed in this section, which is that of Adivasis and Dalits who joined Naxal groupings in the 1990s and 2000s. There are a number of new Naxalite splinter groups (each of probably no more than about twenty people), such as Porrotam (Struggle), the Adivasi Vimochana Samithi (the Adivasi Liberation Front), and the CPI(ML)-Red Flag, which function in contemporary Kerala and occupy a small place in the political scene. The reason I cannot give detailed biographical accounts of activists in these groupings is that since they are followed and sometimes even wanted by the police, establishing contact with them was much more difficult. Usually I could only speak with them for about half an hour before they felt it was no longer safe for them to stay around and for obvious reasons they were usually reluctant to share personal information or open up—often presenting me with rather wooden ideological statements instead. The stories of these contemporary Dalit and Adivasi Naxals showed similarities to those of Janu, Geethanandan, and Soman, except for the fact that they had come to see the CPI(M)'s commitment to parliamentary democracy and the constitution as the main problem and saw the AGMS as complicit in this by searching for agreements with the government.

A Cheruma (Dalit) woman whom I will call Thankamma, a leading activist in the Adivasi Samara Sangam—a branch of Porrotam—told me, "We do not believe in the parliamentary system. We are convinced that, following the constitution, there can be no radical changes. The governments in power have made sure that by following the constitution nothing is possible in terms of changing the existing social setup. We strongly disagree with the Gothra Sabha's decision to work shoulder to shoulder with the constitution. Our ideology is that of Marxism, Leninism, and Maoism." The CPI(M)'s Adivasi Kshema Samithi, likewise, in Thankamma's view, worked "hand in hand with the parliamentary system. It will not be able to liberate the proletariat. Even after fifty years of independence, all these problems still exist. We look forward to a revolution that brings a sea change in society. We want the hegemony of proletarians."

She herself had become part of Porrotam only after breaking with the CPI(M), which in the late 1990s had sent her to Wayanad to organize Adivasis there under CPI(M) leadership. In 2000, she left the party for what she claims were "ideological reasons." Soon enough, clashes with former CPI(M) colleagues became violent—twice they reported her to the police: one time after Porrotam had attacked a mobile food distribution unit (a Mobile Maveli Store of the Kerala State Civil Supplies Corporation) to distribute the food among starving people; the other time after Porrotam besieged a local bank office and destroyed the documents it used to reclaim farmers' loans.

In stark contrast to AGMS activists and sympathizers, the contemporary Naxalites I interviewed would hardly mention issues of caste, identity, or culture and would generally get rather uncomfortable with questions along these lines. Thankamma, when I asked her why Porrotam founded the Adivasi Samara Sangam, was quick to wave the question away saying, "Because Adivasis are a part of the proletarian struggle—Adivasis, Dalits, farmers, women, we are all the same, our party does not discriminate among human beings." When the Naxalites I interviewed did touch on something close to the notion of Adivasi identity, they usually did so entirely along hegemonic lines, with no political reinterpretation. Arruvikal Krishnan,[22] the Paniya leader of the Adivasi Vimoshana Samithi, merely told me when I asked him what it meant to him to be part of the class struggle as an Adivasi, "Adivasis? There are thirty-five different tribal groups, with different customs and traditions; I cannot remember all of them but there is a list."

Being forced to operate underground, being in a very fragmented state, and holding to highly abstract past ideological teachings, there seems to be little ideological innovation going on among these contemporary Naxal groups. Discursively they remain within the hegemony of the political status quo—they state their opposition to it but are unable to do so in ways that simultaneously would challenge the discursive hold that this status quo has over the political interpretation of reality.[23] This then contributes to the fact that, in practice, these contemporary Naxalite outfits come up against the limits of the law much sooner than a movement such as the AGMS does. Activists like Vasu, Geethanandan, Janu, and Soman are also, like the small contemporary Naxalite groupings, much frustrated by the inaction of the established Left when it comes to the concerns of oppressed sections of society but do not only challenge this inaction with action—they also, as organic intellectuals would, articulate their disagreement with the Communist Party into a new vision and a different discourse. Hence their ideas manage to provoke debate in Kerala at large and help mobilize greater alliance and support. The AGMS activists have developed an indigenist vision that clearly—not just practically but also ideologically—distinguishes it from what the Communist Party has become and that processes "past mistakes" ideologically. This difference in vision explains the greater popularity of the AGMS as compared to the small contemporary Naxalite groupings. At the same time, the Naxalites' purely action-centered approach, and swift criminalization by the state, pulls them into a vicious circle where they cannot propagate, nor develop, their ideological visions further.

## Conclusion

Without enquiring into the biographical trajectories of the activists presented here, one could easily arrive at stories merely confirming the idea that the need to organize on the basis of indigenism was always already evident and merely waiting for persons with the right determination to take it forward. One could then read in Janu's encounter with Solidarity, Geethanandan's encounter with Ambedkar's thought, or Soman's encounter with the AGMS itself the trigger that set off the process of indigenist engagement of these activists, with the wider political environment of emergent indigenous movements nationally and internationally as the favorable conditions under which such engagement was possible. Yet even by interviewing them in the present—with their memories transformed by their current experiences—an enquiry into their previous political engagements, before they became convinced of indigenism, reveals the strong commitment all had to Communism. For none of these activists was the turn away from Communism triggered by the positives of indigenism. This is understandable because, as we saw in previous chapters, Adivasi identity is, in fact, a highly complex and difficult notion on which to build an emergent counterhegemonic politics. What pushed activists to nevertheless leave the party—all except Kalan, who in his old age could choose to stand somewhat aloof of the everyday politics of the party and of ideological political debates—were the negative experiences they had within the party or other Communist groupings. Though some of the activists place more emphasis on ideology while others stress practice, their biographies all (except Kalan's) show a combination of practical and ideological reasons to turn away from Communism and towards indigenism.

Ramachandran Guha argues that despite a "bankrupt Stalinist ideology," Communist leaders like E. M. S. Namboodiripad, Kerala's first chief minister and long-time general secretary of the later

CPI(M), retained their popularity because of their "meaningful" Gandhian practice (2003: 212). The biographies I presented here, however, show encounters with a Communist movement that increasingly is both ideologically *and* practically in crisis. In fact, contrary to Guha's perception, the biographical narratives given here show that it was Communist leaders' corruption, rather than their ideological dogmatism, that usually became the first trigger for activists to look for alternatives. The way different activists responded to a crisis of their erstwhile hopes as part of Communist groupings—and the extent to which they rejected Communism altogether—depended on the timing and the nature of their involvement with Communism: the Communist Party C. K. Janu encountered was already a very different one from the one Vasu and Soman had joined in their youth. Rejection of the party was thus easier for Janu than for those who had experienced the party in the days when it still represented a force that was leading unprecedented changes in the lives of the working class. Likewise, it took Geethanandan longer to reject Communism than it did Janu because Geethanandan had been part of a more dynamic and radical Communist grouping—one that was affected by the same kind of ideological dilemmas the mainstream CPI(M) was going through but was less directly part of the move toward practical compromising with the status quo of neoliberal governance.

The story that emerges from the biographical trajectories I discussed here is rather different from the picture usually emerging from studies that focus on the interaction (and sometimes complicity) of indigenous people and the state and do not ask what happened to the alternative venues, other than indigenist organizing, through which many indigenous people were already articulating and resisting their oppression earlier. The Communist Party figures large in every single one of these biographies, as it did in all the life histories I collected of other activists. A major reason for the rise of indigenism in Kerala thus lies with the declining appeal of the Communist Party that, once having decided to stand for elections and effect changes through periodically being in charge of the government, became increasingly torn between its ideological raison d'etre of leading the class struggle on behalf of the working class and its practical need to compromise on this in order to manage its hold on power.

It was not just, however, a question of a declining appeal of the Communist Party: more than that, what started out as efforts to reinvigorate the kind of class struggles that the Communist Party had originally stood for ended up radicalized into mutual hostility between the Communist Party and the new movements, eventually also finding its expression in ideological polarization between Communism and indigenism, Marxist "ideology" and indigenous "culture," "class" and "caste," "human beings" and "identity." In the next chapter, I will take a closer look at this polarizing dynamic that propelled the AGMS to not just critique and transcend the Communist Party, but frame itself in almost diametrically opposite terms.

## Notes

1. The late Sharmila Rege's (2006) work is inspirational in its use of life narratives to document the historical flow of political currents in people's lives. This chapter's life stories, however, are not coauthored "testimonios" like the ones Rege collected, but rather rely on my patching together life stories from the more scattered stories people told me during various interviews.
2. Parliamentary cretinism, a term Marx used in his *18th Brumaire,* describes the belief that a socialist society can be achieved by peaceful, parliamentary means.
3. This was recognizable to me since most Communist party members I interviewed in Kerala during my fieldwork in 2005–2006—including the more critical and well-read ones—still defended Stalin as the hero of the Soviet Union and were convinced that criticism of Stalin's policies was mere CIA propaganda.
4. There was no custom of registering births in his community at the time, or of counting age exactly—hence the vagueness around his exact age.
5. The festival survives till today, held in March every year, but has now become a religious festival cum fun fair.
6. It was then called Coorg, as the British called it, and people still often call it that, though officially this district is now renamed Kodagu.
7. Congress was not only in power at the national level (with Indira Gandhi as prime minister) but also in Kerala itself, though in coalition with the CPI, the Muslim League, and a number of other parties. Chief minister of Kerala between November 1969 and March 1977 was Achuta Menon of the CPI (in coalition with Congress). Kalan's CPI(M), adamantly opposed to an alliance with Congress, was in the opposition and only came to power again in January 1980.
8. A repetition of sorts of the post–World War I scenario of the Left in Germany where the split between social democrats and revolutionaries became so hardened that it undermined their necessary unity against the rise of fascism (e.g., Priestland 2009; Harman 2003).
9. The policeman who shot Varghese, Ramachandran Nair, was himself, in fact, a Communist sympathizer and finally in 1998 publicly revealed the story of how he was forced by his superiors to be the one to pull the trigger on Varghese in a fake "encounter." On 28 October 2010, a special CBI court sentenced the superior officer who ordered the shooting, Lakshmana, to life imprisonment. A fictitious rendering of the Varghese drama, interesting though sharply criticized by former Naxals, is provided in *An Iron Harvest* by C. P. Surendran (2006).
10. The portraits of Lenin and Stalin that decorate Vasu's home also are somewhat misleading—as he himself explained to me, these were simply those that were "available."

11. During the early, exploratory phase of my research in Kerala in 2003, I interviewed K. Venu, notorious among my CPI(M) friends for defending aspects of globalization and, according to them, abandoning Marxist analysis altogether.
12. "Class struggle isn't enough," an interview with Geethanandan by Ka Shaji in *Tehelka*, 12 March 2007.
13. There are interesting parallels between the trajectory of Kerala's fisherfolk/fishworkers activism and the AGMS. The fishworkers' independent organization, the KSMTF (formed in 1980), for instance, prompted political parties' trade unions to focus on fishworkers' rights just as the AGMS prompted them to focus on Adivasi rights. A shift from "class" to "identity" was also apparent among the fishworkers—as Baviskar, Sinha, and Philip (2005: 232) observe, "Caste, community, and economic nationalism now dominate over liberation theology, class, and gender discourses in the way the movement frames justice and ecological issues."
14. I interviewed Mr. Lukose of Hilda and K. Narayanan and Jose Sebastian of Solidarity in 2005.
15. Certainly in the context of the general stereotypes on Adivasi women as "innocent" and "childlike" (*pawam*), I do not think using this odd style of translation (strange spellings, overly simple words, leaving out upper cases) was a good idea.
16. Before the Naxal movement became active in Wayanad, it was common for landlords to pay Adivasi agricultural laborers in kind—in a quantity of rice—rather than in cash. It was common, moreover, for the landlord's middlemen to use bamboo vessels (*nazhi*) that were imprecise and of course adjusted in their favor. Another way they tried to increase their share was by measuring the amount before the chaff and stones were removed from the rice.
17. For some reason transcribed as "Canfed" in Bhaskaran (2004: 22).
18. Often also spelled "Variar," a so-called high caste.
19. Translator's odd style of not using upper cases.
20. Something I certainly expect Janu told Bhaskaran with a hint of irony—note the words "our *own*."
21. George Kunnath's (2006) biographical analysis of a Communist Dalit in Bihar forms an interesting comparison to Soman's story.
22. Days after my interview with him, apparently after talking to a journalist, Arruvikal decided to, under the glare of cameras, stage an attack on me with his small activist outfit (they *gherao*-ed me and hung a placard around my neck that claimed I was a spy). The reasons for the attack seem a complex mix of trying to get back at the owner of the hotel where I was staying, the suspicion that I was indeed a spy or in any case up to "immoral activities", and, probably most importantly, the desire to stage a media spectacle. The attack was indeed extensively covered on Kerala news channels and in local, state, and even national newspapers (e.g., see http://www.thehindu.com/todays-paper/tp-national/tp-kerala/article3095906.ece).
23. For instance, I learned later that the outfit had hoped the attack on me would portray them as "good patriots" who "exposed a spy." Not only are these, paradoxically, rather conformist goals, they were also not reached: except for BJP-related media circuits that told the story as an attack on a "Christian missionary," media generally portrayed the activists in a negative light, and several of the activists were put in jail by the police (something to which I did not lend my cooperation).

– Chapter 4 –

# Widening Circles of Political Disidentification

Whereas the activist biographies that I discussed in the previous chapter, in combination with wider political trends, show a strong inclination for a shift from class-centered to identity-focused politics, the life histories also left a lot of spaces of ambiguity between Communism and indigenism. The dynamics discussed in this chapter, however, show how conflict and competition between the two political blocks increasingly hardened, positioning the two in stark contrast to each other. I look in more detail here at how once a new challenge in the form of indigenism emerged, its interaction with the Communist Party took on a dynamic of its own and magnified the ideological polarization between the two. As we will see, the political split even took on certain ethnicized characteristics. Ethnicization has not reached the point where the split is generally interpreted as an ethnic rather than a political one, though aspects of this can be seen for instance in C. K. Janu's claim that she is not engaged in a political struggle but a cultural one: of Adivasi-Dalit culture versus mainstream culture. As we will see, both political blocks have developed radically different interpretations of history, bordering on different "myths of origin." Both groups, moreover, tend to see each other in diametrically opposed terms. From the side of the AGMS, the Communist Party increasingly comes to stand in for upper castes or Savarnas (caste Hindus) while Dalits and Adivasis—broadly defined (often including Izhavas)—come to be seen as the original "black" race. From the side of the Communist Party, a lot of attention goes to personal comportment and charisma, which gives a lot of space to implicit—that is, naturalized—caste connotations. The ideal Communist leader, for instance, is supposed to be guided purely by intellect and exhibit "sober" and "self-sacrificing" behavior, characteristics that generally belong to the *habitus* of upper-caste men eager to "uplift" their lower-caste comrades (Devika 2010).[1]

It is then perhaps not surprising that notions developed to study ethnic conflict also appear relevant to analyzing the political dynamics of polarization between Communists and indigenists in Kerala. Indeed, Abram de Swaan's (1997: 105) description of "widening circles of disidentification" captures some key processes developing between the two groups. As De Swaan emphasizes, "Identification and disidentification are not each other's opposites" (ibid.). Rather, disidentification is much more virulent where two groups are intimately related and sometimes blur into each other—as between Communist and indigenist activists in Kerala. Identification and disidentification in this sense are "two sides of an emotional triangle, with at its base ignorance and indifference" (ibid.). Identification depends not only on constructing a positive in-group but all the more on constructing a negative "other," a target on which to project the self-serving inclinations that are denied to the self. As we will see in this chapter, it is well possible to capture the rift developing between the Communist Party and the AGMS in terms of such "widening circles of disidentification."

## (Re)reading Kerala History between Communism and Caste

The past is a prime battlefield in contemporary politics in Kerala. The interpretation of the political history of Kerala and in particular the question of the relationship between the caste reform movements and the emerging Communist Party in the early twentieth century has become a key node around which circles of political disidentification have been widening. Both indigenist and Communist activists have by now developed radically different versions of this history. The Communist Party claims to have radicalized the earlier "social reform movements" and broadened their struggle to reform negative traditional customs towards a program of structural social transformation. Indigenist activists argue to the contrary that the rise of the Communist movement took over the momentum of the anti-caste movements and replaced it with an upper caste–dominated project of avoiding radical reform. It is interesting to explore these readings more closely. Though I do check some political sources against academic research, the main aim of such closer exploration is not to arbitrate over the truth value of these claims but to show how the indigenist form of contemporary political mobilization in Kerala is indeed not so much about the fit of notions of indigeneity to political needs but more about explicit opposition to the Communist Party. The polarizing dialogue on Kerala's recent past that I present here is compiled from different partisan sources: my interviews with Communist Party members and indigenist activists as well as official publications by the Communist Party and published writings by indigenist activists.

Apart from specific historical questions and topics, the main polarization starts already with the question of how to approach history in general. It must be noted that Dalit-Adivasi and Communist intellectuals do share a certain take on history wherein present-day fates are not attributed to ontology, timeless antiquity, and the passivity of birth but rather are read as the outcome of circumstance and conjuncture—as V. Geetha (2009) reminds us, the contemporary hegemony of such historiography in itself is a modern product of the struggle against the divine Hindu social order. But beyond this shared basis, there are notable differences in how the two blocks approach history. The writings of E. M. S. Namboodiripad (who was popularly known in India as EMS), which continue to be the main source cited in official Communist Party documents and by party members, emphasize a "scientific" reading of history: seeing things of the past not as moral issues but as signs of a particular form of social organization. In this light, caste is a question of "backwardness," a sign of the feudal relationships that need to be overcome and will be overcome in the rational progression of history. EMS describes the progression of social and family institutions from ancient, Dravidian to feudal society not, he claims, to make an argument about the "superiority" or lack of it of so-called pre-Aryan society—i.e., society before the supposed advent of Brahmins from the North—but simply to "scientifically" describe the course of history. He claims to admire Erode Venkata Ramasamy (commonly known as Periyar or EVR), Tamil Nadu's radical Dravidian thinker, yet argued that, "Dravidian superiority is as unscientific as the theory of Aryan superiority" (in Panikkar 1998). Failing to give an *analytical* reading of history, EMS argued, would only serve to bolster vested interests.

By contrast, indigenist activists I spoke to argued that the crux of the problem with the Communist Party's view of history lay precisely with its supposedly scientific, class-based analysis. This allowed it to disguise as a neutral, "analytical" exercise what was in fact an attempt to recover a role for the Brahmins as the primary movers of history. Such "scientific" reading ignored the achievements of the more egalitarian Dravidian society and excused its violent subjugation to caste hierarchy: it presented what was a cruel turn in history as an inevitable and progressive development, in turn justifying the higher-caste leadership of a proletarian movement. The problem, Dalit activists often told me, was that EMS was trying to do everything to prevent the radical anti-Brahminism that was spreading in Tamil Nadu at the time from reaching Kerala: EMS was in fierce competition with the Dravidian leader EVR, and used a Communist interpretation of history precisely to be able to avoid the moral appeal of EVR's theory that Brahminism was what ruined South India. According to indigenist activists, the right way to interpret history was reading it through a caste lens: how caste hierarchy was imposed, which groups benefitted from it, and how these same groups were now trying their best to find ways of avoiding the problem of caste by labeling it as merely a passing historical moment in the linear advancement of history towards Communism.

### *Early Reform Movements: Sanskritization or Radical Egalitarianism?*

Communist Party documents tend to call the caste-based movements of the early twentieth century (before Indian independence and the unification of Travancore, Cochin, and Malabar) "social reform movements" and it is well known that EMS was involved in one of these himself: the Yogakshema Sabha, an organization he founded to try to introduce reforms to his own Namboodiri caste, the very highest caste in Malabar. EMS wanted to promote reform in the kinship arrangements of his caste—particularly in the traditional practice that only the eldest son of a family would marry while younger sons had informal marriages with Nair women and a majority of Namboodiri women remained unmarried and in *purdah* (total seclusion).[2] He also wanted to awaken a positive attitude towards modern education and abolish certain negative traditional practices, above all the practice of untouchability vis-à-vis other castes—in this, EMS claimed inspiration from the Sree Narayana Dharma Paripalan (SNDP), the Izhava reform movement. EMS is widely acclaimed by Communists to have consistently lived according to his convictions, for instance, dining with people of other castes without any reluctance and no longer wearing the "sacred thread"[3] (see also Namboodiripad 1976: 2ff.). In his own words, EMS wanted to "change Namboodiris into human beings" (see also Panikkar 1998). Other "social reform movements" played a similarly important role in fighting against "superstition and bad customs," "casteism," and "untouchability" (CPI[M] website

2009). These movements were important in "awakening an interest in acquiring modern education," initially introduced by Christian missionaries and thereafter, under pressure from the people, provided by the government (ibid.).

The official history of the party (CPI[M] website 2009) singles out Sree Narayana Guru (of the SNDP), Ayyankali, and Vagbhatananda (a follower of Sree Narayana Guru in Malabar) for praise but all the more so Ramakrishna Pillai (editor of the newspaper *Swadeshabhimani* in Travancore and author of the first Malayalam biography of Marx in 1912) and P. Kesavadev (for introducing the "social renaissance movements" to "ideas of socialism and Soviet Revolution"). Especially noted by many Communists is the atheist Sahodharan Ayyappan, who suggested Sri Narayanan's slogan of "one *jati*, one religion, one God for man" ought to be replaced by the motto "no caste, no religion, no God!" and who argued that the real moral strength of a community lay not in defying caste distinctions vis-à-vis upper castes but in ending untouchability towards Dalits.[4] A Communist Party member told me that even EVR, the great Tamil anticaste ideologue, was inspired by Communism and published a version of the Communist Manifesto.[5]

The Communist version of the history of the social reform movements thus claims that the more revolutionary actors in them drifted towards Communism. For in the course of their existence, the social reform movements, which had initially helped promote a form of public consciousness, became locked within their respective castes. A Communist Party member told me, "These organizations were aiming to encourage Sanskritizing behavior amongst their followers, fighting for temple entry like at Vaikom.[6] They were not interested to address the structural issues." Thus in the Communist reading of history, the social reform movements eventually lost their momentum because they ended up merely challenging existing caste norms in terms of trying to position their own caste higher up in the hierarchy, leaving the hierarchy as such intact—the widespread historical phenomenon in India that Srinivas (1962) famously theorized as "Sanskritization."

Indigenist activists, however, have a very different view on the history of the early reform movements. Rather than lump these movements together as "social reform movements," they emphasize that the main issue was caste and that the upper-caste organizations like EMS's Yogakshema Sabha in the 1920s, but also, for instance, the powerful Nair Service Society (founded in 1914),[7] emerged not so much from the desire for reform but in order to ensure the dominance of these respective castes during a time of radical social change: it was a preparation that allowed them to convert their excessive wealth in land into investments in education and thereby access to the new, salaried sources of wealth when the time came that the descendants of the original Dravidian people—now the lower castes and outcastes—started demanding land. On the other side of the caste spectrum, however, there was Ayyankali's anticaste movement, which was already active in the last years of the nineteenth century and went much further in confronting the caste structure than the Communist movement did. For the Communist Party, caste was only a problem in so far as it prevented workers from uniting but otherwise not an issue to be fought against. Sunny Kapicadu, a Dalit activist involved in the AGMS, told me, "This rigid distinction between base and superstructure allowed Communist leaders to condemn any action that focused on caste discrimination as a distraction from the 'real' issues."

According to him, the strength of an anticaste leader like Ayyankali lies precisely in his ability to combine livelihood issues with issues of "human dignity." Ayyankali fought against the prohibition against lower castes entering particular public spaces so that, by 1900, Pulayas had the right to walk on the public roads in most areas of Travancore.[8] With the founding of the Sadhu Jana Paripalana Sangham (Association for the Welfare of the Poor) in 1905, Ayyankali pushed successfully for the enforcement of a six-day working week for agricultural laborers,[9] and he fought for lower-caste women to be allowed to wear upper garments and go without the bead necklace that symbolized their slave past—the successful Kallumala/bead necklace agitation of 1915–16.[10] Ayyankali's actions and words, Sunny Kapicadu claimed, emerged organically from the lives of Dalits at the time and mobilized them for radical egalitarian visions. It was precisely this momentum that worried upper-caste leaders and prompted them to intervene. As Kapicadu argued, "Not a single man from Ayyankali's movement we find back in the Communist Party leadership. What is the meaning of it? It means the so-called politicization of Kerala society [the emergence of the Communist movement] *de*-politicized this section [Dalits and Adivasis]."

### *The Party: Radicalizing or Impeding the Anticaste Momentum?*

The Communist Party sees itself as having grown organically from the earlier people's movements—both from the social reform movements in Travancore and Cochin and, crucially, from the early peasant movements, mostly in Malabar. In both cases, it claims a radicalizing sequence between these movements and early Communism, whose leaders "propagated a new idea of giving shape to a new man ... formed out of life and experience: a new style which touched the heart of ordinary people" (CPI[M] website 2009). Communist leaders usually have no qualms admitting that in the beginning, they adopted socialist aims without knowing anything much about socialist theory. Communism was, as comrade Krishna Pillai is often quoted, simply seen as the vision that "the whole world belongs to one caste, the human caste." Communist history has early social reform movements like the SNDP gradually, in the course of the 1920s, develop into labor unions—a common example being the first Travancore Labor Association set up in 1922 under the guidance of a new socialist vision, popular with "the oppressed masses" (ibid.). Many ordinary Communist sympathizers express their gratefulness for how Communist leaders helped break all kinds of caste taboos. They came into people's houses, shared food with them, and called both themselves *and* the workers "comrades"—"The Communist leaders did so many things to make people overcome the old caste feelings!" a Pulaya Communist told me. According to such Communist sympathizers, it was the Communists who truly lived Gandhi's ideals of "sincerity and simplicity." The party, moreover, as evidence of its anticasteism, claims to have a much higher number of lower-caste leaders and Members of the Legislative Assembly than other parties.[11] And, as Communists like to point out, it was the only party ideologically committed to maintaining a "genuinely secular stand" including an "uncompromising struggle against caste oppression" that "disassociated itself completely from caste and communal separatism" (Namboodiripad 1976: 3f.).

Indigenist activists hold a radically different view on the relationship between the early anticaste movements and the Communist Party. They argue the latter arose precisely to impede the anticaste momentum, limiting it safely to the symbolic level of interdining and dress codes. This indigenist argument is in line with the critical perspectives of Arundhati Roy, the internationally known activist-novelist from Kerala. Most Communists in Kerala strongly dislike her.[12] Indigenist activists, on the other hand, are generally more generous towards Roy, who also showed herself in strong solidarity with the AGMS after the Muthanga struggle (see her paper in *Frontline*, 15–28 March 2003). In her novel *The God of Small Things* (1997), she includes a passage about the origins of Communism in Kerala: "The real secret was that communism crept into Kerala insidiously. As a reformist movement that never overtly questioned the traditional values of a caste-ridden, extremely traditional community. The Marxists worked from within the communal divides, never challenging them, never appearing not to. They offered a cocktail revolution. A heady mix of Eastern Marxism and orthodox Hinduism, spiked with a shot of democracy."[13]

Indeed, indigenists argue that Communists were always careful not to upset the key caste institution: endogamous marriage. Upper-caste Communist leaders were not prepared to marry outside of their caste: they would publicly present themselves as being against "casteism" and "untouchability" while at the same time retaining the fundamentals of caste practice in their private lives.[14]

On the other hand, indigenist activists also point to the continuing existence of caste in public life. Inspired by this critical perspective, Malayalee scholar Carmel Christy (2015) convincingly demonstrates how caste endures in Kerala's public space, masked—but not eradicated—through (gendered) "cultural codes" (139). For example, the "sincerity and simplicity" that Communist Party members boast in public could easily be read as a cultural code for the otherworldly *habitus* pertaining to Brahmins. Read thus, the *sanyasi* style of early Communist leaders, which the Indian establishment so laments that contemporary Dalit leaders such as Mayawati lack, is another indication of how the Communist leadership was almost automatically assumed to be upper caste. An AGMS activist told me, "Just look at their language, it's always about 'uplifting' the people, all about 'self-sacrifice' ... what does it say? It says the Communist Party per definition sees its leadership as being high caste." Or as Manoj, an RMS activist-intellectual at Kottayam University, said, "When the Dalit speaks he is accused of copying the higher castes, of not being 'authentic' to his caste; 'Sanskritization' is the word invented in academia for this." Indeed, indigenist activists criticized how any attempt by those historically excluded from discursive power to assume its tools were morally condemned as engaging in self-serving and hierarchy-confirming "Sanskritization" behavior—from within this logic, only upper castes (such as Srinivas, who coined the term) would be able to continue to assume discursive power without being condemned for "Sanskritizing" behavior. The Communist Party, who liked to condemn "Sanskritization," was thus criticized for reproducing the typical caste division of labor between manual and intellectual work. For example, another AGMS activist pointed out to me, "Despite his theoretical mediocrity, a Brahmin like EMS was encouraged to become a visionary theoretician of the party, but the scholastic efforts of Marxists born to a lower caste were sidelined. ... Pathrose, a Pulaya Christian who translated Marx's *Capital* into Malayalam, he was thrown out of the party to make way for these high castes posing as great intellectuals. Just look at the leadership of the party: it's all Namboodiripads, Pillais. …"

The abstract theories of Marxism and its air of authoritative intellectualism—"this Marxian Vedanta," as one activist called it (Joe 2010)—many activists hence see as an effort to disguise how Communism in Kerala was about preserving the existing caste hierarchies. C. K. Janu argued that Communist ideology had re-enslaved Adivasis and Dalits: "They were changing into slaves of this ideology." Marxist ideology prevented people from seeing clearly how their oppressed position as former slaves was being produced by the very movement claiming to work for their emancipation.

The general difference of perspective on the role of the Communist Party is particularly controversial when it comes to the history of the two key issues in the reproduction of relations of power in Kerala: education and land reform. The Kerala Land Reform Act and the Kerala Education Act are probably the proudest achievements of Communism in Kerala. Both were introduced by the first Communist government of Kerala (in 1957 and 1958 respectively), were implemented through a lot of struggle in the 1970s, and have been grandly celebrated by the CPI(M) on their fiftieth anniversary in 2007. Yet they are also the two areas where indigenist activists voice their strongest criticism.

### *Education for Emancipation—or Learning Caste?*

The Communist Party claims as one of its key achievements the high level of education and the formal 100 percent literacy rate of Kerala, said to have been attained in 1987 by the CPI(M) government under leadership of E. K. Nayanar (CPI[M] website 2009). The party does acknowledge earlier contributions: the Christian missionary schooling efforts and the demands by "people suppressed so far as untouchables and weaker sections" for schooling in conjunction with access to government employment (through SC/ST reservations) which "imparted a new enthusiasm [for education] among the oppressed masses" (CPI[M] website 2009). But it was the Communist movement that took up this desire of the people and turned it into a priority that every Malayalee would be able to enjoy equal education.[15] According to a Communist MLA I interviewed, "The Communist Party deliberately and methodically invested in education, setting goals so popular with the electorate that even when the Communists lost power, new governments did not dare modify education policies."

In this vein, the CPI(M) website (2009) boasts of the "stellar achievements in … Mass Literacy and Education Development" that have become recognized the world over as cornerstones of the Kerala Model. On top of this, the Communist movement claims to have taught people knowledge that would help in their emancipation. As an Izhava Communist claimed, "They were raising people's consciousness. … or actually, more than that, they were providing a political awareness, political classes … that is the crucial thing."

To "develop political consciousness among the ranks," the Communist Party organized and maintained village reading rooms and libraries (CPI[M] website 2009). The party moreover helped publish accessible scientific and political material, brought out weekly magazines such as *Prabhatham*—later the name of a progressive arts and cultural forum—and a daily newspaper, *Deshabhimani.* It also organized weeks-long "learning and training camps" in which hundreds of people would participate, who, later, back in their villages, educated others in evening schools. Malayalee classics such as P. Kesava Dev's "*From the Gutter*" (1942) or Sivasankara Pillai Thakazhi's "*Two Measures of Rice*" (1948) were all products of this movement. With regard to Dalits and Adivasis, AKS members I interviewed would persistently emphasize the importance of the Communist Party in making education available to them. Babu, a Paniya AKS leader in Kannur, told me about his experience:

> In this country called India there are not many places where the Adivasis and other backward people can sit, walk, eat, and get education with other people, with other communities. Kerala, West Bengal, and Tripura [the three states in India where the Communist Party has been in power regularly] are some of the only places. In other states there are still many practices to keep backward people away … but this is not the case in the states where Communists have the upper hand. Here … any tribal can get his children admitted to school. There is no hindrance for such a thing in the social situation of Kerala. This situation is an achievement and result of the works and efforts by the progressive movements—Communist Party and workers' unions. The Adivasis are people who are not yet up to "that" level of progress. What the CPI(M) and the AKS have been doing is raising them up to that level.

Already in such formulations by Communist Party members, one can, however, sense a certain (in Babu's case internalized) hierarchy that attaches to the question of education ("backward people," "'that' level of progress") and has not really been addressed by the party. Indigenist critics indeed see the educational question in quite a different light. They argue that early missionary efforts helped some Dalits and Adivasis muster the confidence and possibility to acquire education, but that it was above all Ayyankali's movement that cleared the way for their children to start going to school. The agitations he led in the 1910s for the right to education for Dalits were, according to an AGMS activist, "the most revolutionary episode in the history of Kerala. When this village school refused to accept a Pulaya girl, Ayyankali took up the issue and organized a demonstration to assert our right to schooling. He took a brave stance and faced a lot of violence. A group of angry Nairs [upper castes] set fire to the school—just because an untouchable girl had dared to enter it."[16] Ayyankali moreover organized a large strike in which Dalits—almost facing starvation before they won their victory—stood up to their landlords, again demanding education for their children. As a Dalit activist from Idukki told me, "Theirs was not a polite request [like that of the Communist Party]; it was a struggle. Ayyankali told them, 'If you don't let our children go to school, we will turn your schools into fields!'"

Indeed, indigenist activists see education not so much as a tool for "consciousness raising" but as a central pillar of caste. The dividing line of knowledge and ignorance, activists argue, is the central historical dividing line of higher and lower castes. It is, moreover, the key mechanism of caste as well. Kapicadu, a Dalit activist, explained: "Caste is about being locked in one occupation. The Brahminical ideology will make sure an educated Dalit will always be a contradiction; he will always be considered a field worker … and given education only to the extent necessary for such labor."

Hopes and promises were that the Communist movement would make knowledge available to all, but indigenist activists see very little of that materialized. The story told by many activists instead is that while Communist leaders themselves were sending their children off to receive first-class education outside of Kerala, Dalits and Adivasis were suffering the caste prejudices and violence of upper-caste teachers and peers in Kerala's public schools. Many activists claim that schools and universities are the main site where Dalits and Adivasis experience casteism in its most pervasive forms, from subtle everyday caste remarks and exclusions (e.g., during the much celebrated free "midday meal"[17]) to violent "raggings" (bullying and torture by peers). Indigenist activists also have come to interpret the difficulty of Dalit and Adivasi students in getting a student loan as another (institutionalized) form of caste discrimination. Such discrimination easily leads Dalit and Adivasi children to "drop out" (a term that activists claim has a caste connotation) or to even commit suicide, as for instance in the famous case in 2004 of the twenty-one-year-old Dalit student Rejani Anand who jumped from the seventh floor of the office of the entrance commissioner at Trivandrum.[18] Indigenist activists claim that the Communist Party, including its youth wing, the Democratic Youth Federation of India, which has a strong presence on campuses in Kerala, silently condones casteism in schools and colleges or even encourages it so it can maintain the status quo while pretending to make education universally available. The party, according to indigenist activists, has never made an effort to ensure the same quality education was given to Dalits and Adivasis as to members of upper castes. A Dalit AGMS activist told me, "They always made sure that our children, who got education from government schools, would remain poor and ignorant. … While other children were learning English, all our children were learning was how to remain agricultural laborers. And just look at all those 'Communists' sending their children to America for an education!"

On top of this, the "educated" character of Malayalee civil society seems—to indigenist activists—to have become a principal institution ensuring people do not think for themselves, hence perpetuating upper-caste dominance. Having experienced what they came to see as pointless political classes, many indigenist activists, particularly of the younger generation, are thoroughly skeptical of "consciousness raising" in general. In Janu's words, "Adivasis never give classes to others on what they are doing. But if others picked up a stone today, tomorrow they will explain in the news how they picked it up, write a book on it, propagate it, establish it as their own. Adivasis have done all things, but we don't go about lecturing on it."

### *Redistributing Land or Safeguarding Landed Capital?*

The other major achievements that the Communist Party claims it is responsible for are the land reforms in Kerala. While Communist Party documents have become generous in praising "great social reformers," they also note that "these social reform movements … did not address the crucial issue of radical land reforms" (CPI[M] resolution 22 February 2006). It is a common story in Communist Party networks that the most important reform the party (then still undivided) introduced was the package of land reforms laws: first, to make the eviction of tenant farmers from their land illegal; second, to award landless families ownership over their homestead plots (*kudikidappu* land); and third, to set ceilings (of fifteen acres) to landholdings and to redistribute the surplus land among the landless. The first two aims were a tremendous success and have made Kerala, Communists claim, into the Indian state where, by far, the most radical land reform happened. The third component—the distribution of surplus land above a certain ceiling—was less successful because a huge landlord-led and American-backed so-called "liberation movement" emerged against Kerala's first Communist ministry, leading to its dismissal by the federal government in 1959. The implementation of the land reform act was slowed down considerably and moreover muddled by subsequent Congress governments. But still the persistent struggles of the Communist Party to implement the reforms led to significant successes. An AKS member listed some of these:

> It was the Communist Party that took the stand that land should be given to landless workers and peasants. It was the Communist Party that first turned ownership of land by the peasants into a reality, at the time of the EMS government, in 1957. ... it was during EMS's government that the slogan was raised "land to those who work it." It was the Communist government that distributed the land to the peasants in India for the first time. The Communist Party confiscated land from the feudal landlords and distributed it to the peasants and the landless so they had land to love and work and so the landlords were also left with some land for their livelihood. In a country like India where we are bound by a parliamentary and capitalist system, it was a great achievement on the part of the Communist government.

As the CPI(M) website puts it, "It was the Communist Party which raised people of Kerala who were suffocating under the iron grip of landlordism to the pedestal of democratic consciousness." By providing security against eviction to erstwhile tenant farmers and dependent workers, some Communists also claim it laid the necessary basis for these groups to be able to effectively oppose casteist practices and confront the traditional social order.

Indigenists' reading of the historical land question in Kerala diverges strongly from that of the Communist Party. One activist told me, "They [Communists] did not manage to do anything for the downtrodden Dalits and Adivasis. It's the ninth time now that the Communists are going to be in power but they haven't solved even the land issue!" The "tenant" reform, indigenists claim, was actually detrimental to many Adivasis as settlers who had informally taken land from them now claimed to be "tenants" and dubbed the Adivasis "landlords," thus legalizing land-grabbing. For other Dalits and Adivasis who were landless, land reform meant very little—many of them got to own the small piece of land on which their huts stood, a progressive measure no doubt, but it was always made sure they would not come to possess any land that they could use to cultivate and make a steady living from like the rest of society.

It is to Communist Party leaders themselves that many indigenist activists attribute the failure to effectively set ceilings to landholdings and redistribute the surplus. Boban, a Pulaya indigenist activist, complained of this:

> They [Dalits and Adivasis] fought against feudal values, but the party leader was the feudal lord. They initiated agricultural strikes. "The land you work shall be yours," was their slogan. But the party leaders diverted the strikes as they belonged to feudal families themselves. In 1945 EMS organized a meeting of Brahmins in Pallakad at Oomaloor. In that Yogakshema Sabha meeting, he advised the Brahmins to sell their land off and deposit the money in banks—otherwise, EMS told them, workers and labor unions would snatch their land and the Brahmins would become landless people. And for that purpose he himself established a bank called the Dhanlaxmi Bank. Earlier it was Dhanlaxmi Trust, now it's a bank with a nationwide presence. He came into power in 1957, and he has foreseen things much earlier and has saved his community. The Brahmins escaped to the town and started businesses. … They lost nothing.

Apart from converting their landed wealth painlessly into educational and business capital, indigenist activists claim many party leaders warned their relatives to register the family property in separate individual names so that in the end it seemed no family owned above the land ceiling. Boban continued, "EMS was always playing it very intelligently, to keep his own community safe. And *he* was General Secretary of the party, till he died he was chief minister of Kerala twice. And *that* person posed as the savior of the working class?!"

For many indigenist activists, betrayal by the party on the land question lies also in the sacrifices made by Dalits and Adivasis in the struggle, which are largely ignored by the party. The struggle at Punnapra-Vayalar in 1946, which is remembered in Communist circles as part of the Independence struggle and a democratic insurgency against the *dewan* of Travancore's attempt to introduce authoritarian constitutional reforms, is an important point of contention in this regard ("A war over history," P. Venugopal called it in the *Indian Express,* 28 November 1997). According to indigenist activists, it was actually a struggle by Dalits to prevent their eviction and contest the economic hardship imposed by the upper-caste (mostly Nair and Syrian Christian) landlords in the area (see Ayrookuzhiel 1990). The higher-caste Communist Party leaders, they say, took it up and fitted it into the struggle for Independence and "responsible government" but never acknowledged the Dalits who lost their life in the struggle. An activist in the RMS told me, "In 1957 the Left came to power through the Punnapra and Vayalar strikes. But their very first move was to chain the working class. More than five thousand SCs and STs had died at Punnapra and Vayalar!" In reference to the struggle for

Independence he added, "It is hard to be proud of this Kerala that has excluded Dalits and Adivasi for so long."

Drawing lessons from this history, most indigenist activists I spoke to agreed that it made no sense for Dalits and Adivasis to fight in one front with others: after bearing most of the sacrifices for the struggle, they received at most a few cents of wasteland. In fact, they argue, it is only with the rise of the AGMS and the breakthrough at Muthanga that the real struggle for land by all those excluded from Kerala's much-vaunted land reforms has started. As a joint statement by a number of activists supporting the indigenist struggle in Kerala reads, "Kerala was a land of unknown land struggles till the historic land agreement in 2001 October was signed between the protesting Dalits and Adivasis of Kerala and the State government. Since then Dalit and Adivasi land struggles in Kerala attained a new order of practice" (Peoples' Movements Solidarity Team 2007).

The indigenist reading of early twentieth-century activism in Kerala, in sum, is almost the opposite of the Communist story on all major questions—on what the nature of early reform movements was, on what the Communist role was vis-à-vis these movements, on where Kerala's famously high literacy rates come from and what the educational program of the Communist Party meant in this, and finally on the nature of land reforms and the land struggle in Kerala. In all this, the Communist Party equates itself with the "Kerala model" of development, while indigenist activists have come to see the Kerala model as either subtly or rather obviously serving to sustain upper-caste power at the expense of Dalits and Adivasis. And just as Communist Party members continue to mobilize and draw from academic networks behind a defense of the Kerala model (e.g., Dreze and Sen 1997; Franke and Chasin 2000; Heller 2005; Kjosavik 2004; UN 1975), indigenists have been encouraged in their reading by various scholars as well: Chandra Bhan Prasad (1998: 33), who argues that "EMS's Kerala model lags far behind the Congress model of Development" when it comes to Dalits and Adivasis; Gail Omvedt (2005: 4881), who claims that in terms of caste Kerala is simply "part of India"; Chatukalam and John (2006: 182), who argue that "tribals have been largely left out of the gains of the vaunted Kerala model of development"; or Sreekumar and Parayil (2006: 231), according to whom "state projects for the benefit of 'larger' society did not cover Adivasis" and instead often displaced and dispossessed them while "programs intended exclusively for their benefit only marginalized and deprived them further." But though it has gotten a lot of academic support from critical academics, the indigenist discourse is also constantly in danger of being mobilized by reactionary academic forces: the most notable example being how the American Enterprise Institute has twisted themes of the critique of the Kerala model by indigenist activists to argue for the classic neoliberal dogma against government intervention in the market and for "putting the Kerala model to rest" (Shah 2010). Yet because in their everyday political interaction Communist and indigenist activists are each other's most intimate Other, they tend to become more concerned with their differences on the reading of Kerala history than with defending the progressive commonalities of their interpretations. In the following section I will take a closer look at these polarizing political dynamics in the present, out of which these dichotomous views on Kerala's past have arisen—and to which they contribute.

## Revealing the "Real" Other: The Politics of Polarization

The different readings of the past that indigenist and Communist activists uphold should be seen in the context of their interaction in the course of the 1990s and 2000s, when, at almost every major turning point in its rise, the AGMS found itself confronted with the CPI(M). Already during the 1992 Sangamam, the CPI(M), following the example set by CPI(ML), was among the first to argue that the initiative was "foreign funded" and had "unpatriotic" aims (see chapter 2). When the United Democratic Front, led by Congress, was in power from 1991 to 1996, contention between the emerging indigenist movement and the government took place without much mutual defaming. Yet, when in 1996 the Left Democratic Front, led by the CPI(M), came to power, soon the confrontation between the movement and the government again took a more vicious turn, full of mutual defamatory accusations. Towards the end of the Left Democratic Front's term in May 2001, the CPI(M) had clashed with indigenist activist on two more major occasions: both at Kurichy and at Kundala. At Kurichy, the LDF[19] government was seen supporting the contractor against the colony's inhabitants—another proof to many indigenist activists that Communists were only interested in companies. At Kundala, the education minister in charge of the engineering college was the head of Kerala Congress (J), a regional party that had split off from Kerala Congress and joined the CPI(M)-led Left Democratic Front. The conflict again became primarily an indigenist versus Communist one since it was CPI cadres and activists of its trade union wing, AITUC, who supported the *goondas* connected to the Tata estates who came to attack the activists. The consequent reaction of the LDF government to condemn the activists rather than their attackers—and spread rumors again of how the tribals in question were manipulated by "outsiders"—only confirmed indigenist activists' opinion of the Left.

This stands in contrast to developments after the Congress-led UDF had taken over in May 2001 and indigenist activists for the first time were officially invited to talk to the government and reach an agreement. The impact of this symbolic gesture by A. K. Anthony, the Congress chief minister of Kerala at the time, was profound—so profound that despite the fact that it was this same UDF government that ordered the Muthanga police attack, and despite the historical antagonism between Congress and most Dalit and Adivasi communities, many indigenist activists I spoke to in 2005–07 still preferred to deal with Congress rather than with the Left. In 2006, AGMS activists decided to form the Rashtriya Maha Sabha as a political branch of the movement that would possibly give activists a voice in the Legislative Assembly and could strike where it hurt vested interests most: the electoral arena. On her decision to subsequently side with the UDF rather than the LDF during the 2006 municipal elections, Janu told me, "It is true that they [Congress] took a stand against the Muthanga strike. But they were willing to hold discussions with us on the Adivasi land issue, despite that attitude toward the Muthanga strike. We did conduct lots of strikes. But as a government they came forward for discussions, and made an agreement. The Left was never willing to do that." In an interview in 2005, Janu had made a similar point: "The government, be it left or right, they deal with things under the same political agenda. Now the right is in power and the next time when the left comes into power they will do the rest of what the right government has started. They will not make a separate agenda and work for it. One important thing that happened in the history of Kerala is that for the first time the Congress government accepted the Adivasis. None has done that hitherto. They accepted Adivasis, held a discussion sitting with them around one table, made an agreement and maintained that agreement ... to some extent." The sentiment was echoed by many, including, for instance, Mammen, for a while the vice-secretary of the AGMS, who argued, "If one can expect anything it is from the UDF government. It was they who were ready to discuss things when the tribal people protested—they were ready for an agreement."[20]

Many indigenist activists even see the Communist Party behind the Muthanga eviction. They claim the forest officials who had fomented the initial unrest—and gotten themselves captured by activists trying to stop the officials from giving the government an excuse to send in the police—were actually CPI(M) cadres. Just like Janu, Ammini Hamsakkali, a secondary leader of the AGMS, comes from Thrissileri where the CPI(M)–AGMS conflict was particularly intense. Ammini articulates a story that is common in AGMS circles: "A day before the [Muthanga] firing happened, CPM [CPI(M)] people came to set fire to elephant dung and throw it on our huts to create trouble … it was CPM people who did it. Do you know that? Did you know it was the CPM? So now you know who they are. What all they are capable of just to destroy our struggle. … They set fire and cut trees and then went to the collector to blame it on us." Even the death of one of the policemen at Muthanga is blamed on the CPI(M): "It was not Janu or Geethanandan or anybody who killed, but the people of the CPM. It was the people of the party who did it. They did it to destroy the struggle." And they had a reason to, according to Janu (interview, 2005):

> It was the need of the political movements of Kerala, the NGOs, the social organizations and everyone, but above all the Communist Party, that the Muthanga struggle should be pictured as a terrorist struggle. They want it to be pictured like this because … all these years it was with the people here that they nourished their movements … founded the organizations and in the case of NGOs, made the projects. … So if these people go for a struggle, get land, start cultivating things for their living, send their children to school and get educated they will no longer be available for these political movements and NGOs.

Similarly, Communist Party members are usually convinced the AGMS's main goal is to destroy the Communist movement, by "dividing the unity of the struggling masses." Behind all kinds of setbacks the Communist Party suffers, they have come to see the hand of the AGMS, in service of larger "vested interests." When in 2006 the AGMS formed a political branch—though it had earlier claimed not to be interested in elections—and on top of this allied with the Congress-led block and publicly declared it would "work to ensure the defeat of the CPI(M)-led Left Democratic Front" (*The Hindu*, 13 March 2006), most Communists saw all their worst suspicions confirmed.

Both political camps—the Communists versus the indigenists—have hence come to suspect the other intensely, believing it is working for its chief enemies in a perverse, hidden way. Both groups are preoccupied with discovering the "real" other and have become entangled in interactive spirals of suspicion on everything from the question of who the others really are and what their "real" intentions are, to what they are "actually" doing. In the interactive dynamics of such animosity, activists become ever more self-righteous about the maneuvering they engage in to ensure their political survival, projecting the ensuing unease onto the other, whose maneuvering is consistently read as signaling its essentially corrupt and malicious nature. It is precisely in such circles of disidentification that we can start to understand why indigenist activists felt the need to pose their challenge to the status quo in such radically different terms to that of traditional leftist political discourse.

### *Will the Real Adivasi Step Forward?*

One important issue around which disidentification takes place is the problem of defining "Adivasiness." In the face of public scrutiny of whether or not the political formations are representing—and being led by—"real Adivasis," mutual accusations abound. Communist Party members are convinced they are on the side of the real Adivasis as against "variants of identity politics promoted by foreign-funded NGOs that seek to fragment and separate Adivasi identities obliterating the class nature of exploitation" (as Brinda Karat put it in the CPI(M)'s theoretical quarterly *The Marxist* in September 2010). In this vein, a Kurichiya (ST) state committee member of the AKS was at pains to prove his genuine Adivasiness in reference to the heroic struggles of Thalakkal Chandu, the historical Kurichiya leader of a guerilla offensive against the British, and concluded with reference to the AGMS, "This is what is different about the AKS. All *our* leaders are Adivasis." In contrast, he immediately continued in accusatory tone: "Geethanandan set up this *gothra padasala* (clan school) here and just appointed some outside staff. Geethanandan himself is not even an Adivasi. He belongs to the Scheduled Castes."

P. K. Kalan also stressed this point: that Geethanandan, as a Dalit, would never be able to "truly understand Adivasi problems," though he was leading their movement. Kalan was rather suspicious of Geethanandan's leadership: "That is the reason why all these problems [at Muthanga] happened. Keeping Janu at the front of everything and using her as a cover, they exploited the Adivasis. … They are controlling Janu. She can't move on her own."

Written works by Communist members and sympathizers are full of allegations that Janu is not who she appears to be—not a true fighter for the Adivasi cause but rather the embodiment of all the major enemies and competitors of the Communists. For example, Aboo Backer, frequent commentator on Adivasi issues in *The Marxist*, writes, "C. K. Janu has been the creation of the bourgeois politics with the cunning assistance of the naxalite groups of the state in order to tamper with the long enduring solutions to the Adivasi questions introduced by the last [CPI(M)-led] LDF regime" (Backer 2002: 108). And he continues, "The traditional anti-Marxist media lent their full support to this [AGMS] agitation, in the process trying to project C. K. Janu as the real saviour of the tribals. However it was an attempt to thwart the [CPI(M)-led] Adivasi agitation and their demands" (ibid.). According to Backer, the participation of Adivasis in Communist-organized conventions proves that "the paper organizations [the AGMS] sponsored by the vested interests do not actually represent the genuine Adivasis" (ibid.: 109).

An elderly Paniya Communist whom I spoke to in Palakkad added to this line of argument another reason why Janu could not possibly be representative of the "real" Adivasi cause, namely because she did not obey the elderly Adivasi chieftains enough: "This so-called C. K. Janu, where did she suddenly come from? What does she know? If she were a real Adivasi she would know to let the elders lead."

For every Communist suspicion of the genuineness of indigenist activists there are, however, as many counter-suspicions and counterclaims to the effect that underneath Communist Party rhetoric, a divisive and deeply anti-Adivasi and anti-Dalit politics operates. According to Janu, the notion that Adivasis should remain numb is incorporated in the very definition of Adivasiness that most politicians, including Communists, use. In an interview, she explained this to me with regard to the Muthanga struggle:

> When the police started inflicting violence on some of us and the youngsters started fighting back ... we are to study that incident. When someone says "Janu and her friends are violent and they are not Adivasis," they imagine Adivasis as persons who are to bear all possible torture and violence. Even if an Adivasi got brutally murdered, we are not supposed to question it. The Adivasi has to endure all that torture, trauma, and violence with mute consent. Those who react are not Adivasis. So we have to analyze that one particular question itself. When they say that those who react are not Adivasis, actually they are giving the accurate answer of what they consider Adivasis should be.

As most indigenist activists agree, the Communist Party systematically negates any agency on the part of Dalits and Adivasis. Denying the agency of indigenist activists in politicizing the question of caste, these activists are instead accused of having naively caused the specter of caste to rise. Sunny Kapicadu argued, "Now Marxists are claiming to be in favor of the Adivasi, the Dalit. But their very ideology negates us. 'Where is caste?' these materialists ask us. 'Where is caste?' We cannot say to a materialist that caste is a social condition.

He wants to see it: 'No, no, you must show me caste, where is caste? There is no caste. Ha!' And then we came, a true Dalit Adivasi movement. How did these Marxists react? 'Aha, for the last forty years there is no caste in this society, now suddenly there is caste ... who is behind it? Ah, it is the Dalit, it is the Adivasi!'"

According to indigenist activists, though the AKS denies any positive political contribution by Adivasis and Dalits, it itself is the real farce. Geethanandan explained why:

> Now the CPI(M) also has this Adivasi organization, AKS. ... I also talked to their leader ... Vidyadharan Kani [laughs] ... he belongs to the Kani community. ... He is actually the only one from an Adivasi community there. Everything is controlled by the political party leaders. And Kani is not like Janu; he's not representing the different communities of Adivasis. See Janu, she is a nationalist leader, a national leader of the Adivasis. All the different nationalities—Paniya, Adiya, Kurichiya—she is representing them. But in the Kshema Samithi [AKS] they are all represented by party leaders. It's a problem they're facing. But they can rally people anyway because they have money; they have a political apparatus in each and every village.

Another AGMS activist told me about the AKS, "It's not a democratically organized tribal community, it's just a trust, a registered trust ... and all the members ... all seven members who registered this society, not a single one of them is Adivasi!"

### *"If Adivasis Develop They Cannot Play with Them"*

Another mutual suspicion projecting structural contradictions onto the closest political opponent is the notion that the other "wants to always keep Adivasis as a backward group," as an Adiya member of the AKS expressed it. The logic of the allegation is that rather than the oppressed needing leaders, it is leaders who need the oppressed. "They don't let Adivasis achieve good standards of living and culture. They want to keep Adivasis without any social refinement," the same Communist member said. He added, "What Geethanandan and others are trying to do is to make sure Adivasis will always be under them. They want Adivasis to dance according to the tunes they play." A Kurichiya AKS member put it even more forcefully: "Janu and Geethanandan are people who don't want any good to happen to Adivasis. If Adivasis develop they cannot play with the Adivasis."

The idea resonates directly with statements from Communist leaders such as Pinarayi Vijayan. After the signing of the 2001 agreement between the AGMS and (Congress) Chief Minister A. K. Anthony, Vijayan argued in front of a convention of the AKS that the whole

Muthanga strike had been merely an "image-building exercise" for Anthony and Janu: "The Adivasis have earned nothing from the agitation of Janu. It was Janu who earned a good [media] coverage" (*The Hindu*, 18 October 2001).

Most Communists believe that outside of the spotlights of the media, all but neglected, the genuine force pushing for Adivasi welfare was the Communist Party. According to Communist MLA P. Krishnaprasad, who generally refrains from fueling the antagonism between the AGMS and the AKS, "The bourgeois media projected the Gothra Maha Sabha agitation as the only case of resistance put up by the tribals, and tried to suppress the news of AKS struggles." According to Suresh, a Paniya member of the AKS, Janu and Geethanandan were preventing Adivasis from "rising to the forefront of society" by "reviving old superstitious beliefs." Suresh believed that the *poojas* and other rituals he had seen AGMS followers practice were aimed at "mystifying" their thoughts and preventing them from understanding the bigger picture. He clarified: "We don't want Adivasis to leave their ways and rituals. We want the believers to continue in their beliefs. But [unlike the AGMS] the Adivasi Kshema Samithi neither supports nor allows beliefs and rituals that are blind."

AGMS activists in turn are convinced the Communist parties prefer to keep Adivasis in an impoverished, desperate position so that they remain their natural constituency even though the actual constituency of the CPI(M)—the one whose interests it represents—has become the middle class. The key issue for the Communist Party, according to indigenist activists, is to gather "vote banks." According to Kavitha, a Kurichiya activist with the AGMS, party members are so concerned with votes that they start seeing every social initiative as a threat: "I joined with Janu *chechi* [elder sister], to work with her. But I had no ill feeling toward the party at all. I used to give them my vote. But I wanted to work with Janu because of the land issue. Then party people started discriminating against us, calling us 'Janu's people,' saying 'soon she will be giving her vote to Janu.'"

The obsession of the Communist Party with elections was widely criticized, especially where the party was apparently willing to actively block measures that might make Adivasis less needy and dependent just in order not to lose leverage over their votes. Another Paniya activist of the AGMS gave me an example:

> Now there's elections coming up again. So what happens? We were about to get the title deeds [for the land occupied at Aralam farm]. But the CPM [CPI(M)] men influenced the Collector and the Revenue Department and somehow got it stopped. AKS now can promise that with the next elections,

> if CPM wins, all will get land. But how can we trust the CPM? If they win, for five years nothing will happen. Only near elections, they will make a few gestures, just enough to secure their vote. If they wanted, we could all have had title deeds long time ago—but then how to pressurize us to give our vote?

Every move the CPI(M) makes towards Adivasi identity politics—the Communists' appreciation of Ambedkar, their turn to using the notion of Dalit rights, their call for an "intensified struggle for Adivasi rights," and various symbolic gestures such as their role in institutionalizing the "P. K. Kalan Prize" or the "Ambedkar Award"—hence become interpreted as electoral moves and attempts at co-opting the indigenist movement. A Dalit activist even described the Ambedkar Award to me as "the award for Dalits working against Dalits." About the Communist engagement with Ambedkar, Geethanandan said, "Of course Communists argue that Ambedkar is a very good person. Ambedkar fought against caste, didn't he? It's part of democratization and Communists also stand for democratization. ... so Ambedkar who fought against 'casteism' and tried to democratize India is part of Communism ... [they will reduce his thought to] nothing more than that!"

The formation of the AKS is generally interpreted precisely as an attempt to "secure the Adivasi vote bank" in reaction to C. K. Janu's increasing popularity and her exposure of the Communist Party's moral corruption. Maren, one of the Adiya activists I interviewed, explained it this way:

> The AKS is an organization that was formed only after Janu's organization came into action. At the time of Janu's [Muthanga] strike, all the Adivasis stood behind her. So they neglected the Communist Party. Naturally it would lose its Adivasi vote bank. So it became very dissatisfied with Janu's organization and formed the AKS to spread the rumor that "Janu won't get you land. Only we can do that for you." I'm skeptical of that statement. At the time of the previous UDF government we were getting 10 kilos of free ration during rainy season. Now with LDF government we are getting only 5 kilos—even though most Adivasis are now with the AKS, not with Janu! The situation is in their [the Communists'] favor now [they are in government] so they should keep their promises. But all they are interested in is to get the Adivasi vote.

Sajitkumar, a Dalit activist in the AGMS, echoes the same idea, that the AKS was formed not to advance any Adivasi struggles but merely to undermine the AGMS: "The Communists who claim to work for the poor subverted our strikes by forming a parallel organization called AKS. They stole our agenda and plans."

The fact that the AKS was started in order to co-opt the indigenist movement into Communist networks at all costs is all the more noticeable, according to Geethanandan, in how the Communist Party is willing to go against its own ideological line in order to do so:

> Up until 1990, end of eighties, Janu was very acceptable [to the Communist Party], as an "agricultural laborer" and a [Communist] activist. But after 1989 she came out of the Marxist party and started organizing Adivasis in a different way, on a community basis … and they started opposing her. … They initially said Adivasis should not be organized on a community basis … but after two, three years they started organizing Adivasis in the Kshema Samithi. On community basis! This same Communist Party. Generally they are working on a class line … then why are they organizing this Kshema Samithi?

If the Communist Party was really interested in their well-being, indigenist activists argue, it would have acted on their behalf long before Muthanga. As Maren said: "It's just part of their survival strategy that now they are trying to point to all they have done for Adivasis. But it's only after Muthanga that the Marxist party came to stand with us. Did they not realize before that most Adivasis do not even have a piece of land to bury their dead? Were they unaware that we had no land? They knew it … now it's not that they really want to speak for us, they just have their interests to protect."

*Imagined Economies of Exploitation and Betrayal*

The most intensely polarizing views of both camps go even further than to allege the other is hoping to keep Adivasis oppressed, claiming that the other leadership is actively exploiting or oppressing its followers. The structural differences between an institutionalized and well-resourced party, able to pay its staff salaries, and a beginning movement with few resources, whose activists generally lack income, give rise to mutual suspicions of malicious intent. The wildest stories were circulating in Communist Party networks about C. K. Janu having, under false promises, collected money from the poorest tribals to buy herself a "lavish lifestyle." A Kurichiya member of the AKS told me, "Things happened to Janu all of a sudden. She was born to an agriculturalist's family. She was poor like any other Adivasi. Now suddenly she has a huge house[21] and all kinds of luxuries. She built that house in two years' time. How could she do that in two years' time? That is what our question is. We know they are getting foreign money. That is how they get that much money."

Such stories were then often contrasted to the story of P. K. Kalan (the Adiya Communist and Janu's uncle), who had refused, even as panchayat president, to accept money to build a house for himself and had used the money instead to build a school building for children. Unlike those in other movements, the argument went, Communists were not after greed and corruption. A Communist journalist I often spoke to was, as many Communists are, convinced there were all kinds of unscrupulous people, including Naxalites and Janu, making money at the expense of poor tribals: "They will tell foreigners that the Adivasis here in Kerala are so poor and they are starving and so on. They send reports to foreign countries describing the plight of the Adivasis. And they receive money in return for that. They get a lot of money from abroad in name of the Adivasis. The Adivasis don't even know that others are taking money in their name. Is this not exploitation? It's nothing but exploitation."

This line of argument even sometimes stretches beyond the leadership to defame the followers of the other movement as dupes or, in CPI(M) leader Pinarayi Vijayan's words, the few "gullible and apolitical" among the Adivasis (*The Hindu,* 18 October 2001). The AKS in contrast, its members claim, helps, rather than takes from, poor Adivasis. As an AKS member at Aralam farm told me: "Did you see how much money they collected for the Muthanga occupation? Five hundred rupees they collected from each of these poor Adivasis. And nothing did they get in return. AKS is not like that. It is not the way the AKS functions. We do not take money from poor Adivasis!"

AKS members interpreted the "self-help groups" that the AGMS was organizing at Aralam farm (one of its land occupations)—to pool agricultural products and trade them cooperatively—in this same light. An AKS activist I spoke to claimed to be so upset by the "exploitation" going on that they organized to take over the AGMS office at Aralam farm: "Do you know what they are using their office building for? To collect and store coconuts and other stuff for sale. The money they made out of this went straight into their pockets. Leaders like Geethanandan did that!"[22]

Many Communists even blamed the AGMS leadership for the repression that Adivasis experienced at Muthanga. A Communist party member active in Wayanad told me: "Janu played some games for her benefit, using people of that community [Adivasis]. In Wayanad, the people who suffer the most these days are those who stood with Janu."

After the Muthanga violence, it was instead the Communist Party that people could rely on, Communists claim. For example, Suresh Babu, a Paniya AKS member said to me, "When all those Adivasis were in jail, including workers of the Adivasi Gothra Maha Sabha, people of Janu's organization … that organization of Janu didn't do anything to take them out on bail or return them to their homes. It was the Communist Party and the AKS who did all the work of taking them from the jail and bringing them home safely … It was the Communist Party of India that spent money for them. Amongst all the confusion, the only one to help them was the Communist Party and the other Left [party-affiliated] organizations."

Indigenist activists in turn see the Communist Party's large institutional structure as seamlessly blending into local relations of power that oppress Adivasi workers. And since it is often Communist networks that have penetrated deepest into rural areas with a high concentration of Adivasis, the most frequent complaints of direct exploitation tend to be about the Communist Party. Akkati, a Paniya activist from Thirunelli *panchayat* told me, "Men of our community are given toddy and arrack in the nights and girls are seduced. How many unmarried mothers there are in the panchayat! The girls are taken to see films, again and again. Films are a passion for our kids. They are tempted. After seeing the films, the parents are given alcohol and the girls are seduced. The CPM men, they are directly involved. They know they need to cover it all up."

The only reason why some Adivasis still stand with the party, many AGMS activists argued, is as pretense, simply to get some short-term benefits. This, however, does not make committed followers, as Janu points out with reference to the AKS:

> If I give some people 1000 rupees as salary and ask them to partake actively in the works of Gothra Sabha, and appoint someone as a leader, he or she will not necessarily become a leader. That person will come to get the salary. In the eyes of the society, this person is known as the leader. But, that person is not a leader deep inside. … If you decide for yourself to come, then nothing can prevent you. That is the problem with me. Since I joined out of determination, I can't go back no matter what others say. If someone comes to kill me, I'll say, "Kill me if you dare." If I had joined on somebody else's words, I would go back when I stop getting their [financial] support. People must come with a determination that comes from within. … Some come with some selfish interests, to gain some benefits. After some days, when they don't get benefits they will go back.

Indigenist activists thus argue that the ones who are really being duped are Communists who believe they can pay off Adivasis to become genuine followers. To reassert the agency that the discourse of Adivasis always being exploited by leaders denies them, some suggest that it may well be the leaders themselves who are being exploited. The Kattunaikan leader of a smaller, independent land occupation in Wayanad said, "The AKS, this Marxist party's Adivasi wing, they want to gather Adivasis behind them. But if AKS fails to give the Adivasis the promised land, then definitely they will move away from the party. If they *are* working for the Adivasis, good, then definitively they will stand with them. What is even the point in saying they [the Communist leaders] are exploiting?" Or in the words of Maren, "Yes, at the time of election we used to cast our votes. It doesn't mean anything. Our aim is to get land, not to support any political party."

Yet while some stress the need to keep one's eye on the long-term material goals, other indigenist activists emphasize the importance of moral strength in navigating the CPI(M)-dominated landscape of electioneering and political patronage. For example, Kavitha told me, "Two men from the [Communist] party came to my house and offered me money to speak against C. K. Janu in the press conference. They said they would provide for the education of my children too if I spoke against Janu. Janu may not help me in my needs. But I don't want to live with the money gained by betraying someone. So I said I would not speak against Janu and they were offended. The party has been neglecting us ever since."

Spirals of mutual defaming between the AGMS and the CPI(M) thus paint a nasty picture of the political other while simultaneously emphasizing Adivasi followers as likely to be duped and powerless. It is not surprising that in this context, Adivasis partaking in the struggles themselves prefer instead to emphasize their political cunningness and moral fiber.

## Conclusion

To the question of what may have caused the rise of indigenism in Kerala in terms of the political dynamics involved, this and the previous chapter have demonstrated the role of the diminishing appeal of the major alternative to indigenist mobilization in Kerala, that is, the Communist movement. This diminishing appeal does not translate directly into defeat in the arena of parliamentary elections—to the contrary, the CPI(M) in fact claims it "created history" with its election victory in 2006, when it received a "whopping 65 seats and 33 percent votes" (CPI(M) website). This, however, goes together with an increasingly disillusioned working class constituency and intelligentsia who feel that electoral Communism has clearly run its course. Many may still vote for the party to get some practical concessions through its patron–client networks and because there is no realistic electoral alternative, but they no longer believe the party genuinely strives for socialist aims. The demise of the Communist Party in this sense can hardly be considered a sign of democratization. Instead it seems to signal something quite the opposite: the classical social movements' dilemma of how to sustain a popular movement for social reform while at the same time participating in institutions designed to implement such reform as policy (Tarrow 1998). In the course of its continuing participation in power, and all the more so from the 1990s onward when there seemed to be no more scope for state-led socialist reform in a liberalizing economy, subaltern groups in Kerala stopped believing the party still stood for greater social equality and emancipation. This, in turn, lead to a reevaluation of earlier compromises and to critiques of the bias in Indian Communism that had not allowed for a serious engagement with the issue of caste and cultural identity—just as socialist parties in Latin America and Australia are now criticized for having ignored issues of ethnicity and race. Some scholars (e.g., Yashar 2005) believe such emerging critiques show that indigenous people were never really part of socialist initiatives—that also outside of authoritarian regimes, such socialist initiatives were merely imposed on indigenous people by nonindigenous activists and that hence the present moment is one of liberation for indigenous people. As the previous chapter showed, however, many indigenous people in Kerala were closely and personally attached to Communist ideals of fighting for equality and emancipation and only left the party because they were disillusioned by it. The present chapter, moreover, showed how in the process of leaving the party, a rereading of history and an othering of political rivals escalated into widening circles of political disidentification between Communists and indigenists.

The demise of socialism as a force for change was particularly salient in contributing to the rise of indigenism in Kerala. This socialist demise, however, is part of a larger global conjuncture marked by what Wallerstein (2004) calls "the end of a reformist cycle." The reformist cycle, according to Wallerstein, was a long period that began in the mid nineteenth century and that was characterized by the supremacy of the liberal state in combination with "antisystemic" movements demanding inclusion through the mechanism of citizenship. This reformist period was, Wallerstein argues, one of an "optimism of the oppressed" (ibid.: 85)—the idea that history was on their side and that with certain sacrifices in the present, future generations would be facing a better life. By the early decades of the twentieth century, after decades of internal debate within antisystemic movements, the "political option" had become the dominant antisystemic strategy and there was a general agreement on a "two-step agenda of action: first obtain power in the state, then transform the world/the state/the society" (ibid.: 69). In the post–World War II period, antisystemic movements made extraordinary progress in terms of the "first step," and Kerala, the first state to have a democratically elected Communist government, was an example to social democrats across the world. For a while, it was even believed the state might hold the key to a new path to socialism, a "Kerala path," proving that socialism and liberal democracy were not incompatible after all, that even within the frame of a capitalist world economy, there was a route to the kind of democracy both socialists and liberals envisioned as their ideal. As we saw in the previous chapter, this was a period in which many Adivasis and Dalits—like P. K. Kalan—embraced the role of the party in negotiating on their behalf with the powers that be, not because they were blind to the compromises being made but because the results were indeed "progressive," opening up political and economic space for those erstwhile almost entirely excluded.

Yet as popular left-wing movements around the world came to power, a creeping disillusion arose with their apparent inability, once in power, of taking the next step towards social transformation. Including in Kerala, people now found themselves in the position of even being asked "not to make militant demands on what was asserted to be a government that represented them" (Wallerstein 2004: 84ff.). As "the future became the present" many previously ardent militants "began to have second thoughts, and eventually began to dissent" (ibid.). By the late 1960s, the "long-existing anger about the workings of the world-system" combined with a bitter "disappointment with the capacity of the antisystemic movements to transform the world" (ibid.). Two themes were repeated in virtually every context in the protests erupting in the late sixties: on the one hand a rejection of US hegemonic power and criticism of the collusion of the Soviet Union in the American world order; and on the other, a disillusion with the failed promises of antisystemic movements once in power. The long-term certainties that the future would be better had become transformed into "fears that the world-system might be unchanging" (ibid.). The automatic dominance of the liberal center diminished. And this, in turn, formed the context in which the Left (that often did not call itself that anymore) started looking for entirely different forms of organizing and political ideology, triggering the rise of, among others, indigenous rights movements. The kind of clash between these new movements with remainders of the traditional Left, which the present chapter discussed in detail in the case of Kerala, is a general characteristic of the ensuing political dynamics. The antagonism is all the more present where the traditional Left tried to co-opt the new movements through an increasingly hollow rhetoric of socialist developmentalism (Harvey 2003: 168). The infighting and polarization among those who biographically and even ideologically are in fact so close is all the more indicative, however, of the diminishing political space for those currents seeking to resist the ever more unrestrained accumulation and concentration of capital that was unfolding globally from the late seventies. For the crisis of reformism that appeared in the late sixties did not trigger only new social movements—it also triggered a fierce and remarkably successful reaction from the right: the capitalist establishment's counterrevolution of neoliberalism, which made the rise of financial capital to global hegemony a reality. The material effects of this and how they structurally conditioned the rise of indigenism in Kerala is the focus of the following two chapters.

## Notes

1. Projit Mukherji (2009: 93) even argues that "Marxism … in [West] Bengal is no longer a matter of revolutionary praxis … it has instead become a matter of ethnic identity," and that in these contexts one can apparently simply "*be* a Bengali Marxist" as a matter of pride—one need not demonstrate this Marxism by acting in a certain way.
2. Purdah, the concealing of women from men and indeed from all public life, exists in various forms both in Muslim and Hindu communities in India. Namboodiri women did not use a *burkha* but a large palm leaf umbrella to shield their face and generally remained within the walls of the family home (Saradamoni 1980: 129).
3. The *yajnopavita* (sacred thread) is a marker that certain Hindu men wear as sign of having been "twice-born"—a ritual that has historically been restricted to the highest three *varnas* (religious castes).
4. Saradamoni (1980: 146ff.) and Mohan (2008) describe and analyze Ayyappan's struggles in more detail.
5. Mathew Baxter (2009) has done a fascinating study of how EVR vernacularized concepts from the Manifesto in his translation.
6. The Vaikom Satyagraha took place in 1924–25 and was not an actual temple-entry movement but a movement—led by Congress—to establish the right of untouchable lower castes to use the public roads *around* the Vaikom temple (see Raimon 2006). The struggle gained attention particularly for Gandhi's involvement in it. As Raimon's (2006) fascinating collection of documents of the time shows, Gandhi used the occasion primarily to promote the nonviolent, non-"impatient" approach with which he confronted Hindu orthodoxy.
7. By the 1920s, the NSS owned over a hundred acres of land and school buildings and equipment worth over two hundred thousand rupees (Jeffrey 1992: 104).

8. Earlier they had to use special roads or jump off the road and make themselves invisible if someone from a higher caste would appear on the horizon. In the movie *Elippathayam* by Adoor Gopalakrishnan, many such practices are powerfully dramatized.
9. These struggles are documented in detail in Saradamoni 1980 (see 146ff.)
10. Caste-determined dress codes and other everyday rules used to be extreme in Kerala in the nineteenth century. There used to, for instance, be a "polluting distance" for every caste and strict rules on what ornaments particular castes could or could not wear. Even language was caste differentiated and lower castes were forced to use self-debasing words. Names given to people's dwellings differed according to caste (e.g., *chala* for Dalits, *illam* for Namboodiris)—a Pulaya, when in front of a higher-caste person, had to refer to his own dwelling as a "dung-heap" (Saradamoni 1980: 33f.).
11. According to independent researcher Kumar (2009: 402) there are indeed 40 percent more ST and SC party members in the Communist party in Kerala than in Congress.
12. This dislike was fed by suspicion against her cosmopolitanism and rarely was based on having read her book since its Malayalam translation from English only came out in February 2011.
13. Roy goes on to call EMS "the flamboyant Brahmin high priest of Marxism in Kerala" faced with "the extraordinary—critics said absurd—position of having to govern a people and foment revolution simultaneously." Though one can see Roy is not altogether hostile to EMS or the Communist effort, Communists I spoke to in Kerala universally and passionately condemned her for saying such "awful" words about EMS.
14. Chakravarti (2003) works out a similar criticism from a feminist perspective.
15. For an insightful and detailed academic account of the history of literacy and politics in Kerala, with first-hand observations from the 1960s, see Gough 1968.
16. For an academic account of this struggle see Saradamoni 1980: 148.
17. This criticism is beautifully elaborated in *Twinkle Twinkle Little Caste,* a (2009) documentary by Soumya Vincent, about casteism in a nursery school in Kerala.
18. Her case is analyzed from a Dalit perspective in "On Suicides, Caste and Higher Education" by K. P. Girija in *Insight Young Voices* (February/March 2009), a Dalit youth magazine.
19. Two major coalitions emerged in Kerala in the 1970s. One is the Left Democratic Front (LDF), led by the CPI(M). The other, the United Democratic Front (UDF), is led by the Indian National Congress.
20. This perception was nurtured by Congress, which posted page-wide advertisements in all major newspapers in 2001 when the agreement was signed between Anthony and Janu, showing the silhouette of a curly-haired tribal woman with a baby and claiming that Congress had been the first to help the tribals.
21. I've seen Janu's new house and must say it takes considerable imagination, in the context of Kerala, to call it a "huge house."
22. An activist close to Geethanandan within the RMS in fact confided to me worriedly, "He is giving his whole life to these causes. What will happen in his old age? Will people remember his sacrifices when he is old and poor?"

# PART IV

## Conditioning Indigenism: The "Kerala Model" in Crisis

– Chapter 5 –

# Salaried but Subaltern: On the Vulnerability of Social Mobility

In this chapter and the next, I turn to the study of shifts in "structural power" (Wolf 1990: 587) that conditioned the rise of indigenism in Kerala. I focus on the kind of forces that shape the setting in which the political dynamics I discussed in the previous two chapters unfolded and I consider the changing political economy of the Kerala model of development. I hence explore how changes in the context of people's everyday working lives conditioned their attraction to new forms of contention—to indigenist rather than Communist visions thereof. In doing so, I propose an explanation that goes beyond another structural explanation for the global rise of indigenism: that indigenism was a way for indigenous people to defend their communities' cultural integrity, with whatever organizational and legal frameworks were available, in the face of neoliberal dispossession and disintegration (e.g., Niezen 2003, Yashar 2005). This prevalent explanation sees indigenous people's mobilization as simply the most rational response by people culturally attached to their existing, indigenous way of life against the threat that neoliberalism poses to this way of life. Instead of this, I propose a perspective that studies how the rise of indigenism was shaped by the process of economic restructuring itself—by, in this case, the crisis of the Kerala model. I hence do not see economic restructuring merely as an external, future threat that people react to but as an ongoing process that people become part of and that in itself conditions the way they resist. The dynamics of this entanglement add a second explanation—besides the political explanation based on social movement cycles—of why subaltern protest took indigenist rather than Communist forms.

Connecting the political rise of indigenism to economic restructuring means understanding it in terms of everyday, lived experiences. I rely in this on an expanded class perspective that takes class as an analytical concept "rooted in the basic and never frictionless ties and interdependences between ... people as arising from their efforts to survive and maintain themselves" (Kalb 1997: 2). Used in this way, the concept of class helps to relate the daily necessity of securing a living, and the human need for orientation and meaning deriving from this, with the changing regimes of production and appropriation in which such experiences take place. It thereby provides more relational and grounded insights into the process through which people became attracted to the politics of indigenism. I do not take class as yet another factor explaining the attraction of indigenism along with, for instance, the compulsions of "culture," the drive of "self-interest," or the determinants of law: class added in such a manner in fact means depriving class analysis of its synthetic power (Thompson 1965). Cultural, self-interested, or legal determinants are not insignificant in contributing to the rise of indigenism but have more explanatory power when interpreted in terms of a relational and historical class perspective that refuses to disembed people's beliefs, interests, and practices from the everyday conflictive context of living in an evolving capitalist world system. It is precisely by posing the question of the rise of indigenism—for example, by looking at the process of political identification rather than the static question of political identity—that class as a historical relationship of power can be seen to have a determinant role, limiting what is possible and pushing towards what is likely, though never predefining the outcome.

At a global scale, the process through which people's working lives have become transformed has been shaped by the effects of the reaction by the capitalist Establishment to the world revolution of 1968 (Wallerstein 2004: 85f.). The more ferocious of this reaction—the neoliberal counterrevolution—intensified the systemic shift in global capitalism in the late twentieth century towards "accumulation by dispossession" becoming the dominant form of accumulation relative to "expanded reproduction" (Harvey 2003: 153). Whereas expanded reproduction entails deriving profits from the intensification of production—and reinvesting these profits in the productive process (ibid.: 57)—the logic behind accumulation by dispossession is one of intensifying forms of commodification and the privatization of common forms of property rights. Hence it goes accompanied by the expulsion of people from their land and an increasing precariousness as austerity programs re-commodify socioeconomic rights won by labor in previous struggles. These are often, as David Harvey stresses, coercive processes in which the state's monopoly of violence and definitions of legality are key (ibid.: 145). Also in India, struggles over land—the most literal "green field" to be converted into financial profit—intensified after the Indian federal government embraced economic liberalization in the early 1990s. Large areas of land were sold off to mining companies and traded on the stock market (Roy 2010), social and environmental regulations on big dam building were undermined (Khagram 2004: 208f.), and Special Economic Zones occupied ever more space (Banerjee-Guha 2008; Levien 2011). Each of these types of projects relied on the massive deployment of police forces, and even the army, to clear the land of the people living there.

Yet in Kerala the process is subtler than elsewhere. Kerala's government did not allow for large-scale or violent evictions of peasant land nor did it introduce dramatic structural adjustment or austerity policies. What did happen is that with liberalization in 1991, capital further abandoned this state, already famous for its "troublesome" (or "strike-prone") population (see Kannan 1999: 141). A massive "people's planning campaign" was initiated by several key Communist party members in reaction, channeling more than a third of government funds directly to the municipal level to support small-scale productive initiatives in order to revive Kerala's economy. Initiators of the campaign were confident a "new Kerala model" was, in changed circumstances, continuing the old Kerala model of ensuring general wellbeing (Isaac and Franke 2002). The decentralization campaign was not, however, enough to compensate for the lack of manufacturing capital invested in the state and itself became the subject of neoliberal cooptation (Menon and Nigam 2007: 108). The old Kerala model, it became clear, did not merely signal Kerala's exceptional commitment to redistributive and protective programs—it was also intricately part of a world historical period in which expanded reproduction was the dominant form of accumulation. As this part of the book shows, the global economic restructuring driven by neoliberalism did not, as some scholars continue to suggest (e.g., Heller 2007), leave Kerala unaffected. Kerala is not simply one of the few remaining "social democracies" in the global South, isolated from the pressures under which so many other social democracies turned neoliberal. In fact, it turns out the Kerala model pertained more to a particular spatial and temporal conjuncture in world history than to Kerala per se. If the Kerala model was about taming the market through the enforcement of stringent labor laws and land reform, public provision of education and healthcare, a broad range of redistributive welfare measures, and a relatively large public sector in both manufacturing and agriculture, the liberalization of the Indian economy in the 1990s was part of a process that structurally undermined these achievements.

The structural shifts affecting class relations and conditioning the rise of indigenism in Kerala were expressed differently according to the different class positions of those involved in the AGMS. Whereas the next chapter focuses on the experiences of the agricultural workers who form the rank and file of the AGMS's demonstrations and land occupations, this chapter focuses on the AGMS leadership: an upwardly mobile yet vulnerable group of often well-educated, salaried Adivasis and Dalits who experience the effects of intensifying competition that accompany the demise of the Kerala model. This chapter follows the experiences of several such upwardly mobile indigenist activists, pointing out how political-economic changes affecting their lives shaped their turn to indigenist politics.

The activists who form the leadership of the AGMS have certain educational achievements, financial resources, and social networks that facilitated their struggle for the indigenist cause. Minimally they are in a position to combine their unpaid public activism with the need to secure their own livelihood—this being difficult for landless workers who spend their days doing manual labor for minimal wages.[1] Indeed, though strictly economic class differences among Adivasis and Dalits are less than among other groups (Deshpande 2000: 325), the leadership of the AGMS is not in the same position as its followers. The question I look at in this chapter is why, in addition to the ideological reasons discussed in the previous two chapters, the more upwardly mobile among Dalits and Adivasis would be encouraged through structural changes affecting their lives to dedicate their energy and time to organizing an indigenist movement.

This question of the everyday socioeconomic experiences that motivate activist leaders is not often discussed in indigenous studies, as these leaders tend to occupy a complex, atypical position. In the AGMS for instance, apart from C. K. Janu, most leaders have not personally experienced dire poverty and exclusion. Instead, they are socioeconomically close to what might be considered mainstream Kerala—precisely something that allows them to contribute to the movement so effectively. Accepting that leaders' own everyday experiences with maintaining themselves in Kerala society differ from those of followers should not, however, open the door to purely utilitarian arguments about what motivates them: that these leaders would be entrepreneurial or even "exploitative" middle-class men (sometimes women) who are in it simply for financial and cultural/symbolic gain. Such arguments do not explain, for instance, why they did not turn to less risky and more comfortable avenues for personal upward mobility. They, for instance, could have joined the established, well-oiled networks of the major political parties all too eager to incorporate them and their followers. Many indigenist leaders instead run up large debts because of their political activities and get at most an ambiguous social reputation in return. They may be known as defending "poor Adivasis," yet at the same time they usually become the target of vicious smear campaigns, which can be all the more damaging for female leaders. While leaders play a key role in the movement's successes in securing development resources such as land or subsidies from the state, they themselves are seldom eligible to receive any of these resources.

Yet it would also be incorrect to think leaders are motivated purely by abstract concerns to do with ideology or with the situation of the poorest and most oppressed Adivasis in Kerala. As this chapter will demonstrate, leaders do in fact experience the processes associated with the decline of the Kerala model in their own everyday lives. Leaders generally do not dwell on their personal experiences but they do integrate these in their larger political vision. This indigenist vision primarily criticizes the plight of the most marginalized Adivasis and Dalits but at the same time is strongly in line with the way these leaders would prefer to see their own lives in Kerala society transformed. The anxiety and anger that surfaces in their own struggles to maintain their socioeconomic position thus fuels their activism concretely. In this chapter I present vignettes of such everyday struggles in two arenas where many present insecurities take shape: first, the arena of land ownership, professional occupation, and consumption, crucial in representing social status in Kerala today; and second, the arena of education, where middle-class[2] Malayalees concentrate their hopes of carrying over their own social mobility onto their children's generation.

## Pride and Representation in a Bourgeoisifying Society

The initial embourgeoisement of Kerala was arguably a product of the Kerala model of development itself: as land reform gave tenant farmers and even some agricultural workers access to land, it also turned them into small (petit-bourgeois) landowners committed to social mobility within the existing system rather than to revolutionary reform (Morrison 1997; Kannan 1999). The process started already in the 1960s and 1970s. Yet it is in the course of the 1980s and 1990s that successful new small landowners *en masse* started using land not so much for farming but rather as capital to raise money, through sale or loans, to underwrite the costs of setting up off-farm income-earning (Morrisson 1997). Ironically, as the potential of land as a productive resource decreased—as Kerala's agricultural economy was opened up to international competition—land became all the more important as both a sign of social standing and a means toward it by allowing one to draw loans to finance projects of upward mobility. The money made by educated family members who managed to get a salaried job or work in one of the Gulf states—an increasing trend from the 1970s onward—usually became invested in buying more land. Everywhere in key rice-producing regions I visited during my fieldwork in 2005 and 2006, I could see paddy fields being filled up with soil to turn them into ordinary real estate plots. Interest in land as a key form of symbolic capital was also reflected in the sharp rise in land prices—up to 2,000 percent since 1980 (Osella and Osella 2000: 146). As Osella and Osella observed, many people buy land for habitation as soon as enough money is available and only then later start constructing a house on it (ibid.). Agricultural land is bought even later, if at all. Among non-SC/STs in Kerala, landlessness decreased from 12 percent to 7.7 percent between 1982 and 1992 (Omvedt 2006: 192): not due to some belated Kerala-model style land reform[3] but a reflection of the fact that everybody who possibly could was privately investing in land.

The percentage of landlessness for SCs and STs in Kerala, though it has also decreased, still remains more than double that of other communities (Omvedt 2006: 192.). Both Dalits and Adivasis were hard hit by the rising unemployment in Kerala in the 1990s and overall had less access to Gulf money (ibid.). Even those who did manage to progress significantly in comparison to the generation of their parents by acquiring land or a professional job started to see their achievements pale in comparison to the stream of Gulf money—estimated at no less than $150 billion in total between 1980 and 2010 (Oommen 2010: 80)—that was flowing mostly towards other communities, who were in turn investing it in private education and land. They also felt the tensions produced by the increasing competition to express one's self and family name through consumption. As much as production has stagnated in Kerala in the past two decades, consumption thrives. Oommen (2010: 73) has found that since 1993–94, Kerala has had the highest per capita consumer expenditure of all Indian states—and the consumption rate has grown exponentially since then. The divide between the poorest and the richest groups in terms of these consumption figures is growing and Kerala's Gini coefficient has increased tremendously—it is now estimated at 41 percent, second only to Chattisgarth (ibid.). I turn here to studying concretely how such structural processes impacted the lives of those who became indigenist leaders.

### *"It's Not about Earning More. It's about Dignity."*

Sunny Kapicadu has been one of the most important Dalit activists who behind the scenes has consistently supported the AGMS's actions. He is also a major intellectual force behind the indigenist movement.[4] Similar to the activist biographies discussed in chapter 3, Sunny's political trajectory begins with his family: his parents were CPI(M) supporters and his elder brother was a Naxalite. Yet despite being familiar with Marxist theory, Sunny is radically opposed to it. What he hates in particular is how Kerala Communists use class to deny the reality of caste. The focus of his activism and thinking is hence precisely the issue of caste, and he draws his inspiration primarily from the work of Dr. Ambedkar. Sunny is also passionate about relying on the historical experience of Dravidian society, from which both Adivasis and Dalits descend, which was much more egalitarian than the Brahminical caste society that came to replace it. According to Sunny, Adivasis embody the ideals of the Dravidian era even more so than Dalits, as Adivasis escaped to the margins of the new casteist society whereas Dalits became incorporated in it as its slaves.

Sunny's grandparents spent their lives working the paddy fields of upper-caste landlords. Even Sunny worked in paddy fields in his youth and lived just on the edge of these. His family benefitted from land reforms to the extent of being granted a homestead, but, unlike tenant farmers, they did not receive enough land to make a living without engaging also in day labor (*coolie pani*). Sunny was determined not to grow up making a living in agriculture. He pursued his education all the way to college and managed to get an office job. By the time I got to know him during my fieldwork, he lived in a rented house in a mixed middle-class neighborhood in the town of Kottayam. It was not the very best of neighborhoods: it floods so badly every monsoon the water almost comes above my knees when I walk to his house. Yet the houses are fairly large—including two bedrooms, a kitchen, bathroom, and dining room—and many upper-caste families also live in the neighborhood. His neighbors know well that Sunny's family is of

Pulaya background, and numerous quarrels with the neighbors, according to Sunny, boil down to their disdain of his "blackness." Sunny's household includes his wife Jessy, who was his childhood friend and comes from the same community, and their two daughters—their son drowned at a young age when they were visiting Sunny's native hamlet. A small shrine where the family's ancestors are worshipped includes a picture of their young son, as well as a picture of Krishna. Though Krishna is certainly not a Dalit god, his place in the shrine is grudgingly tolerated by Sunny because one of his daughters, as he remarks with some irony, "has taken a liking for Krishna."

Though Sunny Kapicadu articulates his views with the eloquence of a philosophy professor, his job is that of a clerk at the government-run Life Insurance Company of India. It is a fairly prestigious and steady salaried job but without too many exciting career prospects for someone of Sunny's intellectual ambition. It does not earn much in comparison to jobs in the private sector, but it allows Sunny to take a loan with which he bought a piece of land of his own to build a house for his family. However, since a formal loan alone is not enough, Sunny often had to turn to other networks to pursue his project. The rented home his family lived in when I stayed with them had few upper-caste pretentions and chicken happily flocked in and out of it. Yet it did have a few more expensive items, such as a television set, a computer, many books, and a Singer sewing machine.

One of Sunny's daughters one day showed me the family's latest acquisition: a DVD player. Now she would finally be able to play the collection of Malayalam and Tamil films she had been cherishing and singing the tunes of while her more studious sister worked on her homework. Unfortunately, to the skeptical amusement of Sunny, it turned out the DVD player was rather useless as it refused to play any of the DVDs she fed it. Not too surprised or upset about the failing DVD player, Sunny commented that they would have it looked at in a repair shop, and "meanwhile," he teased her, "you could always try doing some homework instead. …"

Another day something more substantial materialized in Sunny's home: the rickety wooden stools and bed surrounding the television were replaced by a sofa set taking up more or less the entire space of the small living room. Sunny was clearly in a good mood about it and told me a little anecdote about the sofa: "These Marxists say in Kerala there is no caste? Let me tell you about caste. A relative and I, we were visiting one upper-caste home some day and there was a sofa like this. And my relative? She was too embarrassed to sit on it. She didn't dare. She sat on the very edge of it, almost fell off!"[5]

In another telling instance of everyday relations and events experienced in terms of caste, Sunny came home one day angry at a confrontation he had at his work. His superior had placed a phone on his desk, and Sunny had immediately noticed the strange looks that some of his coworkers had given him. One of them had eventually said "Oooh, you are getting a phone?!" Sunny said he knew exactly what was implied and had retorted "Who are you? I know who I am but who are you, who are you to make a comment like that?" "He only made that comment because I'm black," Sunny told me. "That is caste. I am willing to die rather than work in the paddy fields. Not as an agricultural laborer in any case. I want to break that tie between caste and labor. Let no one ask 'where is our agricultural laborer now? Oh, he is sitting at a desk, he is getting a phone!' We Dalits need to take on other jobs, in order to have dignity. It's not about earning more. It's about dignity."

Sunny often emphasized this point about dignity to me—also, for instance, when one day he invited me to his native village, hiring a classic "ambassador" car for the occasion. Walking along the small paths beside the paddy fields in his native village, where the car cannot pass, he pointed at the coconut trees and reminded me of the joke in Kerala about K. R. Narayanan, the first Dalit president of India, of the Paravan caste traditionally assigned the task of plucking coconuts: "They say, when the flag hoisting ceremony is going on, they need to hold him down or he will climb the flag post. It's because of the traditional occupation of his caste, climbing coconut trees, tapping toddy [an alcoholic coconut juice]. That is the Kerala mentality!"

The tendency Sunny sees in Malayalees of always perceiving someone according to his traditional caste occupation rather than his present position or capacities is something he most passionately critiques. With a smirk on his face, Sunny added to the story, "I used to climb all these trees in my youth too you know … [then, pointing to his protruding belly] … these days no longer, now I am a so-called *activist*."

Sunny then told me about the history of the paddy fields themselves: "You know they used to say a dike like that [around the paddy field] needs the sacrifice of a Pulaya, otherwise it won't be solid enough? All these dikes are built of our dead bodies.[6] And all these Leftists complaining that there is no paddy cultivation going on in Kerala anymore? I am happy, let the [upper-caste] Namboodiris and Pillais go and do paddy cultivation if they so want to. No Paniya or Pulaya should be doing this."

For Sunny, dignity is something he has come to experience and perceive particularly in terms of caste identity, reinforced in the kind of everyday interactions that accentuate the vulnerability of his upward mobility. Whereas for some this leads to tireless efforts at "fitting in" and keeping up with middle-class status competition, Sunny deals with these dilemmas in a more politicized manner. He has come to be a vocal proponent of what he sees as a Dravidian custom of ancestor worship but tolerates his daughter's "flirtations" with the Hindu god Krishna. The consumption durables trickling into the house are likewise treated with some skepticism—they are certainly not venerated as symbols of belonging to mainstream culture. Sunny is also not particularly obsessed with accumulating wealth by all means possible—the way he spends his money—for example, on hiring a nice car for a day—is not about saving money for the sake of it. The crux for Sunny seems to be neither strict adherence to a particular cultural ideal, nor the pursuit of material affluence, but the desire to be free of relations of dependence and inferiority carried from one generation to the next. Considering Sunny's absolute progress in economic terms and the fact that his frustrations are more about social humiliations than about being particularly exploited at work, it is perhaps logical that his politics stresses the issue of identity—which, according to the political dynamics in Kerala today, is more likely interpreted as Dalit identity than class identity. Moreover, though Sunny is skeptical about the consumer boom in Kerala and related market processes, his anger is understandably more about the existing inequalities this magnifies than about issues such as Kerala's increased dependence on rice imports, which is an issue animating many Communists. Sunny pointed out that, despite the worries of many Malayalees about the decline of their food sovereignty, few are willing to do the kind of manual agricultural work associated with lower-caste status. Like them, Sunny aspires to the security of owning land and a home of his own, if anything to confront the competition for status with his neighbors and colleagues from a more powerful critical position.

### *"Let Their Wives and Daughters Work the Fields!"*

Ammini Hamsakkali, a rather fierce and talkative secondary leader of the AGMS, had a similar critique of Kerala society as Sunny Kapicadu did. She had gained a leading role in the aftermath of the Muthanga occupation when Janu was in jail and had acquired fame for a picture taken during the police confrontation at Muthanga that showed her in a defiant pose, apparently taunting the police to shoot her. She liked telling the story to me, repeating to me what she told the chief police officer: "You there in the front … you do one thing: if you want to attack these people then shoot me first!"

Ammini is of Kattunaikan background—a relatively small "tribe" who used to practice swidden agriculture but lost access to the land they used to work, through a combination of being denied access to it by the Forest Department and settlers taking over the land. Ammini explained to me her community's history with respect to land:

> Our grandfathers possessed land. But suppose I have an acre of land and then a person will come and he would be amiable and he would say "*moopa* [chief], I am from such and such a place. I don't have land to make a shelter. It would be so kind of you to give me a piece of land to put up a house." Then we will allow him a piece of land. Then after some time he will turn up with some money or some paddy. By influencing us like this he will make all the documents about the ownership of the land in his name[7]—we won't have any legal documents to prove that it's our land. Though deep in our heart we know it is our land, the outsider will be powerful enough to influence the government officials to forge the document.

Kattunaikans are generally one of the poorest tribes in Kerala, though they do not have a slave past like the Paniya and the Adiya. Ammini, moreover, is better off than the rest of her family, having married a Muslim contractor who owns a stone quarry. She lives with him and their eight children in a lower-middle-class house with garden. Their social position seems just enough to make them aspire to middle-class status, yet with not quite enough cash income or assets to secure this position. This was noticeable, for instance, in Ammini's preoccupation during our first interview with the fact that AGMS activists had promised her a mobile phone: "They [leading activists] are really happy with me. They had promised me a mobile phone. [Neighboring women from other castes] were upset when they heard it—they asked why I would need a mobile phone." And Ammini continued, only barely hiding her disappointment behind a smile, "They [activists] were joking. They said it as a joke." Despite not being able to afford a mobile phone, Ammini had been able to send all her children to school, and two had already attained their Secondary School Leaving Certificate.

Ammini's story is similar to that of Sunny's in terms of the vulnerability of her slight upward mobility but more clearly demonstrates the gender dynamics involved that in turn reflect the gendered trajectory of the Kerala model of development. Though the decline of matrilineal traditions among the (higher-caste) Nair and other communities in Kerala continued apace during the period of the Kerala model, its heydays were known for the exceptionally high life expectancy of women, as well as their relatively good health and high enrollment in primary and secondary education. Yet these gains of the Kerala model are presently challenged with a vengeance. The competition for prestige, prompted by the increased inequalities and insecurities of the post-Kerala model period, results in women being increasingly treated as status objects. The education that women enjoy is now often an asset on the marriage market rather than a means to employment and independence. The number of shops selling gold chains for women's dowries is visibly on the rise, as are roadside billboards advertising gold. With this, the number of "dowry deaths," a phenomenon that used to be rare in Kerala, is also on the rise (Oommen 2010: 81), and women's sexuality is increasingly guarded and policed as a woman's "reputation" has become all-important in the competition for prestige.

Adivasi and Dalit communities are affected by this gendered competition for status mainly by their stigmatization in society at large as having immoral gender norms and by having to bear the brunt of the excesses that the obsession with women's sexuality and its policing produce on the part of more powerful communities. Angrily Ammini tells how her sister's son was forced to marry a Kattunaikan girl who had been made pregnant by an upper-caste man: "His relatives came to my sister and told her just like that [that her son would have to marry the girl]. She had no choice." Though Ammini herself does not go out to work in the fields, her sisters generally do, and Ammini knows too well the gossip about working women. The gossip angers her because, she says defensively, "it is economic necessity forcing us to go out to work, it is not because we aren't honest women." In a gendered version of Sunny's skeptical remark about upper-caste complaints about the decline of agriculture, she adds, "We plough and work and the *mudalali* (lit. "the one who owns capital"[8]) takes all the profits. We should refuse that kind of work. Let their wives and daughters go out and work the field!"

Thus both Sunny and Ammini, having achieved a steady flow of income and no longer depending on manual labor, continue to be intensely reminded of their social background by the effort it takes to keep up with the kind of consumptive competition—centered on land, but also including consumer durables, jewelry, and gadgets such as mobile phones—that has come to prevail in post-reform Kerala. Where in other parts of India the concern about land among Adivasi groups is triggered by the threat of dispossession, in Kerala such concern seems to be a different, though connected, expression of the increased influence of the free market after India's liberalization in the early 1990s. Its conditioning of identity politics thereby seems even clearer in Kerala: whereas land dispossession by large mining corporations can—and is—contested by Naxalite groups even more than by indigenist outfits in India's central belt ("the red corridor," as it is now known), the kind of experiences encountered by people like Sunny and Ammini seem much more difficult to fit into any of the orthodox class discourses that both the major Communist parties and the Naxalite splinter groups in Kerala espouse. Sunny and Ammini's solidarity with "their" people and the everyday humiliations they experience are more easily expressed in terms of their Adivasi or Dalit identity than in class terms.

## Privileging Education: Adivasi Identification and the "ST List"

Besides land, education is the most important asset Malayalees invest in to ensure—and signal—their upwardly mobile aspirations and avoid being considered backward. Whereas in other Indian states it is often almost taken for granted that the majority of Dalits and Adivasis will be uneducated, in Kerala that is no longer the case. Franke and Chasin (2000: 18) found literacy rates among female SCs and STs in 1997 to be 74 and 51 per cent respectively, and Sreekumar and Parayil (2006: 224), though often critical of the Kerala model's achievements, even show literacy rates of 57 percent for female STs (and 66 percent for ST men; 1999 data)—all incomparably higher than the 24 and 18 per cent for SCs and STs across India in general in the late 1990s (Franke and Chasin 2000: 18). Though Kerala now even claims a 100 percent literacy rate, this does not mean the Kerala model left no educational stratification—still only 16 percent of STs, for instance, reach higher secondary education (see Dilip 2010: 20). On the other hand, a combination of decent public schooling and SC/ST "reservations" (i.e., quotas) in university gave the generations of Dalits and Adivasis growing up in the fifties, sixties, and seventies the feeling that in principle they could be able to achieve a similar standard of education to others. Yet from once being the cornerstone of the Kerala model, education today has become the cornerstone of competition in a liberalizing economy.

The new trend was signaled by the rate of decrease in government expenditure on education during the 1990s. From 1990, the decrease has been 2 percent per year, which means that whereas in the 1970s education took up almost 40 percent of the state budget, it had decreased to barely 18 percent by 2010 (Oommen 2010: 77). Reduced government expenditure has gone hand in hand with the commercialization of education and the mushrooming of unaided schools: whereas in 1990 these still only accounted for 2.5 percent of students, in 2006–07 they accounted already for 8 percent (Oommen 2010: 77). More than half of the richest quartile of households in Kerala is sending their children to private schools, compared to less than five percent of the poorest quartile of households, to which almost all Adivasis and Dalits in Kerala belong (ibid.: 79). As many scholars (e.g., Lukose 2009; Oommen 2010; Osella and Osella 2000: 140ff.) argue, the arena of education in Kerala is hence becoming subject to significant stratification. Not everyone has the money to invest in the widespread practice of extra tutorial teaching and to send their children to private schools more likely to provide the training and contacts necessary to get into the best colleges.

For those who lack such money, the constitutionally ordained reservations (quotas) for STs and SCs in educational institutions receiving government subsidies have become even more crucial.[9] In addition, ST/SC reservations in civil service jobs have also attracted more attention because competition for such jobs has intensified as the number of such jobs has almost stagnated since the 1980s (Kannan 1999: 175). And despite Kerala's rising rates of economic growth since the 1990s, levels of unemployment have remained exceptionally high—private sector jobs are not available to substitute for the increasing difficulty of getting public sector jobs. As being on the ST/SC list has thus become ever more crucial, it has become more politicized and it is usually the more marginalized communities, with fewer resources, who are at a disadvantage in the ensuing political maneuvering.

In some cases, AGMS leaders' engagement with indigenist politics was directly related to the politics surrounding the ST list. An example is Ashogen, another secondary leader of the AGMS, who joined it when his community, the Vedan, became the rather unfortunate object of reclassification. KIRTADS, the government institution responsible, decided the Vedan could no longer be considered a tribe but ought to be considered a caste. This was already a problem for Ashogen's community since competition for the SC quota would be more fierce than for the ST quota (since the levels of educational attainment of STs are generally lower than those of SCs). Yet though removing them from the ST list on KIRTADS's advice, the central government failed to subsequently add them to the SC list. As Ashogen put it, "We're falling in between, we're nothing!" Ashogen joined the AGMS in order to "address the ineptitude of the government's treatment of

Adivasis" and the injustice of his community being removed from the ST list.

Actual ST-SC reclassification is—as yet—still exceptional in Kerala, also because the state's definition of tribal status is not merely economic but also depends on notions of cultural and historical background. The indigenist activists I will now discuss in more detail did not become involved in indigenist politics as the result of being taken off the ST list. What conditioned their turn to indigenism were the shifts in the educational landscape of post-reform Kerala, which did, however, increase their preoccupation with the SC/ST list.

### *"It Is Worthy to Work for Adivasis"*

Mamman *mashe* (teacher) became involved in the AGMS after the Muthanga struggle, when many AGMS leaders were in jail. Being a relatively resourceful person, he soon became catapulted in the media as the movement's "vice-president." I interviewed him in April of 2006 at his home about half an hour from the city of Thrissur. The spacious house fit well with the other middle-class homes in his street: "It's not very much an Adivasi house—people here are very forward," he commented almost apologetically. He built the house himself, he told me, by taking out a loan at the time when he was still employed as a primary school teacher. He had since retired and had recently started putting all his energy into Adivasi politics. It was only recently, therefore, that some of his neighbors had discovered he was Adivasi—it was only recently that he had started publically claiming this identity.

Mamman's story is that of an established yet vulnerable member of the Malayalee middle class, finding in indigenism a way to overcome a previously stigmatized community background in a socially acceptable but also politicized manner. Mamman was born to the Maleria community, originally from a hill area near Kottayam where the famous missionary Henry Baker came in the nineteenth century to set up schools as well as plantations. Mamman's grandfather owned almost a hundred acres of land at the time but was compelled to sell most of it, under pressure from planters wanting to expand their plantations. Two of his grandfather's brothers studied all the way up to the tenth standard—a high level, certainly at the time—and became "writers" (i.e., clerks) at the plantation. Mamman's own grandfather, though also well educated, did not work at the plantation but instead farmed his own land, as many people from his community did. Though Mamman would like to take pride in his grandfather's work, as a school teacher and aspiring member of the Malayalee middle class he is critically aware of the increasing stigma on manual labor, the idea that farming is a debasing, backward practice: "These days it's different: those who study prefer white-collar jobs. There's a negative attitude towards farming and physical work. Some work is considered good, other work is considered bad now. In future people won't even want to brush their teeth—too much exercise!"

Like many other Adivasi landowners, the land Mamman lives on now is not ancestral land of any kind. Rather, it was as part of the great migration wave after WWII that Mamman's father came to the area where they live now: "Some people from our village had come here so that's how we knew there was land here and followed. The government didn't legally give us the land but it gave silent permission. The Forest Department also wasn't too strict: they knew the land was being occupied in order to grow more food. These days almost all the forest is occupied—it's hard now." Mamman's experience of acquiring the land where he has spent most of his life is hence the same as that of non-Adivasi settlers. Education being a key value in his community, Mamman went to college in Thrissur, where the Congress party had just begun organizing a local unit. He joined the party as secretary of the unit and used to do the rounds as a campaigner. He was attracted to Congress because it was "the oldest party" and because the "violence" of the CPI(M) put him off. Congress also supported him in receiving his teacher's training.

Upon his return home Mamman was appointed "recruitment officer" and landed a job as the first primary school teacher in the village—also becoming a member of the Congress Party's teachers' union. For a long time Mamman was the only teacher in the school—only later were three more teachers appointed. It was an area with mostly Adivasi children, from a different community than his. When he heard of C. K. Janu's struggle and reflected upon the condition of some Adivasi communities, he told me he realized their situation was different from his and that it was his "duty" to help "uplift" them: "They were struggling to make ends meet. I also felt then I had to do something to help them advance. C. K. Janu's struggle was a real eye-opener for me." He felt he needed to "take up the issue of social justice." Gradually he also started telling people he was actually an Adivasi himself—he was not used to revealing his background to the general public. Earlier, he had only revealed his ST identity to the necessary bureaucrats in order to access the ST quota. He had been reluctant to reveal himself as an Adivasi partly out of fear for potential humiliation:

> The government and bureaucracy they knew—in job promotions, I experienced this discrimination [of being an ST]. But not from ordinary people—for they did not know. When I joined the school as teacher, the children did not know I am an Adivasi. Only the office worker knew. Some people are very particular about caste and all but I pay no attention to this. The problem is when you see yourself as an Adivasi and take that to be a negative thing—Adivasi is not a bad thing, it is just like all others. Adivasis know two languages but then we hear "Adivasis have no culture"?! Actually they have Adivasi culture.

When I asked whether Mamman himself spoke an Adivasi language he admitted he did not, explaining he was a Christian, belonging to the Church of South India (Protestant). The importance he attached to his Christian identity, in combination with the potential discrimination coming with ST status, earlier had encouraged him to not claim his Adivasi identity at all. Yet this changed when the educational reservations for his community came under threat: "The Maleria are a community that benefitted a lot because of the schooling we got through the Christian missionaries. But that does not mean we are not Adivasis. That is the problem we are facing these days—some groups in Congress are giving us a lot of opposition. They consider us higher, they want to take us off the ST list." Being taken off the ST list would then have grave consequences for future generations of Maleria to access university and civil service jobs. It thus became paramount for Mamman to prove his community's belonging on the ST list. For this to succeed, he had to prove the genuine nature of both his Adivasi and Christian identity. The story he told to emphasize the authenticity of his Christian identity moreover simultaneously stressed how his community had always valued education more than money. Mamman retold the community legend to me:

> Usually people say that those who converted, that missionaries came to them. In our case, we went to the missionaries. A hundred years or so ago, there were five hills where the Maleria lived. There was exploitation then by the Catholics living there. One day a palm reader came to the *moopan*'s [headman's] house and said he should go to the missionaries. He went four, five times but every time the missionaries thought he came only for money, not for education. The final time, moopan insisted he came for education and that they should come to bring education. That's when they went there. So we are double blessed … God choose Israel—but in our case, it was we who choose God. So we are doubly blessed.

Having shared this story on the genuineness of the Maleria "choice for God," Mamman is also emphatic about his true Adivasiness: "The Maleria are Adivasi but became Christian. I know I am Adivasi even though I did not work for them [politically] before. It is worthy to work for Adivasis, so I am taking up the Adivasi issues. There is a Maleria bishop as well. He could have spoken up for Adivasis, but he didn't. He is more interested in Christians than in Adivasis."

Against the negligence of his church in maintaining the Adivasi identity of Malerias, in combination with the Congress Party's efforts to take them off the ST list, Mamman felt called upon to join the indigenist cause. He joined the AGMS and thereby both explicitly identified as Adivasi and took up the task, worthy of a pensioned school teacher, of helping to fight on behalf of "poor Adivasis." As he told me in words that legitimized his personal turn to indigenist politics but did not break too radically with the dominant political culture in Kerala: "Nowadays, without ST reservations, Adivasis will not stand any chance to a better life. Being an Adivasi myself, I felt I had to take up this cause."

### *"To Call Ourselves Adivasis with Pride"*

Mamman's fears and annoyance about the threats to his community's ST status are echoed in the stories of other leading indigenist activists, such as those of Krishnakumar, a Kuruma (ST) leader of the Dalit Panthers in Wayanad. Krishnakumar's parents owned some land but lived mostly on day labor. They were traditionally with the Congress Party, which they associated with Indian independence and Gandhi. Despite not having had formal education themselves, they realized the importance of education and saved up everything they had to make sure their only son would get educated. He recalled, "They had this awareness of the necessity of sending me to school—they had no idea of what I ought to be taught, just that I should be sent to school."

During his college days at St. Mary's in Sultan Bathery, Krishnakumar tended toward Leftist ideology but had little faith in political parties. Instead he joined the Adivasi Renaissance Movement. After meeting a group of Dalit Panthers during his days at Kozhikode Engineering College, Krishnakumar joined their organization. More strongly than his parents did, he identifies as Adivasi, yet not, as he puts it, in a traditional sense: "The world is changing fast now so what's the point of sticking to old traditions? If Adivasis don't change, they won't survive. Take the Brahmins, they have changed and survived. If Adivasis want to survive they have to dance according to a certain tune. Culture is formed by the place where you live—we don't live in the forest now, so we've changed. Though there is something good in their [the ancestors'] way of life … we should be sensible in retaining the good things but embrace modern things."

Like Mamman, Krishnakumar demonstrates a twin preoccupation with, on the one hand, supporting "poor" Adivasi communities—referring generally to communities other than his own—and on the other hand, insisting on the need to resist what he called "a political plot to weaken the Adivasi movement" by taking some of the richer Adivasi communities off the ST list: "It is difficult for Adivasis to organize. I don't agree with these government policies [of reclassification]. What they do is to weaken the Adivasis' vigor to strike. Every time the more powerful groups will become excluded. Kurumas are now fighting for the Adivasi cause—if we get excluded from the list, we won't be able to continue the [Adivasi] struggle."

Krishnakumar also developed a wider vision on the need for an Adivasi movement precisely to counter the stigmas associated with using ST quotas, saying, "There is a need to be able to call ourselves Adivasis with pride." With the increasing importance of reservations in education and the efforts of indigenist activists to make sure SC/ST quotas at colleges and in the civil service (about 8 percent for SCs and 2 percent for STs in Kerala) are filled, the issue has received much coverage in the media. As many activists claim, there is also increasing humiliation—about a supposed lack of merit—for those entering on an SC/ST quota. Indeed, many upper-caste people I spoke to would passionately criticize the fact that SCs and STs could enter college with lower grades, supposedly on less "merit," than they could. Krishnakumar spoke to me of this phenomenon:

> They shout about merit and grades. But just because a person gets 80 percent or 90 percent why should they enter medical college? If an Adivasi gets 50 percent [grade], considering all the oppression that has happened to us for the past centuries, this is as good as 95 percent. Upper castes never understand this. They understand only what they want to understand … they will always bring up this issue to lower our self-esteem.

A pernicious effect of reservations, Krishnakumar argued, was that it pretended the state was historically generous and supportive of Dalit and Adivasi communities, whereas the opposite was true. In this context, is was no longer enough to push for generally improving education or to ensure the technical possibility of using SC/ST reservations—it was necessary for a movement to both expose the continuing oppression of Adivasis, be vigilant about ensuring colleges set the right quota, and enable Adivasis to take pride in their identity.

This concern with identity in Kerala's changing political-economic landscape was so widespread that I even encountered it among Adivasi and Dalit Communist party members I spoke to. Though a concern with identity had not led them to leave the party and organize on an indigenist basis, it did contribute to the pressure on the CPI(M) to also start an Adivasi wing—the AKS. Suresh, a Communist Party member and one of the few prosperous Paniya men I encountered in Kerala, often emphasized the need for Adivasis to remain with the Communist party. Yet he also expressed his relief when the party decided to form the AKS, claiming, "Now we have a chance to rid Adivasi communities of superstitious beliefs and promote the good parts of their culture.[10]"

Suresh himself, despite being highly educated at a prestigious engineering college, had experienced discrimination. "Nothing very serious," he told me, but enough to bring tears to his eyes when he recalled how he had been seated at a distance from others while attending a marriage dinner a few years earlier. The issue had been "settled" by the Communist party—"they [the marriage hosts] did not realize who I was," Suresh explained. The settlement, in other words, had focused on his Communist Party membership rather than the issue of being discriminated as a Paniya. Suresh, perhaps restricted by the party's insistence on putting Communist identity over Adivasi identity, could not articulate exactly why the founding of the AKS had been so important for him. Yet he could not stop telling me how glad he was about the AKS's activities to "uplift" the Adivasis so that "they" could leave behind their stigmatized identity. As an upwardly mobile, educated youth, what preoccupied him most personally regarding Adivasiness was clearly not just the classical Communist themes of class, poverty, and exploitation but primarily the desire to destigmatize Adivasi identity.

## Conclusion

We see from the vignettes presented in this chapter that the increasing uncertainties of social reproduction in contemporary Kerala become experienced and articulated by upwardly mobile but subaltern activists as something threatening them as members of Dalit and Adivasi communities rather than as a particular class experience. The overall picture that emerges confirms the argument by Osella and Osella (2000: 353ff.) that the increasing power of the market, both in the arena of production and in that of consumption, leads to the "substantialization of caste": because their mobility under the Kerala model was merely of an absolute character—rather than of a relative character vis-a-vis other communities—subaltern groups experienced the polarizing effects of the demise of the model as the resurgence of caste discrimination and fell back on—and thus substantiated—their caste identity to confront their increasing social insecurity. As we saw in the vignettes in this chapter, most upwardly mobile Dalits and Adivasis now rub shoulders with members of other communities in many sites—in their neighborhood, at school, at weddings, and at the workplace. Yet as the opportunities offered by public education have started to fall drastically behind those offered by private schools, and as government jobs pale in comparison to those in the global private job market, they are increasingly reminded of their historical vulnerability. Kerala is somewhat exceptional in terms of the considerable number of ex-agricultural workers who, because of relatively smaller family sizes and relatively generous welfare programs, can afford to refuse agricultural work for almost as long as it takes to find educated work (Kannan 201: 165ff.). Yet from a position of no longer being engaged as manual laborers, they are nevertheless increasingly faced with the threat of falling back to the position of a past generation—of needing to do relatively badly paid, low-status labor (*pani*) or face unemployment. This structural bind makes it again understandable why people emphasize their Dalit or Adivasi identity as the primary source of their continuing vulnerability. Though we saw themes of the previous chapter—the conflict and intimacy between indigenist and Communist activists—return in the stories of the activists discussed here, such political dynamics interplay with a more structural conditioning of their turn to indigenism that lies in the kind of everyday relational experiences they encounter in efforts to make a living and secure their children's future.

I have offered a historical-relational interpretation that differs from a purely utilitarian "rational actor" argument. Such a historical-relational perspective is more relevant to understand the politics of the AGMS because, though the movement has at times taken up the issue of SC/ST reservations (quotas) explicitly—for instance in a campaign in October 2007 for the "safeguarding of SC/ST reservations"—it has generally focused on the issue of "comprehensive land reform" to ensure landless Adivasis would receive land (an issue leaders continued to raise, even during this "reservations campaign"). Neither the right of Dalits and Adivasis to retain their position as part of the Malayalee middle class in an increasingly competitive economic environment, nor their concerns about access to educational and civil service SC/

ST quotas have become anything more than secondary demands of the movement. Yet these issues do trigger much of the personal anxiety and anger conditioning these relatively educated and (aspiring) middle-class leaders to turn to a politics of indigenism. These issues shape the "Adivasi dignity" and identity-centered ways in which the struggle is articulated, also when it comes to the question of land. Leaders' lived experience of increased competition and attempted marginalization in education and employment make the movement's emphasis on Adivasi pride something they personally relate to. Meanwhile, they acquire their legitimacy in Kerala—towards followers, wider sympathizers, and also themselves—from the fact that they prioritize the material issues of the poorest among the Adivasis, foremost the struggle for land.

C. K. Janu, the leader of the AGMS, is one of the few leaders whose background is not that of a salaried subaltern: she had no formal education and used to work as an agricultural laborer, without owning any land of her own. Though in the course of Janu becoming a well-known public figure in Kerala, issues to do with Adivasi pride and identity became important for her personally, it is only logical that her main concern from the beginning has been the material emancipation of landless Adivasis out of poverty. As we saw in chapter 3, there were concrete political experiences that encouraged her to break with the Communist vision of such emancipation and instead organize an indigenist struggle for land. Yet this leaves unexplained why the majority of the followers of the AGMS—landless agricultural workers like the Paniya and the Adiya who were aloof from such direct political confrontations—would also become attracted to envisioning their emancipation in terms of indigenist politics rather than in terms of the existing secular-socialist visions of emancipation. It moreover leaves unanswered the question of why, even if the AGMS focused on the poorest Adivasis, the issue of land would take priority over the issue of higher wages. It is hence to this question of what conditioned the popularity of the AGMS's indigenist, land-focused program among so many ordinary Adivasi agricultural workers that I turn in the following chapter.

## Notes

1. A frequent complaint C. K. Janu aired to me was that rank and file would often be unable to come to meetings because they had to spend their time working to ensure they could *kanjikudikkuk* (eat *kanji*, rice soup—i.e., survive).

2. I use "middle class" here in the classic, Weberian sense of the educated, salaried middle stratum (between those performing physical labor and those owning capital)—*not* in terms of the Indian euphemism for the hyper-rich, less than 1 percent of the population, who draw their income from the profits and rents of large private enterprises.
3. Legislatively, land reform in Kerala started in 1957, when the first Communist government of the state immediately introduced its comprehensive Kerala Agrarian Relations Bill (KARB). It was only with the Kerala Land Reforms (Amendment) Act of 1969, however, that implementation finally took off, and it reached a real momentum in 1975 with the simultaneous streamlining of bureaucratic procedures and the need to counter the Naxal "threat" that characterized the Emergency period. By 1981, more than 99 percent of over 3.5 million cases for tenant-farmer ownership of land and over 400,000 cases for workers' ownership of homestead land had been resolved (largely in favor of tenants and workers) by the Land Tribunals (see Radhakrishnan 1981).
4. As such, quotes by Sunny Kapicadu have appeared already in chapters 2 and 4. I thank Sunny for his permission to include the more personal story that follows here, which draws not only on formal interviews but also on informal conversations and observations during the time I lived with his family.
5. There is a beautiful scene in the classic Malayalee movie *Chemmeen* in which the (Dalit) fisherman coming to the *mudalali* (capitalist, upper-caste) home is told to sit on the available chair but hardly dares do so and likewise almost falls off.
6. The collective memory of slavery among Dalits in Kerala contains many stories of the harsh labor, mostly by Pulaya and Paraya workers, involved in the reclamation of the backwaters in the 1930s and 1940s; for a description of such stories see Mohan 2011 (541).
7. The transfer of land from tribal to nontribal ownership is, in principle, illegal, and if a bureaucrat would have conspired in actually transferring the title deeds, he/she would indeed be liable to punishment. Yet, sometimes the land Adivasis were using was not registered under their name to begin with, and many loopholes exist in the prevention of transfer of tribal land. The title deeds as proclaimed by the local municipality (according to whoever has greatest informal influence on its officials) and the title deeds as recorded in official records need not, moreover, be the same. For those with little power to demand transparency, it is impossible to ascertain to whose name land is legally registered. For this reason, in Tamil Nadu, the Right to Information Act has recently been used by Dalit groups to demand transparency on land ownership registration, as land sometimes legally remained with them though the municipality had conspired in proclaiming it transferred to others.
8. An expression workers in Kerala often use to refer to their employers, including small farmers, small-scale industrialists, or traders.
9. Vinod George Joseph's (2005) novel *Hitchhiker,* whose protagonist in a young Dalit-Christian student at a provincial high school, powerfully dramatizes the everyday (caste) experience of such educational competition in contemporary Tamil Nadu.
10. The fact that Suresh, a Paniya, talks of "their" instead of "our" culture suggests a continuing hesitance to openly claim Adivasi identification.

– Chapter 6 –

# ADIVASI LABOR: OF WORKERS WITHOUT WORK

In this chapter, I move to a discussion of the kind of changes in regimes of accumulation and development that encouraged ordinary Adivasi workers to join the indigenist movement from the 1990s onward. The incorporation of these ordinary workers into Kerala's modern political-economy has been in the most precarious low-waged positions. As we have seen in previous chapters, many Paniya and Adiya—among whom we find the largest percentages of agricultural workers—only managed to free themselves of bonded labor relations in the late 1960s with the changing balance of power that settler migrants introduced, the pressure put by the Naxalite movement, and the renewed national-level commitment to ending bonded labor. Their expectations at this time were not of entering college or holding a high-ranking government job but rather of having steady employment for living wages and the chance for their children to do well in school and move away from hard manual labor. In the 1990s, these expectations were starting to pale as Adivasi workers faced a drastic decrease in the demand for their labor following the further withdrawal of capital from Kerala and the difficulty of the agricultural sector to compete with cheaper products from abroad and from other Indian states.

The higher wages for agricultural work that were achieved as part of the labor and land reform movements of the 1960s had already led to a decreasing demand for labor in agriculture and agro-processing industries since the 1970s. As Kannan (1999: 162) puts it, "Once the threat of eviction had gone, laborers became more forceful in demanding higher wages. Landowners responded by giving up their traditional obligation to provide for regular employment" (Kannan 1999).

Yet during the 1970s and 1980s, government mediation, attempts at employment provision, and a host of redistributive and social welfare policies—not least among which a government-subsidized pension scheme for agricultural laborers—had managed to keep alive an idea of progress for most Adivasi workers. Kannan argues these were no more than "poor-relief" programs, yet demonstrates they still had a significant impact in lifting rural households out of poverty (1999: 163). By the 1990s, though the idea of progress was still alive in Adivasi workers' communities, its nature had to be drastically rethought as employment provision and welfare schemes were grinding to a halt through underfunding and mismanagement. There was, moreover, even less demand for rural manual labor: whereas in the late 1980s still about 40 percent of Adivasi workers had more than 200 days of employment per year, in 2003, only 4 percent of them fell into this category (Aerthayil 2008: 69ff.).

The ethnographic vignettes in this chapter will demonstrate more concretely how political-economic changes conditioned the rise of indigenism among the Adivasi workers who became the backbone of the AGMS. I suggest how structural changes in their lives made it more likely for these workers—for different but related reasons compared to salaried Dalits and Adivasis—to turn to indigenism instead of continuing along the path of union struggles and wage strikes. I hence analyze in greater detail the impact of changes coming with the crisis of the Kerala model on two closely related groups of Adivasi workers in Wayanad: those living in rural ghetto-like "colonies," accustomed to making a living through day labor (*coolie pani*) for local landlords and contractors; and second, those living on the government plantations that were originally set up to provide Adivasi ex-bonded laborers with employment.

## An Adivasi Colony Meets the Threat of Absolute Expendability

Kottamurade colony is an exemplary site to study the rise of indigenism among agricultural workers because the entire colony participated in the Muthanga land occupation organized by the AGMS in 2003. Indigenist political themes have since become hotly debated in the colony, leading some people to visibly embrace their "Adivasi identity" while others have grown skeptical of the politics of indigenism.

For instance, one of the women in the colony, Manju, started decorating her home with "tribal" patterns and avoided going to church, preferring, she said, to "stay with our own gods". She also decided to stop voting for non-Adivasi political parties and instead proudly, even if unsuccessfully, stood as a candidate herself—an "Adivasi" candidate. In contrast, others, such as Akkathi, became suspicious of expressions of so-called "Adivasi" culture and even suspected C. K. Janu (the AGMS leader) was "playing a game" with them. Akkathi was even more suspicious, moreover, of Kanavu (Dreaming), the famous alternative school for Adivasi children in Wayanad where they learn "Adivasi" dances and traditions—something Akkathi suspects is a plan by the educated head of the school to "exploit" them. In the following paragraphs, I trace these divergent reactions and the rise of indigenism more generally in Kottamurade by looking at people's everyday working lives and changes therein. I will first give some insight into the history of the colony, after which I discuss recent changes in the local political economy and people's apparent reactions to such changes, first at the level of the colony as a whole, and then more particularly in terms of the experiences of different people within the colony.

### *Kottamurade: Short History of a Paniya Colony*

Kottamurade colony is a cramped, muddy, and poverty-stricken rural ghetto housing forty-four families on two and a half acres of land at the edge of a typically Malayalee "rurban" (sprawling) village of about thirty thousand inhabitants.[1] The village in question is known for having been the site of a successful Naxal-led attack in 1968 against the Special Armed Police force that was camped at the village's famous Sita Devi temple to (unsuccessfully) prevent its land being claimed by the thousands of Christian settler farmers from Southern Kerala moving into the area. By the 1980s, these settler farmers had also made the village famous for producing some of the finest quality pepper in the world: for its booming cash-crop economy the village was known for a while as the "Dubai of Kerala." Though Kottamurade colony is located around the corner of a hill, out of sight from the nearest paved road, it is not at all isolated from the rest of the village. All sorts of visitors frequent the colony, from the municipal "tribal promoter," to the doctor and nurses conducting "medical camps" in the colony (mostly against tuberculosis), the "teacher" of the colony's small *anganwadi* (kindergarten), the Muslim fish seller who drives his motorcycle into the main mud square every

**Figure 6.1** Kottamurade in the rain

other day in search of customers, and journalists (and myself) following up on stories on the Muthanga struggle. Also the occasional big-bellied, white dhoti-clad landowner or contractor can be seen entering the colony looking for skilled day laborers if such were not to be found at the informal labor markets in the larger towns (Sultan Bathery and Mananthavadi), where many men from Kottamurade travel each morning in the hope of being recruited for the day.

The history of the colony itself is closely tied to the village's: it was during the time when Christians from southern Kerala were claiming land around the village from the temple and feudal landlords—the same time when some of the land-owning tribes in the area (mostly Kurichiyas and Kurumas) lost parts of their land—that the older generation of Paniya now living at Kottamurade for the first time gained a place to stay free from the landlord's threat of eviction. According to the elderly Paniya I talked to, Christian settlers were the first to treat them as humans and to oppose bonded labor—out of their "Christian" conviction and the desire to hire Paniya labor themselves.[2] In combination with the Naxalite movement, this opened up many possibilities for these Paniya workers. Their *moopan* (chieftain) when they were still living at Chiralle—a place about half an hour's walk from the village—decided to join the settlers' colonization efforts and settle with his family on the piece of fallow land that is now called Kottamurade. Having claimed the land and received the *pattayam* (title deed) to it, the moopan invited relatives to come and live there too. I was told that originally all the people in the colony were relatives, though now people from outside have come in through marriage. These outsiders who came to live in Kottamurade are mostly Paniya from elsewhere but also, as is usually reluctantly acknowledged, people of other "castes"—mostly Pulayas (SCs)—because of so-called love marriages (cross-caste marriages). When coming to the site of Kottamurade, the moopan's relatives, together with the Chetty, an "indigenous" but not "ST" community who are now the colony's neighbors, cleared the area of trees and decided to call the colony after a fruit that a type of tree there bore. The Paniya called this type of fruit "*kotta*" and, according to an elderly Paniya woman I spoke to, offered it to the deities—an act she said was called "*murade*" in Paniya. The place is hence now known as "Kottamurade colony" ("colony" being the general term used for such residential enclaves).

It is often assumed by outsiders that the moopan is the "traditional" chief and lends his authority by ancient Adivasi custom. Yet in all likelihood the institution of the moopan emerged in the context of the relations of the Paniya to the landlords they worked for. The moopan was often the person described by Thurston (1909: 64) as "appointed by the Nayar Janmi to look after his interests, and be responsible to him for the other inhabitants of the village." Indeed, Aiyappan (1992: 80) claims the moopan is historically a senior Paniya appointed as the "gang leader" of a group of bonded laborers, "bound loyally to look after the interests of the master" (though that is probably an exaggeration of the moopan's true loyalties). According to Aiyappan, these are secular appointments given a "religious color" through certain ceremonies. It can hardly be a coincidence that the contractors who emerged in the 1930s to recruit rural Scheduled Caste workers for the nearby Nilgiri tea plantations were likewise called moopans (Lindberg 2001: 62–63). These moopans were often ordinary workers who sought to improve their lot by providing the plantation owner with work hands, and workers often ran up debts to the moopan (ibid.). It should be no surprise, then, that the living arrangement at Kottamurade is also not one of communal land ownership but rather of rent-obligation to the moopan.

At the time of its founding in the 1970s, the moopan's initiative to establish the colony was certainly experienced as a liberating move. Progress was additionally in evidence when the government—as part of its "one lakh housing" (lakh = one hundred thousand) program—built *pukka* (proper, i.e., concrete) houses on the site. In the stories of their more recent past, people of Kottamurade show no trace of lost glories that "development" may, as some scholars claim, have destroyed. Instead, the older people in Kottamurade will all—often to the surprise of visitors expecting stories of loss and degradation—tell you that "life is much better now" than it was in their youth. Thankamma, a middle-aged woman from the colony, told me that rather than worry about having access to the forest to dig for tubers as was their "tradition," she was glad she could now buy her food in the stores. As she said, "Digging for tubers to eat is hard work, especially after working in the fields all day!" Thankamma much preferred to earn wages and use her government-assigned "Below Poverty Line" (BPL) ration card to get food from the shop. Of course, this involved negotiating with the shop owner and, sure enough, several new families at Kottamurade had not received ration cards yet or, though desperately poor, were not noted as "BPL." The shop owner responsible for the ration cards needed to be constantly pressured to provide the correct ration, and he used the debt that most people at the colony had to him as a lever. Yet such constant bargaining to get what they needed was taken for granted by most people at Kottamurade and did not create nostalgia for a "pre-development" past.

Following people at Kottamurade in their negotiations with the municipality—during meetings and through the "tribal promoter" assigned to their colony—it was clear that they had been used to putting whatever Kerala's development model had to offer to their advantage. There was no doubt to them about the legitimacy of their demands, for instance, for a vehicle to be arranged to take the children of the colony to school, or for better electricity and lavatories to be built at the colony. In this, the recent history of Kerala's land reforms, minimum wages legislation, public distribution system, and Welfare Boards—instituted in the 1970s through the assertion of "workers' dignity," claiming welfare as a "people's right"—seems undeniable. Kerala's rhetorical emphasis on "pro-poor" development clearly did not guarantee such development—certainly not, as we will see, in the present circumstances—but did enable people to expect further progress towards integration as worker-citizens. But even as such claims on the state continue at present, they have started to be undermined by political-economic processes affecting the working lives of people at Kottamurade—processes that, as we will see, made people more prone to follow other routes of emancipation than that of "citizen"- or "worker"-oriented political engagement.

## *"Suffocation" and Expendability*

When I asked people at Kottamurade directly why they joined the AGMS's Muthanga struggle, their answer was usually plainly "We needed land." As Chimbren, the first leader of the AGMS in Kottamurade, told me, "There was no other way—we would have gone with anyone who came to promise us land"—adding "even with you *chechi* [elder sister]."

There were other ways of trying to get land—through political parties or the municipality for instance. Joining the AGMS was not so straightforward a move since it came with a lot of debate in the colony on whether or not there was a need to reclaim their "traditions," and what this entailed, and whether or not they should organize "autonomously" as Adivasis, and what this meant. Yet even after the disastrous breakup of the Muthanga occupation, many people in the colony still passionately advocated the need to organize autonomously as "Adivasis." Since purely utilitarian arguments clearly cannot explain why people took this new route, some scholars are tempted to complement such arguments by a cultural-primordialist reading that beneath the discourses of Adivasiness that are strategically haggled over, there is another, "authentic" Adivasiness that makes it only natural for people to see themselves as Adivasis and articulate themselves politically as such. In that case, however, it remains a puzzle why people at Kottamurade did not do so earlier—why a generation ago they were struggling for higher wages rather than land and why there are still a significant number of people at Kottamurade who are uninterested in talking about "Adivasi" rights and simply want to become less "poor." I want to consider the conditions that made day laborers such as those at Kottamurade turn to a politics of indigenism not through utilitarian, nor culturalist, lenses but rather as part of changes in their everyday working lives.

For both those employed as day laborers as well as those employed in the plantation sector, the 1990s were a time of drastically decreasing demand for their labor following the further withdrawal of capital from production in Kerala and the difficulty Kerala's agricultural sector had competing with cheaper products produced elsewhere. Employment provision and welfare schemes were also grinding to a halt in the 1990s due to underfunding and mismanagement. The large majority of people at Kottamurade whom I spoke to indicated a marked decline during the past decade in their possibilities of finding work. The only people seen working the few paddy fields around Kottamurade colony itself at the time of my fieldwork were Kattunaikans, another small "Adivasi" community who apparently were willing to work for even lower wages than the Paniya (also because they were still more used to trekking into the forest for supplementary food). People at Kottamurade told me as a matter of fact that "they [Kattunaikans] can work for even ten rupees less than we do." Apparently, there were limits to how far one could compromise while retaining a sense of one's self as a Paniya. On road and construction projects in the area, where Paniya did fetch wages that were still considered within their dignity, there was a trend of Tamil migrants being hired. Thankamma, one of the women at Kottamurade, told me, "Nowadays they don't even call the Chettys [the wealthier "indigenous" but not ST neighbors whose women were willing to work for very low wages since their husbands were considered the main breadwinners]. Instead they hire people from outside saying that these [the Chettys and the people from Kottamurade] are asking for too much money. They are not calling us for work anymore." The stress this produces is palpable in Chimbren's words: "If we can't find work, we can't have *kanji* [rice soup]. If there is no work, we won't have *kanji* at home. We have four or five children here, not only mine, my sister's also. Then mother, father, brothers-in-law, we all want *kanji. Chechi* [elder sister], I am saying this out of grief."

Hence while workers at Kottamurade had already been left behind in the course of the 1980s by their upwardly mobile, land-owning neighbors profiting from a booming regional economy in rubber, pepper, and other cash crops at the time, they were in even more trouble when the price of cash crops slumped during the 1990s and the village became known as Kerala's "suicide capital" for the number of farmers committing suicide (Nair and Menon 2007).[3] Debt-ridden farmers could provide even less employment to Paniya workers. The kind of stress that high indebtedness and the threat of losing all status and property produces among small farmers has proven inductive to suicide, prompting the government to implement a host of measures to support small farmers. At the same time, agricultural laborers suffering from hunger—more likely to struggle for survival than to commit suicide—have received little government support. As Mohanakumar (2008) revealed, even the money contributed by agricultural laborers to the Agricultural Workers Welfare Fund Board, which was to provide them with a pension, was diverted to defray the administrative costs of running the board. Particularly in regions with the highest concentration of Scheduled Tribes in Kerala (Wayanad, Idukki, and Palakkad), settlement of due benefits encountered such delays that "a labourer should be considered fortunate if she/he remains alive to avail of the benefit" (Mohanakumar 2008: 28).

While agriculture is in crisis and other sectors are turning to even cheaper sources of labor, the sector that is visibly booming in Wayanad is that of tourism. It is actively promoted as a "growth engine" (Sreekumar and Parayil 2002), with the hope that it will compensate for the collapse of the agricultural and manufacturing sectors. Wayanad has recently been declared a "tourism district" and the number of luxury hotels in the area is visibly on the rise (Jacob 2006: 110). "Adivasi" workers generally have no employment in this sector, though they figure large as an abstract "tourist attraction." The luxurious Brahmagiri hotel in Mananthavadi, the town where the first Adivasi *sangam* was held in 1992, has a huge picture of an Adivasi woman in purportedly traditional dress in the middle of its patio. The "Jungle Retreat" in Thirunelli, an area known for the large number of so-called "unwed Adivasi mothers" whose offspring can often be traced to the military battalion that was stationed there, adorns its homepage with a picture of an exotic-looking "tribal dance" and tells potential tourists that "spending time with these people of the forest is an enchanting and fascinating experience." There's a mushrooming of tourism management courses and institutes in Wayanad (Sreekumar and Parayil 2002: 530). Few of these enroll Adivasis but none of them fails to focus on the Adivasi as an attraction (something my "expert" opinion was several times solicited on—in vain—by students from such institutes). Adivasis also seem to be an attraction for the film industry that is doing well in Kerala. One day I found the set of the shooting of "*The Photographer*," a movie about a photographer of wildlife (and the occasional Adivasi), crowded with people from Kottamurade hoping to get a glimpse of Kerala's movie star Mohanlal in a reenactment of the Muthanga violence. Imaginary "Adivasis" figure prominently in Wayanad but most of the actual Adivasis are standing by on the sidelines.

In order to make a living, people at Kottamurade—like many Adivasis in India (see Breman 1996; Mosse 2005)—were increasingly forced to migrate between their home and places outside of Kerala, particularly to Kodagu (formerly "Coorg"). There they worked on a temporary basis in the privately owned ginger and banana plantations. Many Malayalee farmers and pensioned civil servants were leasing land there from local landlords. The business was quite a gamble, given the fluctuating prices of ginger and other cash crops.[4] People from Kottamurade would be attracted to work on these plantations through advances given to them (usually between five hun-

**Figure 6.2** Inhabitant of Kottamurade, dressed to go out and watch the set of *The Photographer*

dred and one thousand rupees) by the labor contractors working for these farmers. Consequently, the contractors would find many ways of not paying them their full wages later on—for instance, by selling liquor and withholding the money from their wages, or simply through false book keeping. Only when contractors were all too obviously in violation of local norms could workers run off to go back home before the work was done, for the contractors, being no strangers, would know where to find the runaway workers. In Kodagu there was a downward pressure on wages for workers from Kerala, partly because of the presence of other migrant workers, but also because the costs of social reproduction of local workers were absorbed by their families: they needed only one rather than three meals a day at the plantation since they ate breakfast and dinner at home.

As people in Kottamurade told me, the migration to Kodagu started in the early 1990s. Things had become gradually worse. At first they were still able to find work near the village in pepper cultivation when it was the season in February and March. Later they had to move to Kodagu even in those months. Sometimes wages were negotiated before they mounted the jeeps taking them to Kodagu. At other times, the negotiation happened only on the way. The migration experience was stressful because of the bad working and living conditions at the private plantations outside of Kerala but also because migration is highly stigmatized. Kodagu is generally known as a scary and "immoral" place. The one advantage of migration—the chance to take part in less traditionally regulated, more worldly relationships and circuits of consumption (see Shah 2006)—is usually interpreted by villagers as Adivasi workers going to Kodagu only to buy "jeans" and "silly items" such as "Fair & Lovely" (skin lightening cream) and to practice "lax morals," get drunk, and have "affairs." Hence the circular migration Adivasi day laborers like those at Kottamurade are forced to engage in further excludes them both literally and metaphorically from proper Malayalee citizenship. People at Kottamurade would often tell me their land occupation at Muthanga was opposed because "people were afraid that if we would own land, we would no longer come to work theirs." Yet in the changing economic context just described, this statement seems to have a double meaning, pointing not just to their exploitation but also posing a counterclaim to a creeping reality that is worse than that of being exploited: that of being made expendable and no longer being part of local society altogether.

The nature of such political-economic processes is also revealed in a metaphor most often used by people at Kottamurade to describe their situation, namely the idea of being "suffocated." What a generation ago was considered progress—living in *pukka* houses erstwhile only permitted to higher caste communities—is increasingly experienced in the way C. K. Janu generally refers to the founding of these rural ghettoes: as a process of "colonization." "Suffocation" is a product of how the structural processes whereby people are increasingly pushed out of Kerala society are happening also in miniature—and close to the skin—in the colony itself. Kottamurade's land is today registered in the name of Vasi, the son of the deceased moopan, who himself lives outside of the colony. Inhabitants of Kottamurade all pay rent to Vasi, who also profits from the cash crops grown on part of the land the moopan managed to keep uninhabited for that purpose. As Karuppen, one of men of the colony, told me, "This whole colony is under his authority. We all are all living here as coolies." The relation between the moopan and the rest of the people at Kottamurade has, as we saw, never been founded just on "traditional" consensus. Yet, at present it is under particular strain as tensions around the moopan's ownership of the land are escalating under the specter of expendability haunting the colony.

On the one hand, people in the colony often emphasize their "gratitude" to the moopan for having "allowed" them to live on the land. But they thereby also hint at the traditional obligations that come with their respect for the moopan. Vasi, however, seems little interested in such traditional moral claims, or indeed in brokering between the workers at Kottamurade and potential employers—it is not for nothing that the people of Kottamurade did not recognize Vasi as the new moopan when his father died. What Vasi is more interested in is the land on which the houses stand: land that could be used much more profitably than by housing a group of often unemployed distant relatives. If sold or rented out to others, the land could effectively sustain Vasi's narrow escape from the abject poverty of the colony. This is all the more the case since land in Wayanad has acquired a new value as capital investment for corporate resorts and weekend homes of the urban middle classes in Bangalore and Kozhikode. Vasi has hence gradually been trying to get people to leave the colony, which people experience as constantly emphasizing the "suffocating" character of their condition. The pressure comes in the form of an increasing unwillingness on the part of Vasi to allow for late payments of rent (whereas earlier the moopan was happy to have people indebted to him), which in turn increases tensions within families. Often, particularly in the context of alcoholism, this provides the spark for fights in the colony. The pressure also comes in the form of forbidding people at Kottamurade to build new huts on the land or even to take up the scheme approved by the municipality to renovate the houses. Chimbren describes the atmosphere in the colony, telling me, "We can't live here, in this suffocation. … We can't live here. It is choking us. … the house down there … there are six families living in it! We are frustrated. And always we end up in fights." Later, more resigned, he adds, "We have no other way but to live in this suffocating situation. There are people who drink and there are those who don't. But the fact is that no one can live here. There's more people every day. The number never decreases." As the pressure on them in the colony increases, so does the desire of people at Kottamurade to have a piece of land for themselves.

On top of this come changes in the educational landscape that affect people at Kottamurade. Even the Paniya, who are among the very poorest in Kerala, have a literacy rate of about 40 percent for men and 25 percent for women (KIRTADS 2003: 27)—data that are confirmed by my experiences in Kottamurade colony, though the gender gap there seems much smaller as women, rather than men, were among those most committed to attaining literacy (despite the difficulty of combining this with their other "domestic" and labor obligations). Adults at Kottamurade were first introduced to reading and writing during the literacy campaigns of the 1980s, which in turn made many people eager to see their children go to school. Though children I spoke to would dream of becoming "teachers," "movie stars," or—particularly popular—"policemen," parents say they used to at least hope their children would become educated enough to know their rights, to no longer be treated as ignorants ("as we are," they would often say), and perhaps even make it to being assistant to a shop keeper or a public servant. Yet overcrowded living quarters, nightly family fights, and particularly oft-absent or unemployed parents do not create favorable conditions for children to be motivated for school. In the context of increasing unemployment and educational inflation, parents are moreover increasingly considering their erstwhile hopes for their children mere illusions. While some parents continue all the more to struggle for their children's education—keeping the *anganwadi* (kindergarten) running, pressuring the municipality for a vehicle to bring the children to school, making their children promise they won't skip classes—the hope of general, steady emancipation that education held out for a short while has all but dissolved. Many people I spoke to at Kottamurade were torn between extremes when envisioning their children's future, hoping they may make it big through diligent study yet usually expressing the more cynical view that school was at best a place where their children could get a free lunch. This is hardly surprising since not a single child in the colony has yet managed to pass the school-leaving exam, which in itself is no longer enough to acquire a semiskilled job in contemporary Kerala. People at Kottamurade know well that public schooling, just like public health care, is only a façade these days: to have access to real schooling and proper health care, you need money to pay private tutors and visit doctors after hours.

Being made increasingly expendable in their traditional role as agricultural workers, being pushed off the land they still could at least come home to from long periods of seasonal migration elsewhere, and having few prospects of their children being able to integrate with others around them through proper education made people at Kottamurade more receptive to the idea of acquiring a piece of land of their own somewhere and organizing to live "autonomously," apart from the rest of Kerala society. These same processes contributed to the growing popularity of seeing their difference to others in terms of their "Adivasi" identity and the desire to "reclaim" this identity and save it from its present "suffocation." These changes in people's everyday working lives, which in turn shape their outlook on the world, best explain why Kottamurade's inhabitants became motivated to gather their few belongings and move to Muthanga in 2003. After the violent eviction of the Muthanga land occupation, some people in Kottamurade—such as Manju—have become ever more convinced of an "Adivasi" interpretation of their situation. Yet others, such as Akkathi, moved in the opposite direction. In the following section, I will follow the experiences of these two prominent women at Kottamurade to study people's turn to indigenism at a more personal level.

### *Divergent Pathways of Belonging*

The eviction of their land occupation at Muthanga was a traumatic experience for the people of Kottamurade, most of whom had brought with them virtually everything they owned only to see it all destroyed. Many walked for days to escape the police and locals willing to denounce them, all the way from Muthanga back to Kottamurade. Some of them were injured so badly that they sustained lasting handicaps. Two men were tortured in jail and only came back weeks later. One of them returned in such bad health that he died soon after. The other, Manju's husband, continued to be summoned to the local magistrate every month. Many of the local landlords had started hiring other workers, migrants, while the people of Kottamurade were at Muthanga, which made it difficult for them to find any work at all on their return. Children, meanwhile, were refused admission back to school under the pretense that they had "skipped" too many classes. The aftermath of Muthanga was one of total loss. Yet how this had come about and how to continue were topics on which opinions were divided. Two people who were particularly outspoken in their differences were Manju and Akkathi, both literate women in their late twenties, each chairing one of the two "*kudumbashree*" (family luck/prosperity) female microfinance groups in the colony.[5] In the following paragraphs I zoom in on the stories of these two women, treating them to some extent as "ideal-typical" cases—the one, of the conditions leading to an embracing of indigenist politics; the other, of the trajectory of rejecting indigenism.

I first must note, though, that not all people at Kottamurade neatly follow either the indigenist or anti-indigenist paths of Manju and Akkathi respectively. Many people occupy a more ambiguous middle position that demonstrates both the contingencies and the structural determinants involved. Akkathi's friend Vellichi, for instance, was generally skeptical about their participation in the AGMS, which is probably not coincidental with the fact that, even more so than Akkathi, she has a solid foothold in Kerala society as she owns a small plot of land adjacent to the colony. The reason she owns this land is rather contingent, and to some extent of her own doing: after her first husband died, she had an "affair" with a farmer living nearby and gave birth to a son. Being thereby an "unwed mother," and having three brothers and a women's organization willing to help her claim her rights through a court case, she managed to receive a considerable sum of money from the farmer, which she used to buy a piece of land from the moopan.

Unlike Vellichi, Chimbren, who was the first leader of the AGMS at Kottamurade before Manju took over, was much more inclined towards indigenism and pessimistic about the possibility of sustaining a decent living by staying at Kottamurade. This is probably not coincidental with the fact that he was forced to spend months on end at Kodagu and other plantations outside of Kerala in order to sustain his family. Due to this circular migration, he lost his erstwhile public role in the colony. Unlike Akkathi and Vellichi, Chimbren had not received any form of financial support from either the municipality or through neighbors and was often desperate about being able to provide for his family. The improbability of his integration as a worker-citizen made Chimbren more inclined towards a radically different, "Adivasi" vision of his future, though he also resorted to other venues of possible relief, such as listening to Bible readings on the radio and heavy drinking.

Akkathi, whose story I will look at more closely here, ran a tiny shop in the colony, selling rice, soap, and other basics, right beside the *anganwadi* (kindergarten) that she worked for as assistant to the "teacher." As an assistant she earned a salary of a mere five hundred rupees per month from the municipality. Yet, as this is a steady position that gives her access to public connections and information about government support programs, she manages to be significantly better off than most people in the colony. She had her two daughters—six and eight years old at the time of my fieldwork in 2006—both enrolled in the new government savings project for female children,[6] which will ensure a sum of money becomes available to them at age 18. She also arranged a government-subsidized health insurance for her family through the *kudumbashree* (the women's self-help group) and had some money in the bank. In her daily work, she frequently interacted with people outside the colony and was particularly close to some of the Christian neighbors, which may partly have been because Akkathi grew up an orphan. Akkathi's parents both died of diseases (jaundice and tuberculosis) when she was still young, and it was her brothers who brought her up. Her elder brother managed to acquire a job in a local shop and over time invested in a small plot of land about one hundred meters outside the colony, where Akkathi was planning to build a house for herself someday too. Until that time, she and Lalu, her husband, and her two daughters continued to live in a small home in the colony. Lalu went out every day to try to find *coolie pani* (day labor), while both of Akkathi's children, under

**Figure 6.3** Children at Kottamurade, playing on the edge of the colony

her constant monitoring, attended school regularly. Akkathi and Lalu nevertheless decided to join the others to go to Muthanga as they looked forward to building up a less precarious existence and were uncertain about the possibility of indeed living on the land that Akkathi's brother had been acquiring.

In contrast, Manju, who married into the colony, and her husband, Dasen, had no less than five generations living under their roof. At the time of my fieldwork they had three young children—at the time of Muthanga they had just had their first daughter. During my fieldwork, this eldest daughter had just reached school age, but during school time she was mostly found roaming the nearby paddy fields with other kids from Kottamurade. Living next to the kindergarten and the shop, Manju kept an eye on Akkathi's activities but was also herself well-connected to the municipality, among others in her role as chair of the other *kudumbashree.* During *grama sabha* meetings—a regular feature of the Kerala landscape since the "People's Planning" initiative of the 1990s—Manju often was the first to speak up. She was much less shy than Akkathi about voicing her opinions in public. Both Manju and Dasen lived off *coolie pani* (day labor) and often spent weeks in Kodagu, over the border with Tamil Nadu, to work in the ginger plantations there. Manju was not, however, eager to admit this and immediately would add that men and women at Kodagu "always have separate places to sleep … and if there aren't any separate places, then our men will assure that they will sleep separately anyway."

Unhappy and stigmatized by this migratory existence, both Manju and Dasen wished to build up an "Adivasi" life on a piece of land to call their own. They got into contact with C. K. Janu through the organization that initially used to organize literacy campaigns in the colony and eventually became local leaders of the AGMS at Kottamurade. They visited Janu a number of times to receive "political classes." They also mobilized a number of other colonies[7] to join the AGMS in preparation of Muthanga.

Whereas Manju led the preparations for Muthanga and took on a leadership position during the occupation, Akkathi left for Muthanga hesitantly, worried about leaving behind her small shop, her job in the kindergarten, her good connections to neighbors, and indeed her children's school. Soon enough, tensions between Manju and Akkathi erupted at Muthanga. Akkathi—as others from Kottamurade who had been less intensely involved in the preparations—could not understand why the leaders had selected a wildlife sanctuary for them to claim land in. Living under the threat of wild elephants with no running water or shops, let alone schools, nearby was about the last thing she had hoped for. Akkathi also complained to me that Manju and Dasen suddenly "changed into different persons than they were in the colony." With some rhetorical excess she claimed, "Here [at Kottamurade] nobody will dominate the other. When we reached there, Dasan and Manju were there to dominate and rule us. What we said was not given any importance; what they said was considered important. That had to be obeyed. We were not ready for it. We went there for land, not to live like their slaves."

A conflict also developed over the issue of "Adivasi" traditions. Akkathi described how one day she was told by the AGMS leaders that she was to give up going to church and stick to her "original Adivasi deities." This upset her as she was used to going to church and to temples and had no desire to "go back to the old traditions"—she and most people in the colony considered themselves people of "many faiths." Akkathi felt looked down upon by the leaders and eventually claimed she preferred to live surrounded by Christian farmers than in an "Adivasi" community such as that of Muthanga. Tensions further intensified when some of the children at Muthanga fell ill and Akkathi wanted to leave the occupation to get health care for them: "One day we had picked a quarrel with Dasen and Manju. All our children were having some or other kind of illness. Perhaps because of the climate. … Children were infected with scurf. And also cold and fever. … we went and told them that our children were sick and that some of us would go out to get medicines for them. Then they said that was not ok with them. They asked us not to go out!"

Considering the rivalry between Manju and Akkathi, it should not surprise us that Manju relished the fact that at Muthanga she became the more influential of the two—nor is it surprising that Akkathi was particularly sensitive about this. Akkathi's frustrations and the tensions that were developing at Muthanga should, however, be contextualized as foremost the result of the activists' difficult task of sustaining the occupation against the backdrop of fierce opposition from both political parties afraid of the rise of a rival political movement and local notables preoccupied with Adivasi workers becoming all too assertive and taking over the land these notables consider theirs. As I described in chapter 2, the discursive tactics used by the opposition, focusing on discrediting the "authenticity" of the participants' "Adivasi" identity, intensified tensions among leaders and participants in the occupation. Understandably under such circumstances, AGMS leaders felt the pressure to "educate" participants in ways of conforming to the discourse of authentic indigenism they had become trapped in. It was also important to make sure participants would stay at the occupation at all times in order to be able to defend it in case of attack. Leaders tried to keep participants committed to the ideal of living in a self-sustaining, self-organized community rather than venturing out for government services or day labor. As the outside threats to the occupation increased, one can easily imagine how the pressures within the land occupation became intense.

On 19 February 2003, after almost two months of living at Muthanga, the occupation was violently evicted. Most people of Kottamurade were camped some distance from the direct frontline and hence most of them escaped the worst of the violence. They did, however, lose all they took with them to Muthanga. On his way back to Kottamurade, Dasen—Manju's husband—was caught by a group of local people and handed over to the police. They tortured him and held him—and his young daughter—in the central district jail for over two months. Manju, on returning to Kottamurade, fell ill and was unable to go for work for a long time, leaving the household dependent on the income that Dasen's mother could contribute. Dasen's mother worked as a household servant for one of the neighboring families. She resented the job intensely because servant work, even though less back-breaking than planting rice, is extremely low-paying and informal, and rather

**Figure 6.4** Manju's home

than working in groups, one works alone as the "personal slave" of a household's matriarch. Manju hardened her resolve to fight to attain a piece of land on which her family would be able to establish the kind of dignified, autonomous life that she had come to associate with "Adivasi" culture. One of the actions Manju undertook after Muthanga was to stand as a candidate during the local elections—not in the vain hope of actually winning the elections but, as she told me, "to make a point: that we Adivasis will only give our vote to parties that work for us, that we can withhold our vote if we wish to."

When I visited Manju again in 2009, it struck me that she had now decorated her home with "tribal" patterns I had not seen anywhere in the colony before. Manju did not see Muthanga purely as a failure and looked forward to a new opportunity of claiming Adivasi land. She took pride in having participated in the struggle and saw the renewed attention that Kottamurade colony was getting by that time from the municipality as a victory by the AGMS.

Akkathi looked back to Muthanga with much more bitterness even though she escaped the violence relatively unscarred; her elder

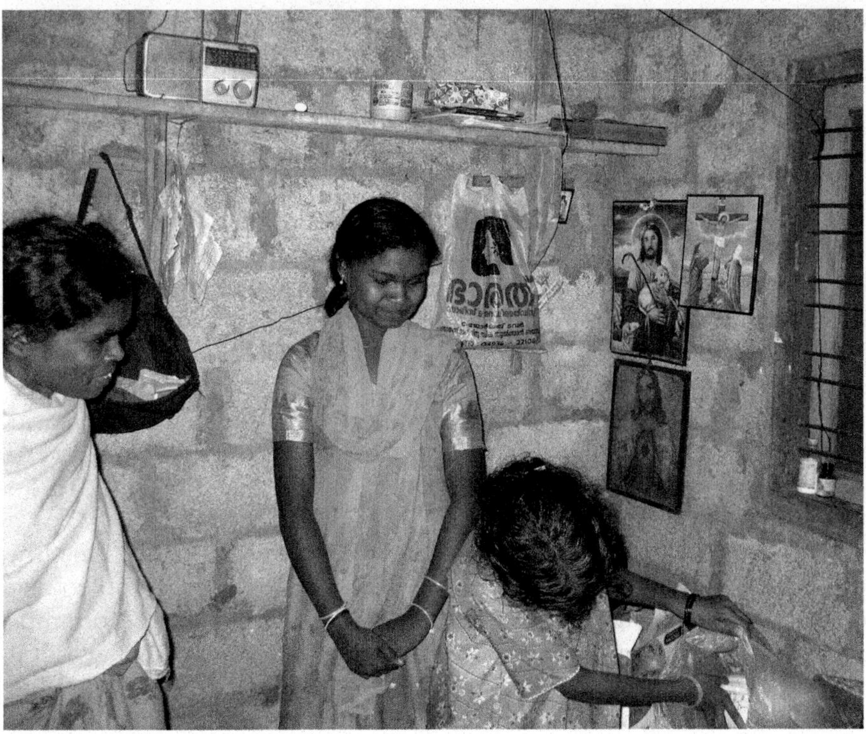

**Figure 6.5** Akkathi's home

brother, having heard of the impeding police assault, had come to take her family away from Muthanga just in time. A number of NGOs that had come to Kottamurade after Muthanga to hand out blankets and clothes moreover helped restart the *anganwadi* (kindergarten), and the municipality sped up Akkathi's application for a housing grant that would allow her to build a *pukka* house on the land her brother had acquired. When I visited Akkathi again in 2009 the house had been completed and she now lived outside of the colony, though still working there in the shop and the kindergarten. Where Manju's walls had become decorated in "tribal" patterns, pictures of Jesus had come to decorate those of Akkathi. Her daughters were diligently attending school and there was a strikingly different atmosphere in her composed, nuclear-family home with two children than there was in Manju's household in the colony where children ran in and out and looked like they had more exciting things to spend their childhood on than school. Unlike Manju's hardening indigenist resolve, the experience of Muthanga had led Akkathi to no longer want to have anything to do with "Adivasi" politics.

One of the developments after Muthanga was that to honor its commitments to redistributing land to landless Adivasis and under pressure from the AGMS, the government had proposed distributing land at Aralam farm—a seven-thousand-acre government-owned farm about nine hours by bus from Kottamurade colony. It was not so much Manju but Akkathi who was fiercely opposed to the idea of moving so far away from her native place, where all the connections through which she sustained her family were and where her children were going to school. Akkathi was suspicious that all this talk of "Adivasis" was in fact a "game" set up to "exploit" them. This was confirmed to her even more since the tourism boom in the area had picked up steam and women in all kinds of "Adivasi" dress could be seen decorating hotel billboards. Whereas Manju claimed this was part of the victory of the AGMS in redeeming Adivasi culture and making people proud to be Adivasi, Akkathi saw it as an attempt to portray them as "animals of the forest" and wanted nothing to do with it.

The story of Kottamurade, in sum, is a story of the conditions under which Adivasi day laborers turned to indigenism in the course of the 1990s. The story demonstrates how those people at Kottamurade who most intensely experienced the process of footloose capital forcing them to become "footloose labour" (Breman 1996: 13) were often also those who became most attracted to indigenist solutions. A sense of absolute expendability loomed over workers at the colony and prepared the conditions under which the politics of indigenism became attractive to many of them. Indigenism allowed them to turn a process of economic exclusion into a political assertion: as contemporary capitalist configurations worked to push people not just out of the realm of proper Malayalee citizenship but even literally off the land where their homes were located, the attraction of occupying a piece of land of their own and starting an "Adivasi" life grew. Rather than being able to integrate into society through stable employment and secure rights to education as "workers," people started to envision that by owning a piece of land, they might be able to eschew fading social institutions and instead organize an "Adivasi" way of life on their own. For some, participation in the actions of the AGMS and the experience of violent state repression led to even greater attachment to the vision of indigenism. However, those who still considered avenues of integration open to them started to become skeptical of the Adivasi movement and placed renewed hopes on strategies of integration. By analyzing the story of Kottamurade from an expanded class perspective (Kalb 1997)—rather than from the perspective of strict rational self-interest or cultural histories alone—I thus capture the diverging pathways of belonging of people at Kottamurade. I thereby draw attention to how people's everyday experiences, and the political identification these experiences allow for, connect to larger political-economic processes. As we saw, there were structural tendencies in these processes that—in combination with the political dynamics discussed in previous chapters—encouraged people to see their pasts and futures as depending not on class struggle but on Adivasi assertion.

## (Dis)Possession among Adivasi Plantation Workers

The story of Kottamurade showed the trajectory towards indigenism of people depending on day labor, primarily in the agricultural sector, and the impact of the "sense of expendability" they were facing. The following stories are closely related: the people whose experiences I will discuss now are likewise manual laborers in agriculture. Yet they differ in one aspect: the workers discussed in the following paragraphs used to have fixed employment in cash crop plantations in Wayanad. They had a guaranteed number of days of work per week and a free place to live in the plantations' workers' quarters. Yet this changed in the course of the 1990s as the plantation sector in Kerala entered a crisis. The outcome of this crisis is that almost all of the projects set up as so-called "tribal rehabilitation" projects in earlier decades in Wayanad to provide employment to ex-bonded Adivasis, including the Cheengeni coffee project (founded in 1958), the Sugandagiri Cardamom Project (1978), and the Girijan Collective Farming Cooperative (1979), are now defunct (Wayanad Initiative 2006: 10). Of government-run estates in Wayanad, it is only the Priyadarshini Tea Estate that was still running at the time of my research, yet it did so at a loss, had not paid the wages it owed its workers, and was using less than half of its hectares.

The reasons for the crisis were first of all related to diminishing subsidies to government plantations as Kerala's budget deficit reached record levels in the late 1980s. The Kerala government was forced to cut spending in order to abide by the conditions of the loan it received from the Asian Development Bank to manage the budget deficit. Moreover, almost all plantations in Wayanad, including privately owned ones, got into trouble in the course of the 1990s due to the collapse of the price of cash crops.[8] Subsequent mismanagement of the plantations and the suspension of welfare benefits that may have otherwise provided relief only further "alienated workers from a sense of belonging to the plantation" (Raj 2013: 15). What the stories I present here emphasize in particular—and more clearly than the stories of people at Kottamurade—is how older working regimes crumbled and, with them, the basis for class-based, unionist politics. Out of the crisis of these older working regimes, indigenist visions—particularly of Adivasis receiving land ownership—eventually seemed the only solution.

### *"We Can Complain Perhaps … but There's No One Who Will Hear It!"*

The Sugandagiri (Fragrant Hill) project was set up in 1978, in the wake of Indira Gandhi's "Eliminate Poverty" campaign, a twenty-point program that included a serious attempt to enforce the abolition of bonded labor. The Sugandagiri project was designed to employ and "rehabilitate" Adivasi laborers that were liberated from such bondage. They would be given the chance to integrate as full citizens in society with steady employment in cooperative cultivation under the supervision of the Wayanad Cooperative Farming Society. The project was assigned fifteen hundred hectares of forestland—land that many of these same Adivasis earlier used to supplement the meager diet provided to them by the landlords they were tied to. While destroying this safety net for Adivasis, the clearing of the forest also provided them with work. Eventually 850 hectares of cardamom,

133 of hectares of coffee and 160 hectares of pepper were planted at Sugandagiri. In all, the project provided work and accommodation to about 750 Adivasi families—mostly Paniyas, though also quite a few Kurichiyas, and also Pulayas (SCs). The project was not initially intended for these latter groups, since they had not been bonded laborers, but they came in when Paniya families dropped out, often because the poorest Paniya families did not have enough reserves to cope with monthly rather than daily wages offered by the project. Though initially quite successful, the project started to run at a heavy loss in the course of the 1990s, and by 2003 the project was disbanded and the land allocated to 438 families, each Adivasi family receiving five acres of land, while Dalit families received one acre. This is the abbreviated history as it is generally known in Kerala.

The story suggests that parceling up the plantation was the only logical and just solution to the crisis. The actual story of how and why the cooperative project was parceled up rather than given support to continue is, however, more complex and more revealing of how structural political-economic processes worked to condition the rise of indigenism. I got a first hint about the complexity of Adivasiness in the politics around the demise of the Sugandagiri project when I asked one of the workers I met when walking through the plantation whether he was Adivasi and whether I could speak to him. With an air of cynicism he retorted: "Adivasi? I don't know about that. You should probably speak to K. V. Raman. He seems to know exactly who Adivasis are." As he pointed me to Raman's home and walked on, he hesitated and added, "But actually you should talk to Paniyas—we are the real Adivasis."

It turned out K. V. Raman was the leader of the "Samara Samithi" (Struggle Committee), the organization that had led the strikes that had been taking place at Sugandagiri to force the government to parcel up the farm and redistribute the land to Adivasis as a solution to the crisis. Raman belonged to the Kurichiya "tribe," most of whom were traditionally—and still are—land-owning and many of whom are now well-educated. From my interview with Raman on the veranda of his comfortably large house—in the middle of the banana fields he was cultivating—I learned that though his family used to support the Communist Party, Raman had been a member of Congress since 1984. The first thing Raman emphasized to me during the interview was that the Sugandagiri project "was given to the Adivasis by Prime Minister Indira Gandhi." He said that ever since the start of the project they had been told they would get five acres of land and had agitated for it but had gotten no support from the government.

He said, "It was only when this wage crisis came, when people were starving and the government had run out of funds that the government started listening. But still somehow they managed to pay out wages by collecting from some other tribal fund. It is mostly the upper-caste staff that benefits from this—workers get only five hundred rupees or so while the officials here get ten thousand rupees."

On top of policies increasingly less favorable to supporting government-subsidized cooperative farms, the rise of the AGMS itself also contributed to Raman's success in finally getting the demand for the estate to be parceled up heard: "In 2001 C. K. Janu also came with a strike program and managed to have an agreement with Anthony [the then chief minister]. Then the government also decided to redistribute the land here to Adivasis. But due to the opposition of some officials and other parties there was some delay." In reaction to the delay, Raman's organization decided to go to the High Court and finally got the order that the cooperative society was to be dismissed. Raman told me, "We didn't want a cooperative in which we don't have representatives. We want land, nothing else." Finally the land got distributed among the workers and plots were assigned through a lottery system. According to Raman, "There was a box with plot numbers, that's how people got their plot. There was no malpractice, just an open system."

There was, however, some room for negotiation as some people were invested in the plot where they had already been living and hence had built up a claim to that particular plot. The room for negotiation this provided, I discovered, seems to have been just enough for almost all the good land ending up with the Kurichiyas. Raman, meanwhile, had now turned to the struggle for infrastructure since without this it was impossible to properly cultivate the land. He legitimized the struggle particularly in terms of those Adivasi workers whose land—unlike his own—remained uncultivable because of a lack of facilities: "Under the Sugandagiri project the idea was not just land redistribution but also roads, facilities, irrigation, electricity. … the situation of some of the Adivasis up in the hills is really pathetic, they are getting no government aid at all." Apart from struggling for better infrastructure at the defunct Sugandagiri plantation, Raman had also become the Wayanad district president of the Kerala Adivasi Congress[9] and hoped to continue his struggle not just for Adivasis at Sugandagiri but all over Kerala.

The Paniya and Pulaya workers I spoke to, however, were often skeptical about the way the struggle had been waged and about its outcome. It turned out that most of them had initially demanded that the government step in to call the management of the project to order and give financial support so that workers would continue to get at least four days of work a week. Many workers continued to work on the plantation, even though they had not been paid wages for months, in order to build up pressure on the government to continue the project and to lay a moral claim to receiving the wages. The block of workers demanding the project to continue to provide employment was initially strong. Yet as the strike dragged on, many families had to leave the estate because they could not do without wages for so long. Since those who left were mostly those who had nothing to fall back on and who had belonged to the block demanding wages and employment rather than land, this block was gradually weakened. The block of workers demanding the project to be parceled up into individual plots was meanwhile gaining support and had started to claim that the project's actual aim all along had been to provide not employment but land to Adivasis. The SCs working on the estate, most of whom were more interested in being employed on the estate and living on a small plot near the roadside than on receiving a piece of land to live on and farm somewhere in the interior of the project, at that point decided to split off from the Adivasi workers altogether as they realized they would, in any case, have a different legal right. One of the Pulaya (SC) men who did stay on and eventually received one acre of land (as opposed to the five acres most STs got) said, "Suddenly there came this rumor that the government considers SCs as a forward caste, so they might not give us land. That's when we decided to fight separately as Dalits." However, with an eye on one of the Paniya men standing nearby, he added, "Dalit includes all the Adivasis. It just means an organization for all lower-caste people. All Adivasis come under the umbrella term Dalit. Dalit stands for lower-caste people; see, compared to Paniyas, Kurichiyas are forward."

Eventually there were only about 450 of the original 750 families left at Sugandagiri and even those who had initially struggled to keep the project running saw their demand was hopeless and eventually joined the call to divide up the land. One of the Paniya women told me about the decision:

> "All this five-acres story is organized by this Raman. But we were having problems all this time and some people started thinking if we stop working and give in to this five-acre story we will at least get the provident fund. Because there were so many wage problems arising. So people supported the five-acres-of-land man. All those who demanded one acre and four days of work got isolated. Actually life here was good, we had work, we had maternity leave, we had insurance, allowance, clothes, blankets. Then all of a

sudden this man comes up with a five-acres story and exploits the wage crisis. It was a crisis, but it was manageable. Look at the [managerial] staff: they are still working and getting salary."

The tensions that had been building up during the years of mismanagement and later the strike had made most of the workers weary of a collective undertaking and favorably inclined toward receiving an individual plot instead. Yet, as, Prabhagan, one of the Paniya workers still at Sugandagiri, told me, "When finally the strike was settled, almost all the forward Adivasis [Kurichiyas] got fertile lands. Paniyas and Kattunaikans got worthless lands so we're all living in a pathetic condition now. But we can't complain. ... We can complain perhaps but there's no one who will hear it!"

The land most Paniyas and Kattunaikans ended up with was officially still forestland, so they were not given titles to it, only a certificate of possession. Even if they would be able to buy the resources needed to work the land and somehow get it irrigated, they would be officially forbidden to do so by the Forest Department. The Forest Department was even preventing them from felling the trees on the plots they supposedly owned. As one of the Paniya men I spoke to at Sugandagiri told me: "They are not letting us cut anything. We need to go out for *coolie pani* (day labor) to survive. At least if we were allowed to work the land perhaps the next generation could make a living from it."

In airing their frustration at this situation, many Paniyas and Kattunaikans employed a discourse of indigenism that had become popular in the course of the struggle, claiming they were the real Adivasis, as opposed to other STs, who were more wealthy and cunning. One Paniya said to me, "We Paniya became Adivasis because we are the primitive people, we came here first. Sugandagiri was intended for Paniyas and Kattunaikans, but now Kurichiyas are getting all the best land." At the same time, Paniyas and Kattunaikans would point to how wealthier and better-educated Adivasis like the Kurichiyas seemed best at articulating the indigenist discourse in their favor. A Paniya cautioned me, "But you should not think we can talk about being Adivasi; we are the least aware of what this project was really intended for. We just know one thing: in order to eat we need to work." With some vengefulness, one of the Paniya workers who was originally in favor of demanding work rather than land told me, "People [referring here to Paniyas] became divided in two: the ones who wanted land, and those who wanted work. Now after they got land, they have started thinking it would have been better to have work." A Pulaya (SC) woman, with tears in her eyes, described the internal conflicts that arose once the decision was made to distribute the land:

> "I have been working here for twenty-eight years and now I get one acre of land, on top of a hill, with no irrigation, impossible to cultivate. So we demanded land with an irrigation facility, we approached the collector and he promised us ten cents[10] somewhere else. But he never gave us the title and, anyway, other people are living there! So now these people who got five acres of land are teasing those who received one acre of land. And on that 10 cents we got, another family is living there—that man owns five acres, and he will be pestering us. The day before yesterday we had a huge quarrel with him [cries as she speaks]. This man planted coffee on the land. … actually he had been living there for a long time already but now the authorities designated it to be redistributed to the SCs. This Kuruma ["forward" Adivasi] got five acres of land elsewhere but it is bad land. So he has been searching out those who were assigned his land [the land he lives on now] and has started to pester them. We are still only living in the workers' quarters."

For the poorest Adivasi workers, the appeal of indigenism—of placing Adivasi identity centrally and focusing on land ownership—had not been the attractiveness of the indigenist political vision as such but the reality of how desperate earlier labor arrangements had become. In the absence of actual involvement of the AGMS, the indigenist solution that was reached at Sugandagiri had merely reproduced existing categorical inequalities—in many cases by right of law, in almost all cases *de facto*.

### *"Then the Promise Came That Adivasis Would Be Given Land."*

The supposed success of the strike and subsequent parceling up of Sugandagiri, one of the largest government-run cooperatives in Kerala, sent a signal to other plantations in crisis. Many of the activists I interviewed at other occupied plantations mentioned Sugandagiri and how it led political parties and organizations to focus on occupying land for Adivasi workers. At Plantation "Seventy-Three," I interviewed Api, a Kattunaikan worker at the (ex-)plantation and leading activist in the occupation initiative. About two hundred Paniya and Kattunaikan families were occupying the 250-acre plantation and had agreed that the sixty or so original workers of the project would all get two acres each, while Adivasis who had not worked there but joined from a colony nearby would get one acre. Api explained the decision:

> "The problems at this plantation were getting worse. We were laborers at this plantation. Actually this plantation was set up by the government for our good. But they [plantation's management] were being reluctant to give us the

> workers' concessions that the labor law provides—like the provident fund, medical aid, wages even ... only five, eight or ten working days were available per month. When we asked for our Onam [Kerala's main holiday] bonus they would not give it in time. Then we *gherao*-ed [encircled] them. We seized their office. After that the collector and the police interfered to sanction all those concessions to us. And then we realized that at this plantation we would not get much work and we would not be able to improve our living conditions. So at that critical juncture we occupied the land. More so, if we didn't seize the land, other organizations would occupy it ... there was the strike going on in Muthanga and before that, in Sugandagiri—a plantation was given to Adivasis. So we occupied it [Plantation Seventy-Three] all, because we didn't want other organizations like AKS or Gothra Maha Sabha to seize the land. More so, we have no land of our own and we had a feeling that if we get land, things will be better."

The belief that indigenist politics would lead to emancipation comes almost as an afterthought in Api's story, which instead highlights the impossibility of reviving the earlier work arrangements and the fear of others coming to take ownership of the land instead. Hence a strike that had begun as one to demand the plantation management fulfill its obligations to its employees gradually, against the background of the wider political dynamics of the rise of the AGMS, transformed into a land strike. Api explained further: "There was no clash with the police here. Actually, this project is modeled after the Sugandagiri project. When we *gherao*-ed the field assistants the district collector came with a lot of [police] vehicles. We thought they would beat us black and blue. But the collector took the decision then to sell the pepper harvest and distribute our benefits. At that time as far as my understanding is concerned it was a strike, like Janu's strike in Muthanga—we could have held it anywhere, including in front of the secretariat. But then the promise came that Adivasis would be given land."

Since the initial occupation they held was intended to be symbolic and a way to claim their wages and benefits rather than to redistribute the land, little conscious effort had been made to divide the land fairly. Now the ones who happened to have set up in a fertile part of the plantation were much better off that those who got stuck with less productive areas. There was talk of trying to get those who had more productive pieces of land to share their profit with others, but the problem was that whenever a formal meeting was called by a district collector or other authority to negotiate on the plantation, it were those who already had the better pieces of land who could afford the transportation charges and hence solidify their position. Api complained, "They won't provide a penny for those with less productive land."

Api's story hence reveals how he had been unprepared for the transformation of what was at first a symbolic land occupation—intended as a strike to make certain claims—into a real land occupation, meant to take possession of the land in question. The story, however, also reveals a more general pattern that the AGMS itself was caught up in. For as we saw in previous chapters, the demand for land was not the only demand the AGMS put forward, nor was Muthanga selected for the attractiveness of actually living there.[11] The general pattern was that, as other demands related to social rights or employment proved chanceless, land became the overriding political concern, backed up by visions of "Adivasi autonomy", and symbolic land occupations turned into claims to the particular land in question.

The pattern became even more clear at a nearby plantation-in-crisis occupied by the CPI(M)'s Adivasi Kshema Samithi. At this plantation—Marianade estate—Adivasi workers were actually a minority—most workers were Christian settlers. The solution here was thus more complex than simply calling for the estate to be parceled up among its Adivasi workers. The AKS had dealt with the issue by dividing the estate in two, having Adivasi workers and Adivasis from nearby colonies claim one half of the land, while on the other half of the land the non-Adivasi workers clamored for compensations while sustaining themselves by cultivating the land. Most of the Christian workers I spoke to were primarily concerned with financing their children's education in Kozhikode (the nearest city) and doing so through the forced retirement benefits they expected to receive from the government to buy them out and redistribute the plantation's land among landless Adivasis. The AKS leader managing the occupation—a settler from a nearby Christian neighborhood—was eager to stress the cultural difference between the Adivasis and the Christians at the plantation: "They have a very different culture; they are the primitive people of this place. Government should buy the land for them. Have you heard them at night playing their drums?"

On the "workers' side" (the non-Adivasi side), however, there were also those belonging to a community of Kunduvadians, who used to be STs but had recently been taken off the ST list. Theirs was an all the more complicated situation since they were lobbying to get back onto the ST list to access ST quotas in education and civil service but at the same time were on the non-Adivasi side of the land occupation.

At the Adivasi side of the Marianade plantation, there were people from many different so-called tribes (Urali, Mullu Kuruma, Paniya) and from many different parts of Wayanad, encouraged by the AKS to come and occupy the plantation. Generally it was only one member of each household that could be found at the plantation itself, the others being away for work in Kodagu (Karnataka) or other farther away places. Usually it was a sickly member of the household who could not work anyway who could be found occupying the land which, in combination with the lack of facilities and lack of experience and resources to continue cultivating the coffee plantation, gave the Adivasi side of the occupation a rather bleak atmosphere. One of the few "complete" families I met there was an Urali family surviving on the AKS's occasional support. Their son had a serious accident when working for a building contractor and could no longer work, while the man and woman were too old to work. All the other children they had were dead. A Paniya woman, Thankammana, was the local AKS leader and one of the few healthy people I met at the site. Her husband, however, had chest pain and therefore was unable to work—they sustained themselves by collecting wood and other material from the plantation and selling it as well as by receiving some support through the AKS. Even for Thankamma, however, the last time she remembered having had enough to eat was in jail, when they had just started the occupation and the police came and kept them in custody for two months. Life is hard at the plantation, she admitted: just a week before her neighbor had a baby, but it died after a few days because they had no money to go to the hospital. The mere mentioning of Kodagu fills her with fear—she told me it is a place from which people return with diseases or never return. Unlike the stories the Christian AKS leader told me, Thankammana saw little cultural difference between Adivasis and others. "Adivasisi are the poor ones," she tells me. Yet every time she mentions Kodagu, she emphasizes that "it's better if Adivasis live on their own, without interference from others."

What becomes particularly clear from the story of Marianade is that it was especially the most powerless workers who were left with no other option but to demand land. We already saw at Sugandagiri that management staff continued to receive wages despite the crisis. Here at Marianade, we saw it was the less impoverished workers who could claim social rights and benefits instead of having only land to claim. All in all, it becomes clear that the emphasis on land rights did not emerge from an a priori political consensus that land ownership is the best road to Adivasi empowerment. Rather, the political emphasis on land ownership, initially promoted by indigenist activists but soon becoming a political consensus with regard to Adivasis, evolved in the course of struggle. That the demand for land became particularly pronounced among Adivasis is not simply because Adivasis lack land and hence need it but because Adivasis are generally at the bottom of the social hierarchy in Kerala and do not have the power to sustain other claims. This, then, can hardly be considered the victorious coming of age of an "Adivasi" wish to repossess "their" land, nor is it the most useful outcome for all concerned. Instead, in each case we saw initial differences in wealth, which were kept in balance through employment in a cooperative project, become enlarged as soon as the project was disbanded and Adivasis were given individual plots through which to make a living. While those Adivasi families who historically possessed land (for instance those of Kurichiya or Kuruma background) can then embrace indigenist visions of land because they resonate with their desire to "reclaim Adivasi land," Adivasi families who have a history of bonded labor struggle to attain fertile land and often lack the means to cultivate the land they get. Even when they do attain land, many of these families are thus at the same time forced back into a life of day labor and migration. This creates much ambivalence about indigenist politics. But sometimes it actually reinforces the more general appeal of indigenism, which, as for the day laborers of Kottamurade colony, is not only about owning a piece of land, but also about being able to build up an autonomous "Adivasi" life regardless of the closed avenues of integration into mainstream Kerala.

## Conclusion

In the nineteenth century, Travancore (the southern part of what is now Kerala) was frequently labeled "the Model State" (Baak 1997: 135) It was not human development organizations who gave it that label then but British administrators, impressed by the Travancore government's exceptionally lenient attitude towards planters' efforts to acquire land, control labor, and make the local state bear its infrastructural costs (ibid.). In other words, Kerala was a model in facilitating corporate profits at the expense of investments in general wellbeing. Luckily, the epithet "model state" in reference to Kerala by now has come to signify the opposite. Nonetheless, as we have seen in this chapter and the previous, a crisis of the egalitarian model is palpable, not just in figures on government spending and Gini coefficients but also in the everyday experiences of people. Though it might seem logical to interpret the rise of indigenism exactly in the context of people's anxieties about how to sustain themselves, most commentators look only at the current position of Adivasis at the bottom of the social and economic hierarchy of Kerala and conclude that their uprising must be about the Kerala model having bypassed them altogether.

I have argued, instead, that it is precisely the changes coming in the "post-reform" period of Kerala's model of development that have—in interaction with political dynamics discussed earlier—not just triggered but also shaped a new wave of resistance focusing on issues of pride, identity, autonomy, and land. It was not automatic, for instance, that the difficulties that Adivasis experienced in an increasingly commercialized educational field would lead to an emphasis on ST quotas and "Adivasi" identity rather than a movement to resist the rise of private schools, allowing "Adivasis" to remain unmarked, unexceptional citizens. It was only when the momentum of private education seemed irresistible, considering the general direction of political-economic change in Kerala—but also considering resistance against it was led by a no-longer-credible "Communist" Party—that many "Adivasis" started rediscovering their "roots." It was likewise not automatic that the collapse of the cooperative plantation sector would lead to the call for Adivasi land rights rather than for government intervention to restore these cooperatives' role of providing employment and social benefits. The emphasis on land only came with the defeat of the latter demand due to Adivasi workers' relative powerlessness to challenge a government structurally pushed toward discontinuing employment projects and cutting social benefits.

What I have offered is a class analysis but not one that reproduces the Communist Party's line. Indeed, as we saw in earlier chapters, class analysis of that type would probably imply arguing that indigenism is a problem of activist leaders "misleading" their followers and promoting a form of "false consciousness." What a relational or "expanded" class analysis does instead is show that it is not just the kind of political dynamics described in chapters 3 and 4 that have given rise to indigenism, but that this process has been structurally conditioned by changes in people's everyday experiences in making a living. With such a focus, it becomes all too clear that despite producing a highly politically aware population and despite leaving few untouched by the commonly shared, cultivated, and almost hegemonic desire to focus on making life better for the poor, the "Kerala model" cannot in itself withstand the myriad ways in which an intensified capitalist logic penetrates into society and reinforces endogenous capitalist processes that were erstwhile so diligently tamed.

The Kerala model is best understood as a more radical and more consistently implemented version of general Nehruvian social democracy, flourishing at a time when Keynesian economic policy dominated in the West and developmentalism in the South. The new situation in Kerala concomitantly seems to be no more than a milder version of neoliberalism, with certain path-dependent eccentricities. One eccentricity is the extent to which a majority of Kerala's population, because of how redistributive policies made land ownership and education generally available, participates in the bourgeois competition for prestige and mobility. In Kerala, even many Dalits and Adivasis participate in the competition for social status that centers on land and educational achievement. And, as we saw in the previous chapter, particularly for those Dalits and Adivasis for whom aspirations to middle-class ownership and education have come within reach, the vulnerability of their position in an increasingly consumerist and at the same time polarizing society produces anxieties more easily translated into a language of caste-determined or ethnically determined "culture" and "identity" than into a language of class. Being already somewhat upwardly mobile and experiencing tensions primarily in the sphere of consumption rather than production, it is more their historical background than their fragile present condition that presents itself as a source of potential humiliation or pride. Being constantly reminded of this historical background, through the stress of maintaining their position as well as by the derogatory remarks of others, they are constantly reminded of those who have not experienced such mobility at all. The combination makes it easier for them to turn to a community of ethnic descent as a basis for political mobilization and to see injustice primarily in terms of caste discrimination. For these persons, Dalit and/or Adivasi identity combines the desire to pursue their own concerns for mobility, for breaking the negative grip of the past on them, and the wish to eliminate the inequalities of that living past altogether.

This path to identity politics that characterizes the trajectory of activist leaders of the AGMS is different from that of ordinary workers who joined the AGMS. Adivasi workers have generally enjoyed absolute material progress under the Kerala model but have seen their relative position vis-à-vis the middle class unchanged and therefore are not particularly stressed about living up to a higher status. Their everyday lives hold out few pretenses of equality: most of them live in ghetto-like colonies or workers' quarters and take orders from those willing to employ them. What the Kerala model meant for them is the ability to work and live independently of a particular landlord who can treat them as his personal slaves. They have consequently, however, become all the more dependent on selling their labor power, and it is here that life has become increasingly stressful in post-reform Kerala. As government-run cooperatives collapse, as migrant labor comes to compete with local labor, as basic avenues for integration such as education and health care are hollowed out, and as the sector they are traditionally dependent on—agriculture—goes into crisis, these workers see themselves increasingly excluded from Kerala society. These processes of precarization, which reveal a society pushing them to the absolute margins, clearly make it more likely for them to believe in a politics of autonomy than one of social integration. In the course of political mobilization, then, the two trajectories—of leaders and rank-and-file—start to connect and strengthen each other. Adivasi workers' turning to struggle for land, which as we saw appeared more out of necessity than as a deliberate choice, receive further encouragement through the importance that more socially mobile activists attach to land ownership as a way to get rid of the historically stigmatized identity of "agricultural laborer."

Cultural or utilitarian perspectives are not irrelevant in studying the structural conditions leading to the rise of indigenism. Yet pulling such considerations apart from the ways they express, reflect, and shape everyday life under changing relations of production and appropriation leads to sterile theorizing. Dalit and Adivasi activists turn to their past not out of a primordial reflex but because they need new inspiration on how to deal with the problems of the present. To call this a "cultural revival," as is often done, is a simplification that reduces our understanding of what the movement is a reaction to. The discourse of indigenism has certain advantages that fit the present—the demand for land, for instance, as this is what is most likely to receive government attention. People indeed act on what is best for them, but how particular courses of action become interpreted as in people's best interest depends on larger social processes and people's experiences in everyday life. Proudly claiming "Dalit" or "Adivasi" identity and demanding land is not simply the most rational political reaction to confront changing circumstances but the outcome of processes of identification shaped by the increasing insecurities of everyday life in post-reform Kerala.

Legal structures also play a role in the rise of indigenism, yet should also not be divorced of class processes. Being a "Scheduled Tribe" or not and acting according to legal opportunities and limitations is something people think about and act on in particular ways. Yet it is more interesting to look at how laws start playing a role in people's lives than it is to assume their a priori determining role. For a long time—and still today to some extent—upwardly mobile "SCs" and "STs" have avoided these categories for the shame that attaches to them of not being "meritorious" enough. The fact that legal categories of SC/ST play such an important role today—though these categories have existed since independence—and are now being politically transformed into a source of pride rather than shame forces us to look for what has changed in the wider context.

Using an understanding of the changing tendencies of global capitalism helps discern changes in people's everyday working lives. The experiences that people shared with me in turn allowed me to rethink these global processes and how they shape—and are shaped by—local dynamics. Kerala governments are still generally more committed to social equality and to resisting dramatic commodification than other Indian state governments are: those in power in Kerala know all too well that they will not easily get away with dispossessing ordinary people of their land or taking away social rights that were so passionately fought for. Yet changes happened in Kerala nonetheless. The remittances that are said to keep the Kerala economy afloat reinforced a status competition unfolding in the sphere of consumption, aside from a productive sector that was stagnant. A steady job in the government sector, unless at a high-ranking position, started to pale in comparison to the opportunities offered in the private sector and abroad. Those employed as workers in the agricultural sector increasingly felt the pressure of being made expendable. Indigenism grew out of these changing conditions of people's lives. But it is more than simply an adaptation. It is at the same time an obvious challenge to these processes. In the indigenist program, opposed to the Communist Party and its emphasis on "class"-based mobilization, we nevertheless see strong substantive continuities with the historical struggle of the Left in Kerala—I discuss this further in the following chapter.

## Notes

1. To prevent all too facile recognition of the village, I will not mention its name here.
2. A pattern we know from earlier anti–bonded labor campaigns, notably by British colonial administrators and missionaries eager to access labor for their plantations (Kooiman 1989).
3. For a compelling analysis of how industrial agriculture and, later, speculative agribusiness created the political-economic and environmental context for these farmer suicides see Muenster 2011.

4. As the farmers leasing land in Kodagu told me, there is significant financial stress on them since the price of leasing land is constantly increasing and stands at more than thirty thousand rupees an acre (in 2009) while the price of ginger fluctuates as much as from two thousand to three hundred rupees per sixty kilograms. According to these farmers, the ones really benefiting from it all were the large landowners in Karnataka who leased out their land.
5. These *kudumbashree* projects were part of a state-wide female-oriented poverty reduction campaign initiated in 1991.
6. Presented as an emancipatory policy aimed at providing women with the necessary funds to pay for education, the program is seen by most people in Kerala today as a policy to help people save up for the rising costs of dowries.
7. They also tried to organize Manju's native colony, which stayed with the CPI(M) instead.
8. The collapse of the price of cash crops was in turn related to the disintegration of the USSR, which made the United States no longer eager to sustain international trade agreements with quotas to regulate prices, particularly of tea and coffee (Neilson and Pritchard 2009).
9. Adivasi Congress, an arm of the Congress party, was established in Kerala on 19 October 2005.
10. One acre of land = 100 cents of land.
11. Muthanga had been strategically selected by AGMS leaders with the idea that as it was a nature reserve, an occupation there would have the potential of drawing attention also from the central Indian government (see chapter 2).

# PART V

## CONCLUSION

– Chapter 7 –

# THE (DIS)PLACEMENTS OF CLASS

Explaining the rise of indigenism as a new form of political mobilization by looking at what happened to the political programs that attracted people previously and by analyzing the locally experienced, yet globally induced, changes in people's working lives is an approach that is more common in studies on right-wing, neonationalist politics. When it comes to the rise of Hindutva and its nativist "sons of the soil" rhetoric, for instance, ample attention has been paid not only to historically deconstructing its core formal concepts ("Hindu-ness," "nation"; e.g., Ludden 2005) but also to addressing the question of how class conflict becomes displaced onto cultural frames (e.g., Breman and Shah 2004; Shani 2007); to analyzing the complex and contradictory relationship of the rise of Hindutva to processes of democratization (e.g., Hansen 1999; cf. Jaffrelot 2003); and to looking at the kind of socioeconomic changes conditioning the spread of Hindu nationalism (e.g., Froerer 2007). When it comes to indigenous people's movements, however, such perspectives are less popular. Indigenous movements usually carry forward more inclusive and progressive ideals, making the deconstruction of their political form and the explanation of their popularity less urgent. However, the hesitation to explain the rise of indigenism with the tools of critical social analysis ultimately isolates indigenous movements from a more general critique of relations of power within the contemporary world system. The aim of this book has been to study the rise of indigenism, asking similar questions to those usually posed about the rise of nativism: what political dynamics existed that prevented the underlying conflicts to be articulated in the existing modern-secular repertoire of class and what more structural changes prepared the ground for this political shift. In other words, I studied what caused the displacement of class conflict and the shift from Communist to indigenist political frames. Crucial to this question has been the notion of class—not just the emic notion of class as referring to the Communist party's political focus but particularly class as a theoretical tool within the Marxist analytical tradition where it helps to link global relations of power to people's everyday experiences of making a living.

I started this book demonstrating the problematic historical baggage and difficult political dilemmas that a politics centered on the notion of Adivasiness invites. It became all the more pertinent, then, to explain why Dalit and Adivasi workers turned away from Communism as the most obvious and hegemonic means of articulating the issues now taken up by indigenism in Kerala. My theoretical research program and the empirical clues I found during my fieldwork complicated ideas on the rise of indigenism that tend to dominate the literature on indigenous movements. At the level of political interactions, the prevalent idea is that indigenous movements arise where there is a process of liberal democratization. This did not make sense in Kerala as liberal democracy has been the only mode of governance there since independence. Not much evidence could be found, moreover, for the argument that it is primarily international networking that induces people to emphasize their indigenous identity. International networking with indigenous movements has been very limited and often more of a political liability than a benefit for the Adivasi Gothra Maha Sabha. Following activist biographies and looking into the political dynamics producing an indigenist narrative, I found that not democratization, nor international contacts, but encounters and interactions with the existing Left had played a major role in shaping the rise of indigenism. There were clear signs that the Communist Party's increasingly alienated rhetoric of "class struggle," combined with its practical compliance with the pressures of neoliberal reform, was the main trigger for the rise of indigenism in Kerala.

This disillusionment with antisystemic movements centered on "workers and peasants" after the Communist Party had come to power and lost its commitment to confronting structural relations of power was not, however, a phenomenon confined to Kerala. It is a process developing throughout the late modern capitalist world, and I argued that rather than being a step forward in a progressive trajectory towards ever-greater freedom for historically oppressed peoples, my findings in Kerala suggested a different perspective: that the rise of indigenism within the current world system signals the end of a reformist cycle in world history. In other words, indigenism signals the end of an "optimism of the oppressed" (Wallerstein 2004: 85) —the end of an era in which oppressed people could feel certain that history was on their side and could believe in—and muster some patience for—the possibilities of progress within the framework of the liberal-secular nation-state.

The second level at which I subsequently explored the rise of indigenism was that of the more structural shifts that shaped the conditions under which various groups in Kerala turned to indigenism. I noted that interpreting the turn to indigenism as the strategic mobilization of cultural attachments in the face of the threat of neoliberalism—the most prevalent structural explanation given for the rise of indigenous movements in the last quarter of the twentieth century—did not fit the case of Kerala well. The strategic benefits and cultural attachments of Adivasiness were not givens, waiting in abstract to be relied upon in the face of threats to people's livelihood. Rather, my fieldwork in Kerala suggested that it was the gradual process of neoliberal restructuring itself that had determined the attractiveness of demanding land rather than wage labor and had enticed people to start interpreting their social position and historical experiences as determined by their being Adivasi. For the recently upwardly-mobile subaltern leadership of the indigenist movement in Kerala, the increasing fragility of their middle-class position was understandably interpreted as resulting not so much from the general injustice of privatization and competition within a capitalist system but as a legacy of the stigma they carried of belonging to a culturally despised social group. Among the Adivasi agricultural workers forming the rank and file of the Adivasi Gothra Maha Sabha, the turn to indigenous over class identity was, on the other hand, encouraged by their growing desire to claim a piece of land and envision building up a life determined by themselves. It was a reaction that grew out of the experience of becoming increasingly expendable in the local economy in the wake of the agricultural crisis and the collapse of employment and workers' protection schemes. The case of Kerala suggested that neoliberalism was not simply an external threat to subaltern communities but a process gradually shaping people's everyday lives and, in doing so, triggering different political imaginations.

These arguments on the rise of indigenism emerge from the specificities of the case of Kerala. The more prevalent argument in indigenous studies is that democratization and greater tolerance for ethnolinguistic diversity on the one hand, and politically strategic and culturally emancipatory strategies of dealing with the threat of accumulation by dispossession on the other, triggered the rise of indigenism. This argument arises particularly from the literature on indigenous movements in Latin America, which tends to prevail in the field of indigenous studies. The same argument can garner some evidence in the central tribal corridor of India. Yet this is not to argue that Kerala is, as is said so often, simply an "exceptional" case. Suggesting alternative explanations for the rise of indigenism in Kerala—stressing the demise of the traditional Left and the gradual disappearance of the political-economic bases of working-class identification—can also help illuminate aspects of the history of the rise of indigenism in various parts of Latin America and elsewhere.

Looking at the case of the Zapatista movement in Chiapas from the perspective developed here, for instance, highlights parts of the movement's history that are often neglected in analyses focusing on how the movement forced the Mexican state to become more open to ethnocultural diversity or on the key role played by the international networks supporting indigenous resistance against globalization. A historical-political and world-systems perspective would draw attention to the fact that the demise of the Institutional Revolutionary Party (the PRI)—the long-time hegemonic party that carried on the legacy of the Mexican revolution—was not simply a sign of "democratization" (it was always formally democratic) but more a sign that the party had, as in Kerala, lost its commitment to the emancipatory ideals that had once attracted the loyalty of Mexico's poor. Also, though many international activists came to Chiapas, the early phases of the Zapatista movement, as in Kerala, involved not the international indigenous movement but urban intellectuals joining up with indigenous leaders (Harvey 1998). Moreover, though symbolically launched in 1994 at the beginning of the enforcement of the NAFTA free trade treaty—and hence often perceived as trying to prevent neoliberalism—local relations in Chiapas had already become shaped by neoliberal reform at least from 1982 onwards, when, following the financial crisis, the government had drastically deprioritized land reform and started retracting its support to agrarian cooperatives functioning on communally owned so-called *ejido* land. In fact, whereas earlier accounts of the Zapatista movement often elaborated the movement's claims that it was heading a wave of democratization and resisting the government's plans for neoliberal reform, later accounts have paid more attention precisely to the shift from class to indigenous rights that the Zapatistas represented and the intertwining of neoliberal reform and new forms of political protest (e.g., Speed 2008). Even from Latin America, the argument can now be heard that the global so-called third wave of democratic transition was in fact a "combination of democratization and neoliberal development policies" and that while "universaliz[ing] the language of rights" it "at the same time ... constricted the ideological and structural space for the political expression of class identities" (Young 2008: 151).

I could go further and suggest that the perspective emerging from Kerala is relevant even for Ecuador, a country that, because of its corporatist dictatorship until 1979 and the obvious threats by oil companies to indigenous land, would seem a perfect fit with the dominant frame in indigenous studies so far. Indeed, Yashar (2005) has argued strongly that indigenism in Ecuador arose due to the democratization of an erstwhile culturally homogenizing authoritarian state in combination with the growing need to resist the threat that indigenous communities were facing of being dispossessed of their basic means of existence (Yashar 2005). We see that even here, sensitivity to an alternative perspective will highlight historical evidence that shows parallels with Kerala—for one, the fact that Ecuador's indigenous movement so explicitly grew out of Leftist organizing (Becker 2008). But also the fact that in its early years ECUARUNARI, the major indigenous movement that arose in Ecuador, was dominated by a class-based *campesino* (peasant) focus that only changed to a more exclusively ethnic focus in 1985, after years of emergency measures during the presidency of Hurtado (Hey and Klak 1999: 70ff.). The Hurtado presidency was Left in rhetoric but neoliberal in policy and had formed the basis of structural adjustment in Ecuador. A study by Petras and Veltmeyer (2005: 139) shows that indigenism came to dominate class-based mobilization as the political repression of protests increased with every subsequent popular revolt in the 1980s—an indication that not democratization but repression was what led to the rise of indigenism. A parallel to the rise of indigenism in Kerala that can be found in Petras and Veltmeyer's study of Ecuador is that indigenism became particularly popular after labor unions had become politically defective in the mid-eighties due to soaring unemployment. All this indicates that a perspective that combines attention to systemic movement cycles and the demise of traditional class politics, with a focus on the entanglement of indigenist forms of protest with actual neoliberal restructuring, is relevant also to many places outside Kerala where class-based mobilization was overtaken by indigenism.

In order to draw attention to this different perspective on the rise of indigenism, it was necessary for me to make a clear formal distinction between Communism and indigenism—a formal distinction that could be convincing since it is one generally acknowledged in Kerala, if under different headings such as "identity politics" versus

"Marxism," or "Dravidian culture" versus "Communist ideology." I chose the heading of "indigenism" as a concept uniting these political references to Adivasi belonging as it also tied these local references to the international phenomenon of indigenism. I preferred the term to simply "indigenous politics" because it emphasizes political form over existential being, which is important because one of the main problems in the study of indigenous movements that I wanted to avoid was the frequent collapsing of formal political expression and substantive historical experience. The clear formal distinction between indigenism and Communism matters precisely because I was determined to historically and politically challenge the substantive distinction between indigenous people and workers and instead, from a Marxist perspective, emphasize the unity of the cultural and economic conditions of indigenous working lives.

Making the formal distinction between the two political currents had the advantage of being able to point to certain trends not always observable within the complex ethnographic realities on the ground. As I was working on this research in June 2010, an email from a Malayalee PhD student reporting on how two public intellectuals[1] had just challenged the Communist party to open the discussion on "identity politics" (*swathwa rashtriyam*) confirmed my intuition on this. The student wrote to me, "It is in this background that I came to know that you have observed [in an article in the *Journal of South Asian Development*] that this particular political strategy [identity politics] is at work in this state since the 90s," continuing that in fact it was only at the recent CPI(M) conference he attended that the reality of the emergence of identity politics was explicitly discussed. The emic term "identity politics" indeed was not yet prevalent in public debate during the time of my fieldwork, and the Communist party had been trying to, publicly at least, turn a blind eye to the challenge posed by indigenism. Nevertheless, combining ethnographic observation with formal analytical distinctions, it was not difficult to see a social trend from "class" to "identity" before it became a prevalent emic reference to the process. Ending my analysis on this confirmatory note about the rise of indigenism, however, would be unsatisfactory. Social scientists, after all, may foresee the relations and conditions under which people make history but cannot foresee the making of history itself. Rather, they can play a role in that, and for this reason I would like to end this book by warning against any closure—either on the question of indigenism and Communism as contrasting currents or on the question of how the rise of indigenism relates to cycles of world history.

### *Hidden Histories in the Making?*

C. K. Janu once gave me an allegory for the unacknowledged appropriation of Adivasi heritage by Hindu art:

> If we plant two plantains, and don't fertilize one of them, that one will soon die. Say that this plantain tree then decays at the base of the other one and becomes compost; the other will certainly bear more fruit then. If the two had grown alike, both would have less fruit—if one decays at the base of the other, the other will have better fruit. But we say the one tree was no good, and marvel at the fruit of the other one. We never think why and how it got those great fruits. We see only one thing: the fruit on this tree is good, and the other one decayed. (25 June 2005).

Janu's allegory would be equally relevant to a critique of how the Communist movement appropriated the campaigns for social justice carried on by some of the earlier anticaste movements and grew in popularity at the same time that these movements declined. It would also apply to how, in turn, indigenist activists often claim their success is based on formulating a whole new political agenda where in fact their success depends also on the work done by the Communist movement before them. It is precisely my awareness of the substantive continuities between Communist and indigenist initiatives that made me wonder why the shift in formal articulation had taken place. Yet in focusing on formal contrasts, I did not mean to contribute to the process by which the continuities between the two are turned into a hidden history—a history no longer recognized through contemporary lenses. From the stories told in this book—and especially from the words of different activists and from their life histories—it should be clear that there is a strong continuity between what is now called the "traditional Left" and the new indigenist activism.

Continuities between Communist and indigenist politics can be seen particularly clearly in what is a key issue in both movements: the issue of land. According to the AGMS, land ownership is about reclaiming ancestral territory. For many of those participating in the AGMS's land occupations, however, it is just as much about laying claim to the promises of land reform that were extended to them a generation ago by the Communist movement but never materialized (cf. Nieuwenhuys 1991). Likewise, owning a piece of land is usually represented by the AGMS as the basis from which Adivasis can start to live a more autonomous life and gain greater independence. Yet for many of the people claiming land through the AGMS—and indeed for some of its leading activists[2]—owning land is at the same time a claim to what is historically and culturally of primary significance in proper Malayalee citizenship. Both indigenist and Communist views on land, moreover, are today articulated under the shadow of a neoliberal "model of empowerment based implicitly or explicitly on property rights" (Rajagopalan 2004: 229f.; see also Humphrey and Verdery 2004). Though land ownership is a key point of both Communist and indigenist politics in Kerala, both at the same time try to critique the neoliberal model, either by emphasizing the emotional attachment to land so that it is not just another commodity that can be substituted by monetary compensation (see also Ghosh 2006) or by framing access to land as a right that the state has a duty to implement in support of the emancipation of the oppressed.

The strong continuity between Communism and indigenism in Kerala is certainly apparent when viewed in comparison to indigenous movements elsewhere. Vernacular versions of international indigenist discourses in Kerala generally bring these discourses closer to socialist visions than to the visions circulating in indigenous networks in countries less influenced by democratic socialism. The fact that in Kerala almost all indigenist leaders started their political engagement in Communist movements clearly has had its effects on the form indigenism has taken in Kerala. As Sunny Kapicadu, one of the few indigenist leaders who had not himself been a Communist but only had parents involved in the Communist movement, complained to me, "Even our [Dalit and Adivasi] leaders still have Marx in their heads!" When I subsequently pressed him on why the AGMS in Kerala has, in contrast to most Dalit and Adivasi movements elsewhere in India, hardly suffered from subcaste competition and a bias toward the needs of the "creamy layer" (subaltern elites) over those of ordinary workers, even he admitted this may well be related to what he called the "hegemony of class-thinking in Kerala."

In other parts of the world, socialist-indigenist continuities are often less obvious. In Australia, a country where socialist movements have generally—as in the United States—remained marginal, the extent to which the aboriginal struggle for rights was supported by and built on the Communist Party remains almost entirely unacknowledged (Boughton 2001).[3] Even in Latin America, where socialist movements have historically been much stronger, continuities between socialist and indigenist organizing are not always noted. Marc Becker's work on the indigenous *levantamiento* (uprising) in June 1990 in Ecuador explicitly sets out to examine the preceding cross-fertilization between urban left-wing intelligentsia and rural indigenous activists and the fluidity in activist thinking on indigenous and class issues. In doing so, Becker's work is an important and still necessary critique of the many histories that look only abstractly at the "five-centuries-old" indigenous struggle against colonization in Latin America and leave out the whole history of socialist organizing in the more recent past. This relates to the problem in many analyses of indigenous movements—that an analytical leap is made from the here and now of indigenist mobilization to a deep history of indigenous belonging and culture, with little interest in the concrete and more contingent social processes that have taken place in more recent decades. As Becker argues, if we actually do pay attention to this more recent history, it is striking how much indigenous organizing in Latin America has been shaped by Leftist visions. In Kerala, this is so obvious that the alternative—that Adivasi movements could have been shaped by Rightist visions (e.g., see Froerer 2007)—is hardly even contemplated. Lest we mistakenly assume subaltern populations are automatically more inclined towards structural social reform than towards authoritarian attempts to fix the status quo, the fact that the AGMS is so left-inclined is clearly an outcome of the actual continuity (despite the polarization) between Communist and indigenist mobilization in Kerala.

Whereas substantively the politics of Communism and indigenism are closely related, even the formal distinctions sometimes break down, certainly outside of the front line of political battle between old Left and rising indigenous movements. "Adivasi identity" is in fact a complex and contested signifier to do with being downtrodden, poor, pushed to the margins, and in need of protection from the state. It is only in transmission—when the need for quick "consciousness raising" arises—or in confrontation with dogmatic elements within the Communist Party that Adivasi identity suddenly is articulated as being about culture to the exclusion of class. In Kerala, emic notions of "class" are in turn entirely open to being read as "caste." As we saw, early Communists were prone to understanding Communism as the idea that "all human beings belong to one caste." With the Communist Party slowly trying to come to terms with indigenist challenges, its speeches are increasingly filled with references to "Dalits" and "Adivasis." When not in explicit opposition to Communism, indigenist activists likewise will stress their concern for "the poor" even more vehemently than their concern for Adivasis. It is interesting to note in this respect that from its initial focus on "the unity of all tribes" and on "recovering our Adivasi culture"—phrases that arguably were borrowed from the ethnographic state—the AGMS after Muthanga has increasingly focused on "the right to live," "land for the landless" and "dignity." In the process, we may well see "culture" and "identity" taking on much more relational and dynamic meanings than their dominant interpretation was at the beginning of the indigenist wave of protest in Kerala. Though the change in the meaning of notions remade in the process of political struggle will be influenced by scholarly debates, the academic consensus on the meaning of such concepts as "class," "identity," "caste," or "culture" will be all the more influenced by the political struggles outside academia. One may hence wonder what political frames will be mobilized at various critical junctures of local political history and global transformation. Likewise, we may also ask how the influence of an ongoing indigenist challenge will affect the meaning of different political keywords through which social conflicts have been addressed. In this respect, what I want to turn to finally is a consideration of how the substantive continuities and even formal blurring of Communist and indigenist movements in Kerala also show how even though it takes place under structural pressures and limitations, the indigenist struggle is nevertheless an expression of the contingency introduced through human action in the course of world history.

### *Critical Struggles Continued*

The main reasons for the rise of indigenism in Kerala presented in this book—the demise of modern political platforms of economic integration and changing regimes of (re)production and accumulation—align with Jonathan Friedman's view on indigenism as a dominant trend under phases of "hegemonic decline" in the world system. According to Friedman (2000), the contemporary world system is disintegrating and fragmenting into a few nationless cosmopolitans versus a mix of fanatic identities among other core populations, desperate consumptive stabs at a vanishing "modern" in the third world, and exit-strategies in the "fourth" (indigenous) world. This process is part of the fact that US imperialism has reached the limits of its economic dominance in the world. With the decline of US hegemony comes the demise of the global homogenization and ranking of difference it sustained, leading to intensified identity politics. In all of this, the politics of indigeneity "is not so much about concrete indigenous groups" as about "a process of identification in the contemporary global arena that is a powerful expression of the transformation of the global system" (Friedman 1999: 408). According to Friedman, "class polarization," together with the related decline of the nation-state, is the driving mechanism behind the process of indigenization. It is what fuels the desire for "rooting" among the majority of the world's populations and the cosmopolitanization of the world's elites. Hence, says Friedman, "the rise of indigenous movements is part of this large systemic process" (ibid.: 398), though he adds that "this is not to say that it is a mere product in a mechanical deterministic sense."

Yet, though not "mechanically" or "deterministically" produced, the historical inevitability in Friedman's view is palpable. It has sometimes led to the idea that Friedman is particularly pessimistic about indigenous movements—a mistaken reading since Friedman in fact stresses that though indigenization is indeed a structural process, it takes on very different forms: "In certain conditions it produces alternative identities against the state, in other conditions it can produce extreme nationalism within the state" (Friedman 1999: 401). In this sense, Friedman agrees with the proponents of indigenous movements who argue against criticism of the potential exclusivist political tendencies of indigenism by arguing for the crucial difference between subaltern and majoritarian indigenist movements (e.g., Kenrick and Lewis 2003 against Kuper 2003). Friedman in fact ridicules the fears that cosmopolitan liberal elites—"the global cocktail circuit" (1999: 406)—harbor of the indigenizing tendencies of the majority of the world. He debunks elite attempts to deconstruct notions of territorial belonging or cultural coherence as efforts to shape the world according to these elites' own worldview from "above it all." He criticizes moral judgments against the "practice of a particular kind of identity, an identity of rootedness, of genealogy as it relates to territory," and points out that such identities are in fact logically (though not necessarily empirically) prior to the nation-state (1999: 398). Friedman thus comes down squarely in defense of indigenous movements and even of culturally coherent indigenous identities. What is problematic, however, about Friedman's vision is that despite defending indigenous movements, we are still—with caveats against mechanical analyses and determinism—left with the notion that these movements necessarily signal a path back to a survivalist reliance on more local, territorially rooted ways of life, a regression from the moment of modern democracy and class reformism (see also Rata 2003). This leaves little room for the Marxist insight that people make their own history—even if not under conditions of their own choosing (see also McMichael 2008). To keep an open mind about where history is heading, it is therefore important to end with a "critical struggles" perspective (McMichael 2010).

A critical struggles perspective calls for attention not just to the global systemic context of the rise of indigenism but also, dialectically, to the epistemological challenges posed by movements like the

AGMS and the role that these movements play in an ongoing global class struggle. From a critical struggles perspective, analysis of the emergent politics of indigenist movements should not become restricted by the dominant liberal dichotomy of class versus culture. As we have seen in this book, though there is a formal tendency for "indigenous culture" to replace "class" as the political master frame in Kerala and though there are lived reasons for people to connect to this formal shift, there are myriad ways in which leaders and participants in the AGMS undermine the formal opposition of class and indigeneity in practice and consistently focus their actions on pushing against the tendencies of contemporary capitalism in Kerala. The AGMS does not simply reproduce the systemic tendency towards cultural reification and economic disintegration; on the contrary, it creates a solidarity of laboring classes that defies these tendencies in new ways. If Kerala is a place that complicates the romantic interpretation of indigenism as the next step in a global forward march of liberal emancipation, it is at the same time a place where we see how historical struggles of labor endure. Notwithstanding the progression of world capitalism and the manifestations thereof in Kerala, the AGMS combines giving priority to the needs of the most oppressed with a tendency to leave the category of "Adivasi" much more open than any movement before it has. In this we can see glimpses of how a collective good sense to overcome capitalism is progressing. The struggle continues.

## Notes

1. K. E. N. Kunhammed and P. K. Poker.
2. E.g., see Kapicadu 2008, "Beyond Just a Home and a Name."
3. Bob Boughton (2001) also acknowledges the problems in this relationship—for instance in the Communist Party's hesitance to acknowledge aboriginal workers as anything more culturally particular than "the lowest rung of the proletarian ladder."

# GLOSSARY

| | |
|---|---|
| Adiya | Name of a Scheduled Tribe in Kerala, mostly landless, ex-slave agricultural laborers (lit. "slave"). |
| Adivasi | Lit. "aboriginal." In common language often used interchangeably with "Scheduled Tribe." |
| AITUC | All Indian Trade Union Congress, affiliated to CPI. |
| AKS | Adivasi Kshema Samithi, CPI(M)'s Adivasi wing in Kerala founded in 2001. |
| AGMS | Adivasi Gothra Maha Sabha, the name adopted in 2001 by the most prominent new Adivasi movement in Kerala (lit. "Indigenous Clans Grand Council"). |
| Ambedkar | Dr. Bhimrao Ramji Ambedkar (14 April 1891 – 6 December 1956), also known as Babasaheb, the most prominent Dalit leader of India, and chief architect of the Indian Constitution. |
| Ayyankali | Early Dalit (Pulaya) leader of Kerala. Became a Member of Legislative Assembly (MLA) in 1910. Lived from 1863 to 1941. |
| bahujan | Lit. "majority". A political term originating in Maharashtra to refer to subordinated Hindu castes but often extended to include any caste, tribe, or religious group in India who shares a history of subordination by Hindu upper castes. |
| BJP | Bharatiya Janata Party, a Hindutva/Hindu nationalist party, part of the Sangh Parivar, the umbrella group that includes the paramilitary anti-Muslim RSS and the international VHP organization, active in fundraising among the Indian diaspora. |

| | |
|---|---|
| Cochin | A city (renamed Kochi), but also the name of the former Princely State in Southern Kerala. |
| CITU | Center of Indian Trade Unions, affiliated to CPI(M). |
| C. K. Janu | Adiya woman leading the AGMS. |
| Communalism | Generally refers to attempts to create antagonism between communities, usually meaning Hindu versus Muslim communities. |
| Congress | Indian National Congress or INC. |
| CPI | Communist Party of India. Name of the original party formed at Kerala level in 1939 out of the Congress Socialist Party, and the name, after the 1964 split, of the party in favor of cooperation with Congress. At a national level, according to the (now) CPI, the original party was formed in 1925; according to the CPI(M), the original CPI was formed in 1920. |
| CPI(M) | Communist Party of India (Marxist). Name of the party that split off from the CPI in 1964 under the leadership of EMS Namboodiripad. (Periods in government after 1964: 1967–69; 1980–81; 1987–91; 1996–2001; 2006–11; 2016–present). |
| CPI(ML) | Communist Party of India (Marxist-Leninist). Party founded by Kanu Sanyal on 22 April 1969 in Calcutta in the wake of the Naxalbari uprising. |
| Dalit | Lit. "crushed," referring generally to those oppressed by the caste system. Often used interchangeably with "Scheduled Caste." |
| EMS | Initials by which Kerala's first Chief Minister EMS Namboodiripad (1909–98) is known. Chief Minister from April 1957 to July 1959 and again from March 1967 to October 1969. General Secretary of the CPI(M) from 1977 until 1992. |
| gherao | Encirclement. Political protest tactic whereby activists encircle a government functionary or "capitalist" (*mudalali*), prevent him or her from leaving, and shout slogans. |
| goonda | Thug. |
| gothra | Clan—exogamous unit within a *jati*. |

| | |
|---|---|
| INTUC | Indian National Trade Union Congress, a trade union affiliated to Congress. |
| Izhava | Known in Malabar as Tiyya. Listed as Other Backward Class (OBC). A community/caste treated as untouchables in nineteenth-century Kerala (religiously considered "Shudras") that experienced great vertical mobility in the twentieth century. |
| janmi/jenmi | Big landlord of Nair or Namboodiri caste. |
| jati | Commonly translated as "community" or "caste," used in reference to the thousands of exclusive, endogamous and regionally-specific communities existing in India. Jati names usually refer to a particular traditional occupation. Jatis differs from *varna* (see below). |
| Kattunaikan | Scheduled Tribe, generally landless, with a background of making a living by collecting forest products. |
| KIRTADS | Kerala Institute for Research, Training and Development Studies of Scheduled Castes and Schedules Tribes. Governmental organization set up in 1979 under the Ministry of SC/ST Development. |
| Kunduvadian | Formerly Scheduled Tribe, now "Other Eligible Community." |
| Kurichiya | Scheduled Tribe, mostly small farmers. |
| Kuruma | Scheduled Tribe, mostly small farmers. |
| KSKTU | The Kerala State Karshaka Thozhilali Union, i.e., Agricultural Workers' Union, affiliated to the CPI(M). |
| LDF | Left Democratic Front, a coalition lead by CPI(M) in Kerala. |
| Malabar | Northern part of what is now Kerala. During the colonial period under direct British rule from Madras (Chennai). |
| Malayalam | Dravidian language formally spoken in the territory of what became, with the States Reorganization Act of 1956, Kerala. The language has many regional dialects as well as (caste-specific) sociolects. |
| Malayalee | Person originating from Kerala (speaking Malayalam), popularly known also as "Mallu." |

| | |
|---|---|
| MLA | Member of Legislative Assembly. |
| moopan | Generally considered the name for a tribal chieftain. |
| Muthanga | Name of a wildlife sanctuary established in 1973 under the Forest Department in Wayanad. Site of the most prominent land occupation organized by the AGMS in 2003. |
| Nair/Nayar | Name of a prominent so-called "forward caste" in Kerala (according to Hindu religious interpretation, considered warriors/Kshatriyas). |
| Namboodiri | "Highest" Brahmin caste in Kerala. |
| Naxal/Naxalite | Generic term used for antiparliamentary, militant Communist groups in India, mostly tracing their origin back to the CPI(ML), though other groupings include the Maoist Communist Center and the People's War Group. |
| Nehru | Jawaharlal Nehru (14 November 1889 – 27 May 1964). First prime minister of India from 1947 to 1964. |
| OBC | Other Backward Class. Communities formally considered better off than SCs and STs yet still labeled "historically disadvantaged." |
| Paniya | Name of a Scheduled Tribe in Kerala, mostly landless ex-slave agricultural laborers (lit. "worker"). |
| panchayat | In common parlance refers to the village or municipal government. With the "Kerala Panchayat Raj Act & Municipality Act" of 1994, administration in rural areas was divided into four levels: *grama sabha* (ward level, "direct democracy"), *grama panchayat* (village level), *taluka panchayat* (block level) and district *panchayat* (district level). In urban areas there is only the Municipality or Municipal Corporation. |
| Pillai | Nair subcaste in Kerala (and last name). |
| Pulaya | Name of a Scheduled Caste in Kerala historically consisting of agricultural laborers. |
| RMS | Rashtriya Maha Sabha. Name of a political party attached to AGMS, launched on 19 February 2004. |

| | |
|---|---|
| Savarna | The so-called "twice-born" upper castes, the first three varnas in the Hindu religious caste hierarchy: Brahmins, Kshatriyas and Vaishyas. |
| SC | Scheduled Caste, i.e., a community listed as a caste eligible for affirmative action. In daily language used as synonym for "Dalit" (or harijan). |
| Secretariat | Name given in Kerala to the government complex housing the highest echelon of the state's administrative structure. |
| SNDP | Sree Narayana Dharma Paripalana yogam, organized by Sree Narayana Guru, an Izhava spiritual reformer. The organization was founded in 1903 and is still active today. |
| SSLC | Secondary School Leaving Certificate. |
| ST | Scheduled Tribe, i.e., a community listed as a tribe eligible for affirmative action. In daily language used as synonym for "Adivasi" (or girijan). |
| Syrian Christians | "Forward" community of Christians (considered of upper-caste origin) said to have been converted in the early days of Christianity by St. Thomas, as opposed to later "lower-caste" Christian converts. |
| Travancore | Former Princely State in what is now southern Kerala. |
| UDF | United Democratic Front, a coalition under the leadership of Congress in Kerala. |
| varna | Caste (or lit. color) in Hinduism's fourfold scheme of priests/Brahmins, warriors/Kshatriyas, merchants/Vaishyas and artisans/Shudras. Untouchables fall outside this scheme. |
| Wayanad | Northern hilly district of Kerala (in former Malabar) with the highest concentration of STs (17 percent; roughly a third of all STs in Kerala according to 2006 KIRTADS data). |

# Bibliography


Abrams, Philip. 1982. *Historical Sociology.* Ithaca: Cornell University Press.

Aerthayil, Mathew. 2008. *Impact of Globalization on Tribals in the Context of Kerala.* New Delhi: Rawat Publications.

Aiyappan, A. [1973] 1992. *The Paniyas: An Ex-Slave Tribe of South India.* Calcutta: Institute of Social Research and Anthropology.

Aiyer, Ananthakrishnan. 2007. "The Allure of the Transnational: Notes on Some Aspects of the Political Economy of Water in India." *Cultural Anthropology,* 22 (4): 640–658.

Ajitha. 1990. "Reminiscences from Wynad." In *A Space within the Struggle: Women's Participation in People's Movements,* edited by Ilina Sen, 19–24. Delhi: Kali for Women.

———. 2008. *Kerala's Naxalbari: Ajitha—Memoirs of a Young Revolutionary.* New Delhi: Srishti.

Anderson, Benedict. 1983. *Imagined Communities: Reflections on the Origin and Spread of Nationalism.* London: Verso.

Ayrookuzhiel, A. M. Abraham. 1990. *The Dalit Desiyata: The Kerala Experience in Development and Class Struggle.* Delhi: USOCJ.

Baak, Paul Erik. 1997. *Plantation, Production and Political Power: Plantation Development in South-west India in a Long Term Historical Perspective, 1743-1963.* Delhi: OUP.

Baby, K. J. 1993. *Nadugadhika.* Bangalore: W. Q. Judge Press.

Backer, Aboo. 2002. "Adivasis on War Path." *People's Democracy: Weekly Organ of the Communist Party of India (Marxist),* 26 (28), 21 July.

Banerjee-Guha, Swapna. 2008. "Space Relations of Capital and Significance of New Economic Enclaves: SEZs in India." *Economic and Political Weekly.* 22 Nov: 51–59.

Banerjee, Sumanta. 1984. *India's Simmering Revolution: The Naxalite Uprising.* London: Zed Books.

Bates, Crispin. 1995. "'Lost Innocents and the Loss of Innocence': Interpreting Adivasi Movements in South Asia." In *Indigenous Peoples of Asia,* edited by R. H. Barnes, A. Gray, and B. Kingsbury, 103–19. Michigan: The Association for Asian Studies.

———. 2007. *Subalterns and Raj: South Asia since 1600.* London: Routledge.

Baviskar, Amita. 2005a. *In the Belly of the River: Tribal Conflicts over Development in the Narmada Valley.* Oxford: Oxford University Press.

———. 2005b. "Red in Tooth and Claw? Looking for Class in Struggles over Nature." In *Social Movements in India,* edited by R. Ray and M. F. Katzenstein. Lanham, MD: Rowman & Littlefield.

———. 2007. "Indian Indigeneities: Adivasi Engagements with Hindu Nationalism in India." In *Indigenous Experience Today,* edited by Marisol de la Cadena and Orin Starn, 275–303. Oxford, New Yok: Berg Publishers.

Baviskar, Amita, Subir Sinha, Kavita Philip. 2005. "Rethinking Indian Environmentalism: Industrial Pollution in Delhi and Fisheries in Kerala." In *Forging Environmentalism: Justice, Livelihood and Contested Environments.* New York: M. E. Sharpe.

Baxter, Matthew. 2009. "Non-Brahmin Political Thought and the Communist Manifesto: Reception and Projection." Einaudi Center for International Studies seminar, 23 November.

Bayat, Asef. 2010. *Life as Politics: How Ordinary People Change the Middle-East.* Amsterdam: Amsterdam University Press.

Bayly, Susan. 1999. *Caste, Society and Politics in India: From the Eighteenth Century to the Modern Age.* Cambridge: Cambridge University Press.

Becker, Marc. 2008. *Indians and Leftists in the Making of Ecuador's Modern Indigenous Movements.* Durham: Duke University Press.

Beteille, Andre. 1998. "The Idea of Indigenous People." *Current Anthropology* 39 (2): 187–92.

Bhaskaran. 2004. *Mother Forest: The Unfinished Story of C. K. Janu.* Trans. N. Ravi Shanker. New Delhi: Kali for Women and Women Unlimited.

Bijoy, C. R. 2006. "Adivasi Groups vs. Coca-Cola." *Ghadar: A publication of the forum of inquilabi leftists.* 10. http://ghadar.insaf.net/September2006/pdf/Bijoy.pdf.

———. n.d. "The Southern region." Document obtained from the author.

———. 1993. "Emergence of the Submerged: Indigenous People at the UN." *Economic and Political Weekly* (June 26): 1357–60.

Bijoy, C. R., and Ravi Raman. 2003. "Muthanga: The Real Story—Adivasi Movement to Recover Land," *Economic and Political Weekly* (May 17): 1975–82.

Bindu, K. C. 2003. "Constructing the Adivasi identity: Reading the Dominant, Reading the Adivasi." Doctoral dissertation, University of Hyderabad, School of Humanities.

———. 2009. "The Tribe in the Early Census Reports: Constructing the Nation, Hindu and Outside Hindu." Paper presented at BASAS Conference, 30 March–1 April, Edinburgh.

Borras, Saturnino, Marc Edelman, and Cristobal Kay. 2008. "Transnational Agrarian Movements: Origins and Politics, Campaigns and Impact." *Journal of Agrarian Change* 8 (2, 3): 169–204. Knowledge. Delhi: Naudin Prakasha Kendra.

Bose, Sateesh Chandra, and Shiju Sam Varughese. 2015. Introduction to *Kerala Modernity: Ideas, Spaces and Practices in Transition.* New Delhi: Orient Blackswan.

Boughton, Bob. 2001. "The Communist Party of Australia's Involvement in the Struggle for Aboriginal and Torres Strait Islander Peoples' Rights 1920–1970." In *Labour and Community: Historical Essays,* edited by R. Markey, 263–94. Wollongong: University of Wollongong Press.

Breman, Jan. 1996. *Footloose Labour: Working in India's Informal Economy.* Cambridge: Cambridge University Press.

Breman, Jan and Parthiv Shah. 2004. *Working in the Mill No More.* Amsterdam: Amsterdam University Press.

Breman, Jan. 2007. *The Poverty Regime in Village India.* London: Oxford University Press.

Burawoy, Michael. 1989. "Two Methods in Search of Science: Skocpol vs. Trotsky." *Theory and Society* 18: 759–805.

———. 2000. "Introduction: Reaching for the Global." In *Global Ethnography: Forces, Connections, and Imaginations in a Postmodern World,* edited by Michael Burawoy, Joseph A. Blum, Sheba George, Zsuzsa Gille, and Millie Thayer, 1–40. Berkeley: University of California Press.

———. 2009. *The Extended Case Method: Four Countries, Four Decades, Four Great Transformations, and One Theoretical Tradition.* Berkeley: University of California Press.

C. K. Janu and M. Geethanandan. 2003. "The Return to Muthanga." PUCL Bulletin. Translated from the original Malayalam "Muthangayilekkulla Thirichhupokku—Oru."

Cederlof, Gunnel, and Deborah Sutton. 2005. "The Aboriginal Today: On Indigeneity, Exclusivism and Privileged Access to Land in the Nilgiri Hills, South India." In *Indigeneity in India,* edited by Bengt Karlsson and Tanka Subba. London: Kegan Paul.

Chakrabarty, Dipesh. 2000. *Provincializing Europe: Postcolonial Thought and Historical Difference.* Princeton: Princeton University Press.

———. 2005. "Politics Unlimited: The Global Adivasi and Debates about the Political." In *Indigeneity in India,* edited by Bengt Karlsson and Tanka Subba. London: Kegan Paul.
Chakravarti, Uma. 2003. *Gendering Caste: Through a Feminist Lens.* Calcutta: Stree.
Chathukulam, J. and M. S. John. 2006. "Issues in Tribal Development: The Recent Experience of Kerala." In *Tribal Development in India: The Contemporary Debate,* edited by C. R. Govinda, 82–202. New Delhi: SAGE.
Chatterjee, Partha. 2004. *The Politics of the Governed: Reflections on Popular Politics in Most of the World.* New York: Columbia University Press.
———. 2008. "Democratic and Economic Transformation in India." *Economic and Political Weekly* (19 April): 53–62.
Cheria, Anita, K. Narayanan, C. R. Bijoy, and Edwin. 1997. *A Search for Justice: A Citizen's Report on the Adivasi Experience in South India.* Bangalore: St. Paul's Publications.
Chibber, Vivek. 2003. *Locked in Place: State-Building and Late Industrialization in India.* Princeton: Princeton University Press.
———. 2009. "On the Decline of Class Analysis in South Asian Studies." In *Whatever Happened to Class? Reflections from South Asia,* edited by Rina Agarwala and Ronald Herring. Lanham: Lexington Books.
Christy, Carmel K. J. 2015. "The Politics of Sexuality and Caste: Looking through Kerala's Public Space." In *Kerala Modernity: Ideas, Spaces and Practices in Transition,* edited by Satheese Chandra Bose and Shiju Sam Varughese, 126–45. New Delhi: Orient Blackswan.
Clastres, Pierre. 1977. *Society Against the State.* Oxford: Basil Blackwell.
Clifford, James, and George Marcus. 1986. *Writing Culture: The Poetics and Politics of Ethnography.* Berkeley: University of California Press.
Conklin, Beth. 2002. "Shamans Versus Pirates in the Amazonian Treasure Chest." *American Anthropologist* 104(4): 1050–61.
Cooper, Frederick, and Ann Laura Stoler. 1997. *Tensions of Empire: Colonial Cultures in a Bourgeois World.* Berkeley: University of California Press.
Cooper, Frederick. 2008. "Possibility and Constraint: African Independence in Historical Perspective." *Journal of African History* 49: 167–96.
Damodaran, K. 1985. "The Tragedy of Indian Communism." In *The Stalinist Legacy: Its Impact on Twentieth Century World Politics,* edited by Tariq Ali, 345–73. Boulder: Lynne Rienner Publishers.
Davis, Mike. 2001. *Late Victorian Holocausts: El Nino Famines and the Making of the Third World.* London: Verso.
Deshpande, Ashwini. 2000. "Does Caste Still Define Disparity? A Look at Inequality in Kerala, India." *The American Economic Review* 90 (2): 322–35.
Devalle, Susana B. C. 1992. *Discourses of Ethnicity: Culture and Protest in Jharkhand.* New Delhi: SAGE.
Devika, J. 2010. "Egalitarian Developmentalism, Communist Mobilization, and the Question of Caste in Kerala State, India." *The Journal of Asian Studies* 69 (3):799–820.
Dilip, T. R. 2010. "School Educational Attainment in Kerala: Trends and Differentials." Thiruvanathapuram: CDS Working Paper.
Dirks, Nicholas. 2003. *Castes of Mind: Colonialism and the Making of Modern India.* Delhi: Permanent Black.
Dreze, Jean, and Amartya Sen. 1997. *Indian Development: Selected Regional Perspectives.* Oxford: Clarendon Press Oxford.
Dumont, Louis. 1972. *Homo Hierarchicus.* New York: Harper Collins.
Edelman, Marc. 2001. "Social Movements: Changing Paradigms and Forms of Politics." *Annual Review of Anthropology* 30: 285–317.
Elkana, Yehuda. 2009. "Freedom and Interdisciplinarity: The Future of the University Curriculum." *Social Research* 76 (3): 933–42.

Fic, Victor. 1970. *Kerala: Yenan of India. Rise of Communist Power,* 1937–1969. Bombay: Nachiketa Publications Limited.

Foucault, Michel. 2007. *Archaeology of Knowledge.* London: Routledge Classics.

Franke, Richard, and Barbara Chasin. 2000. "Is the Kerala Model Sustainable? Lessons from the Past: Prospects for the Future." In *Kerala: The Development Experience,* edited by G. Parayil, 16–39. London: Zed Books.

Frankel, Francine. 2005. *India's Political Economy, 1947–2004: The Gradual Revolution.* New Delhi: Oxford University Press.

Fraser, Nancy. 1995. "From Redistribution to Recognition? Dilemmas of Justice in a 'Post-Socialist' Age." *New Left Review* I/212

Friedman, Jonathan. 1994. *Cultural Identity and Global Process.* London: SAGE.

———. 1999. "Indigenous Struggles and the Discreet Charm of the Bourgeoisie." *Journal of World-Systems Research* 2 (summer 1999): 391–411.

———. 2000. "Globalization, Class and Culture in Global Systems." *Journal of World Systems Research* 6 (3): 636–56.

Friedman, Kajsa Ekholm, and Jonathan Friedman. 2003. *Global Anthropology.* Walnut Creek: Altamira Press.

Froerer, Peggy. 2007. *Religious Division and Social Conflict: The Emergence of Hindu Nationalism in Rural India.* New York: Berghahn Books.

Gailey, Christine Ward. 2006. "Community, State, and the Question of Social Evolution in Karl Marx' Ethnological Notebooks." In *Politics of Egalitarianism,* edited by Jacqueline Solway, 31–52. New York: Berghahn Books.

George Joseph, Vinod. 2005. *Hitchhiker.* Bangalore: Books for Change.

Geetha, V. 2009. "Bereft of Being: The Humiliations of Untouchability." In *Humiliation: Claims and Context,* edited by Gopal Guru, 95–107. New Delhi: Oxford University Press.

Ghosh, Kaushik. 2006. "Between Global Flows and Local Dams: Indigenousness, Locality, and the Transnational Sphere in Jharkhand, India." *Cultural Anthropology* 21 (4): 501–34.

Ghurye, Govind Sadashiv. 1943. *The Aboriginals - So-called - and Their Future.* Poona: D.R. Gadgil.

Gidwani, Vinay. 2008. *Capital, Interrupted.* Minneapolis: University of Minnesota Press.

Gingrich, Andre, and Richard G. Fox. 2002. *Anthropology, by Comparison.* London: Routledge.

Girija, K. P. 2009. "On Suicides, Caste and Higher Education." *Insight Young Voices* (February/March)

Gordon, Kathleen. 2009. "Questioning the Indigenous in Bolivian Politics." CASCA presentation, Vancouver.

Gough, Kathleen. 1968. "Literacy in Kerala." In *Literacy in Traditional Societies,* edited by Jack Goody, 132–60. Cambridge: Cambridge University Press.

Gramsci, Antonio. *Selections from the Prison Notebooks of Antonio Gramsci.* Ed. and translated by Quintin Hoare and Geoffrey Nowell Smith. New York: International Publishers.

Guha, Ramachandra, and Juan Martinez-Alier. 1997. *Varieties of Environmentalism. Essays North and South.* London: Earthscan Publications.

Guha, Ramachandra. 1999. *Savaging the Civilized: Verrier Elwin, His Tribals, and India.* Chicago: University Of Chicago Press.

———. 2004. *Anthropologist among the Marxist and Other Essays.* Delhi: Permanent Black.

Guha, Ranajit, ed. 1982. *Subaltern Studies I: Writings on South Asian History and Society.* Delhi: Oxford University Press.

Guha, Sumit. 1999. *Environment and Ethnicity in India, 1200–1991.* Cambridge Studies in Indian History and Society. Cambridge: Cambridge University Press.

Guilhot, Nicolas. 2007. "Reforming the World: George Soros, Global Capitalism and the Philanthropic Management of the Social Sciences." *Critical Sociology* 33 (3): 447–77.

Gupta, Akhil, and James Ferguson. 1997. "Beyond Culture: Space, Identity, and the Politics of Difference." In *Culture, Power, Place: Explorations in Critical Anthropology*, 33–51. Durham: Duke University Press.

Gupta, D. N. 2008. *Communism and Nationalism in Colonial India, 1939–45*. New Delhi: SAGE.

———. 2009. *The Caged Phoenix: Can India Fly?* Penguin Books India: Viking.

Halliburton, Murphy. 2001. "Rethinking Anthropological Studies of the Body: Manas and Bodham in Kerala." *American Anthropologist* 104 (4): 1123–34.

Hann, Chris. 1993. *Socialism: Ideals, Ideologies and Local Practice*. London: Routledge.

Hansen, Thomas Blom. 1999. *The Saffron Wave*. Princeton: Princeton University Press.

Hardiman, David. 2004. *Gandhi in His Time and Ours: The Global Legacy of His Ideas*. New York: Columbia UP.

Hardtmann, Eva-Maria. 2003. *Our Fury Is Burning: Local Practice & Global Connections in the Dalit Movement*. Stockholm Studies in Social Anthropology. Stockholm: Stockholm Universitet.

Harman, Chris. 2003. *The Lost Revolution: Germany 1918–1923*. Chicago: Haymarket Books.

Harvey, David. 2003. *The New Imperialism*. Oxford: Oxford University Press.

Harvey, Neil. 1998. *The Chiapas Rebellion: The Struggle for Land and Democracy*. Durham: Duke University Press.

Heller, Patrick.1999. *The Labor of Development: Workers and the Transformation of Capitalism in Kerala, India*. Ithaca: Cornell University Press.

———. 2005. "Reinventing Public Power in the Age of Globalization: Decentralization and the Transformation of Movement Politics in Kerala." In *Social Movements in India: Poverty, Power and Politics*, edited by R. Ray and M. Katzenstein, 79–107. New York: Rowman & Littlefield.

Herring, Ron. 2008. "From 'Fanaticism' to Power: The Deep Roots of Kerala's Agrarian Exceptionalism." In *Speaking of Peasants: Essays on Indian History and Politics in Honor of Walter Hauser*, edited by William Pinch, 277–320. New Delhi: Manohar.

Hey, Jeanne, and Thomas Klak. 1999. "From Protectionism towards Neoliberalism: Ecuador across Four Administrations (1981–1996)." Studies in Comparative International Development 34 (3): 66–97.

Hoare, Quintin, and Geoffrey Nowell Smith, eds. 1971. *Antonio Gramsci: Selections from the Prison Notebooks*. New York: International Publishers.

Hopkins, Terence. 1978. "World-System Analysis: Methodological Issues." In *Social Change in the Capitalist World Economy*, edited by Barbara Hockey Kaplan, 199–217. Beverly Hills/London: SAGE.

———. 1979. "The Study of the Capitalist World-Economy: Some Introductory Considerations." In *The World-System of Capitalism: Past and Present*. Beverly Hills/London: SAGE.

Humphrey, Caroline, and Katherine Verdery. 2004. *Property in Question*. Vol. 2, *Value Transformation in the Global Economy*. English Edition. New York: Berg Publishers.

Isaac, Thomas and Richard Franke. 2002. *Local Democracy and Development: People's Campaign for Decentralized Planning in Kerala*. New Delhi: LeftWord Press.

Isaac, Thomas, Richard Franke, and Pyaralal Raghavan. 1998. *Democracy at Work in an Indian Industrial Cooperative*. Ithaca: Cornell University Press.

Isac, Susamma. 2012. Perceptions and experiences of development: a study of two tribal communities in Wayanad district, Kerala. Doctoral dissertation, Tata Institute of Social Sciences.

Jacob, T. G. 2006. "Wayanad: Misery in an Emerald Bowl." *Essays on the Ongoing Crisis in the Cash Crop Economy—Kerala*. Mumbai: Vikas Adhyayan Kendra.

Jacob, T. G., and P. Bandhu. 2002. *Reflections on the Caste Question: The Dalit Situation in South India*. Bangalore: Nesa.

Jaffrelot, Christophe. 2003. *India's Silent Revolution: The Rise of the Lower Castes*. New edition. London: Hurst & Company.

Janu, C.K. and M. Geethanandan. 2003. "The return to Muthanga". *PUCL Bulletin.* Http: http://www.pucl.org/Topics/Dalit-tribal/2003/muthanga.htm.

Jeffrey, Robin. 1992. *Politics, Women and Well-being: How Kerala Became "A Model."* New Delhi: Oxford University Press.

Joe, M. S. 2010. "Sree Narayana Guru, The Left, and Chitralekha." Countercurrents.org. Accessed 10 January 2016. http://www.countercurrents.org/joems180310.htm

Joseph, K. V. 1986. *Migration and Economic Development of Kerala.* Trivandrum: University of Kerala.

Jung, Courtney. 2008. *The Moral Force of Indigenous Politics: Critical Liberalism and the Zapatistas.* Cambridge: Cambridge University Press.

Kalathil, Mariamma. 2004. "Withering Valli: Alienation, Degradation, and Enslavement of Tribal Women in Attappady." CDS discussion paper no. 66.

Kalb, Don. 1997. *Expanding Class: Power and Everyday Politics in Industrial Communities, The Netherlands, 1850–1950.* Durham: Duke University Press.

Kannan, K. P. 1999. "Rural Labour Relations and Development Dilemmas in Kerala: Reflections on the Dilemmas of a Socially Transforming Labour Force in a Slowly Growing Economy." *Journal of Peasant Studies* 26 (2): 140–81.

Kapicadu, Sunny M. 2008. "Beyond Just 'a Home and a Name.'" Translated from Malayalam by J. Devika. Originally posted on Kafila. Accessed 10 January 2016. Https://kafila.online/2008/06/14/beyond-just-a-home-and-a-name/

Karat, Brinda. 2010. "Towards Intensified Struggles for Adivasi Rights." *The Marxist* 26 (3), 19–38.

Karlsson, Bengt. 2003. "Anthropology and the 'Indigenous Slot.'" *Critique of Anthropology* 23 (4): 403–23.

Kaviraj, S., and S. Khilnani. (2002) *Civil Society: History and Possibilities.* Cambridge University Press.

Kenrick, Justin, and Jerome Lewis. 2004. "Indigenous Peoples' Rights and the Politics of the Term 'Indigenous.'" *Anthropology Today* 20 (2): 4–9.

Khagram, Sanjeev. 2004. *Dams and Development: Transnational Struggles for Water and Power.* Cornell University Press.

Khilnani, Sunil. 1997. *The Idea of India.* London: Hamish Hamilton.

KIRTADS. 2006. "Wayanad Initiative: A Situational Study and Feasibility Report for the Comprehensive Development of Adivasi Communities of Wayanad." Kozhikode: Centre of Excellence and Management.

Kjosavik, Darley, and N. Shanmugaratnam. 2007. "Property Rights Dynamics and Indigenous Communities in Highland Kerala, South India: An Institutional-Historical Perspective." *Modern Asian Studies 41* (6): 1183–260.

Kjosavik, Darley. 2004. "Integration or Exclusion? Locating Indigenous Peoples in the Development Process of Kerala, South India." *Forum for Development Studies* 2: 231–73.

Kooiman, Dick. 1989. *Conversion and Social Equality in India.* Delhi: Manohar.

Krishna, Iyer, L. K. A. 1925. *Lectures on Ethnography.* Calcutta; University of Calcutta.

Krishna, Sankaran. 2009. "Globalization and Postcolonialism: Hegemony and Resistance in the Twenty-First Century." Lanham: Rowman & Littlefield.

Krishnan, T. V. 1971. *Kerala's First Communist: Life of "Sakhavu" Krishna Pillai.* Communist Party Publication.

Krishnakumar, R. 2001. "The Adivasi Struggle." *Frontline* 18 (21), 13–26 Oct.

Kumar, G. Gopa. 2008. "Socio-Economic Background of Legislators in Kerala." In *Rise of the Plebeians? The Changing Face of Indian Legislative Assemblies,* edited by Christophe Jaffrelot and Sanjay Kumar, 393–408. New Delhi: Routledge.

Kunhaman, M. 1985. "The Tribal Economy of Kerala: An Intra-Regional Analysis." *Economic and Political Weekly* 20 (11): 466–74.

Kunnath, George J. 2006. "Becoming a Naxalite in Rural Bihar: Class Struggle and Its Contradictions." *Journal of Peasant Studies* 33 (1): 89–123.

Kuper, Adam. 1996. *Anthropology and Anthropologists: The Modern British School.* London: Routledge.

———. 1988. *The Invention of Primitive Society: Transformations of an Illusion.* London: Routledge.

———. 2003. "The Return of the Native." *Current Anthropology* 44 (3): 389–95.

Lee, Richard Borshay. 2006. "Twenty-First Century Indigenism." *Anthropological Theory* 6 (4): 455–79.

Lerche, Jens. 2008. "Transnational Advocacy Networks and Affirmative Action for Dalits in India." *Development and Change* 39(2): 239–261.

Levien, Michael. 2011. "Special Economic Zones and Accumulation by Dispossession in India." *Journal of Agrarian Change* 11 (4): 454–483.

Li, Tania. 2000. "Articulating Indigenous Identity in Indonesia: Resource Politics and the Tribal Slot." *Comparative Studies in Society and History* 42 (1): 149–79.

———. 2009. "Indigeneity, Capitalism and the Management of Dispossession." *Current Anthropology* 51(3): 385–414.

Lindberg, Anna. 2001. "Experience and Identity: A Historical Account of Class, Caste and Gender among the Cashew Workers of Kerala, 1930–2000." Lund: Lund University Press.

Logan, William. [1887] 2006. *Malabar Manual.* Asian Educational Services. Facsimile of 1887 edition.

Lukacs, Georg. 1923. *What is Orthodox Marxism? History and Class Consciousness.* Cambridge, MA: MIT Press.

Lukose, Ritty. 2005. "Empty Citizenship: Protesting Politics in the Era of Globalization." *Cultural Anthropology* 20(4): 506–33.

———. 2009. *Liberalization's Children: Gender, Youth and Consumer Citizenship in Globalizing India.* Durham: Duke University Press.

Madsen, Stig Toft. 2001. "The View from Vevey." *Economic and Political Weekly* (29 September): 3733–42.

Mannathukkaren, Nissim. 2010. "The 'Poverty' of Political Society: Partha Chatterjee and the People's Planning Campaign in Kerala, India." *Third World Quarterly* 31 (2): 295–314.

Marcus, George. 1995. Ethnography in/of the World System: The Emergence of Multi-Sited Ethnography. *Annual Review of Anthropology* 24.

Marx, Karl. [1852] 2008. *The Eighteenth Brumaire of Louis Bonaparte.* Rockville: Wildside Press.

Mathew, George. 1989. *Communal Road to a Secular Kerala.* Delhi: Concept Publishing Company.

Mathur, P. R. G. 1977. *Tribal Situation in Kerala.* Thiruvanathapuram: St. Joseph's Press.

Mauss, Marcel. [1934] 1973. "Techniques of the Body." *Economy and Society* 2 (1): 70–88.

Mayaram, Shail, M. S. S. Pandian, and Ajay Skaria, eds. *Subaltern Studies.* Vol. 12, *Muslims, Dalist and the Fabrications of History.* New Delhi: Permanent Black.

McMichael, Philip. 2000. "World-Systems Analysis, Globalization and Incorporated Comparison." *Journal of World Systems Research* VI 3. http://jwsr.ucr.edu/archive/vol6/number3/pdf/jwsr-v6n3-mcmichael.pdf.

———. 2008. "Peasants Make Their Own History, But Not Just as They Please." *Journal of Agrarian Change* 8 (2): 205–28.

———, ed. 2010. *Contesting Development: Critical Struggles for Social Change.* New York: Routledge.

McMillan, Alistair. 2005. *Standing at the Margins: Representation and Electoral Reservation in India.* Oxford: OUP.

Meillassoux, Claude. 1981. *Maidens, Meal and Money: Capitalism and Domestic Community.* Cambridge: Cambridge University Press.

Menon, Dilip. 1994. *Caste, Nationalism and Communism in South India: Malabar 1900–1948.* Cambridge: Cambridge University Press.

———. 2006. *The Blindness of Insight: Essays on Caste in Modern India.* Pondicherry: Navayana.

Menon, Nivedita, and Aditya Nigam. 2007. *Power and Contestation: India since 1989.* Halifax: Fernwood Publishing; London: Zed Books.

Menon, Sreedhara. 2007. *A Survey of Kerala History.* Kottayam: D. C. Books.

Menon, Vineetha. 2009. "Problem of 'Knowledge' in Applied Anthropology." *Journal of Social Sciences* 11 (1): 101–14.

Middleton, Townsend. 2013. "Scheduling Tribes: A View from Inside the 'Ethnographic State.'" *Focaal- Journal of Global and Historical Anthropology* 65: 13–23.

Mohan, Sanal. 2008. "Social Space, Civil Society and Dalit Agency in Twentieth Century Kerala." Paper presented at The Dalit Studies Conference, Center for the Advanced Study of India, University of Pennsylvania, Philadelphia, PA, 3–5 December.

———. 2011. "Narrativizing the History of Slave Suffering." In *No Alphabet in Sight,* edited by K. Satyanarayana and Susie Tharu. Delhi: Penguin Books.

Mohan, K. T. Ram, and K. Ravi Raman. 1988. "Kerala Worker Rises against Indian Big Capital: Report on Rayons Workers' Struggle." *Economic and Political Weekly* (July 2): 1259–364.

Mohanakumar, S. 2008. "Kerala's Agricultural Laborers: Victims of a Crisis." *Economic and Political Weekly* (May 10): 27–29.

Morris, Brian. 1982. *Forest Traders: A Socio-Economic Study of the Hill Pandaram.* New Jersey: Athlone Press.

Morrison, Barrie M. 1997. "The Embourgeoisement of the Kerala Farmer." *Modern Asian Studies* 31 (1): 61–87.

Mosse, David. 2005. "On the Margins of the City: Adivasi Seasonal Labour Migration in Western India." *Economic and Political Weekly* (July 9): 3025–38.

———. 2012. *The Saint in the Banyan Tree: Christianity and Caste Society in India.* Berkeley: University of California Press.

Moynihan, Daniel Patrick, with Suzanne Weaver. 1975. *A Dangerous Place.* Bombay: Allied Publishers.

Muenster, Daniel. 2011. "From Farming to Speculation: A Neoliberal Mode of Production in Hill Produce Agriculture?" Paper presented at the Agrarian Transformation in India seminar, Oxford University, Oxford, UK, 13 July.

Mukherji, Projit Bihari. 2009. "'Communist' Dispossession Meets 'Reactionary' Resistance: The Ironies of the Parliamentary Left in West-Bengal." *Focaal* 54 (2009): 89–96.

Mukundan, C. M. 2001. "Tribal Dies Due to Starvation: Kundala Tribals to Occupy Minister's Land." Dalit e-forum. Accessed 10 January 2016. http://ambedkar.org/news/tribaldies.htm.

Nair, K. N., and Vineetha Menon. 2007. "Distress Debt and Suicides among Agrarian Households: Findings from Three Village Studies in Kerala." CDS Working Paper 397.

Namboodiripad, E. M. S. 1976. *How I Became a Communist.* Trivandrum: Chintha Publications

Nanda, Meera 2003 *Prophets Facing Backward: Postmodern Critiques of Science and Hindu Nationalism in India.* New Brunswick and London: Rutgers University Press.

Nash, June. 2001. *Mayan Visions: The Question for Autonomy in an Age of Globalization.* New York: Routledge.

Neilson, Jeff, and Bill Pritchard. 2009. *Value Chain Struggles: Institutions and Governance in the Plantation Districts of South India.* Oxford: Wiley-Blackwell.

Nelson, Diane M. 2003. "'The More You Kill the More You Will Live': The Maya, 'Race,' and Biopolitical Hopes for Peace in Guatemala." In *Race, Nature and the Politics of Difference,* edited by Donald S. Moore, Jake Kosek, and Anand Pandian. Durham: Duke University Press.

Nieuwenhuys, Olga. 1991. "Emancipation for Survival: Access to Land and Labor of Thandans in Kerala." *Modern Asian Studies* 25(3): 599–619.
Niezen, Ronald. 2003. *The Origins of Indigenism.* Berkeley: University of California Press.
Nossiter, T. J. 1982. *Communism in Kerala: A Study in Political Adaptation.* Berkeley: University of California Press.
Omvedt, Gail. 1993. *Reinventing Revolution: New Social Movements and the Socialist Tradition in India.* New York: M. E. Sharpe.
———. 2005. "Capitalism and Globalization, Dalits and Adivasis." *Economic and Political Weekly* (19 November): 4881.
———. 2006. *Dalit Visions: The Anti-Caste Movement and the Construction on an Indian Identity.* 2nd ed. New Delhi: Orient Longman.
Oommen, M. A. 2010. "Reform and the Kerala 'Model': A Critique Based on Sen's Capability Approach." In *Development, Democracy, and the State: Critiquing the Kerala Model of Development,* edited by Ravi Raman. London: Routledge.
Osella, Filippo, and Caroline Osella. 2000. *Social Mobility in Kerala: Modernity and Identity in Conflict.* London: Pluto Press.
Panikkar, K. N. 1978. "Agrarian Legislation and Social Classes: A Case Study of Malabar." *Economic and Political Weekly* 13 (21): 880–88.
———. 1992. *Against Lord and State: Religion and Peasant Uprisings in Malabar 1836–1921.* Oxford University Press.
———. 1998. "EMS as Historian." *Frontline* 15 (7) 4–17 April.
Patil, Sharad. 2009. "Search for Aborigines, or Sudra Varna, or Caste-Ending Equality?" *Mainstream* 47 (11).
Peoples' Movements Solidarity Team. 2007. A Report on Chengara Land Struggle in Kerala. Http:// http://sanhati.com/articles/535/.
Petras, James, and Henry Veltmeyer. 2005. *Social Movements and State Power: Argentina, Brazil, Bolivia, Ecuador.* London: Pluto Press.
Philip, Kavita. 2003. *Civilising Natures: Race, Resources and Modernity in Colonial South India.* New Delhi: Orient Longman.
Plowden, W. C. 1883. *Report on the Census of British India.* London: Eyre and Spottiswoode.
Postero, Nancy. 2006. *Now We Are Citizens: Indigenous Politics in Postmulticultural Bolivia.* Chicago: Stanford University Press.
Povinelli, Elizabeth A. 2002. *The Cunning of Recognition.* Durham: Duke University Press.
Prasad, Archana. 2003. *Against Ecological Romanticism: Verrier Elwin and the Making of Anti-Modern Tribal Identity.* New Delhi: Three Essays Collective.
Prasad, Chandra Bhan. 1998. "EMS Is No More: Long Live Socialism." *Communalism Combat* 5 (5): 33–34.
Priestland, David. 2009. *The Red Flag: A History of Communism.* New York: Grove Press.
Puthucherril, Tony George, and Lekshmi Vijayabalan. 2001. "Tribal Land Alienation in Kerala: A Tale of Promises and Betrayals." *Cochin University Law Review* 25: 1–24.
Radhakrishna, Meena. 2001. *Dishonoured by History: "Criminal Tribes" and British Colonial Policy.* New Delhi: Orient Longman.
Radhakrishnan, P. 1981. "Land Reforms in Theory and Practice: The Kerala Experience." *Economic and Political Weekly* 16 (52): 129–37.
Raj, Jayaseelan. 2013. "Alienated Enclaves: Economic Crisis and Neo-Bondage in a South Indian Plantation Belt." *Forum for Development Studies* 2013: 1–26.
Ray, Rabindra. 1988. *The Naxalites and Their Ideology.* Delhi: Oxford University Press.
Raman, Ravi. 2004. Muthanga: "A Spark of Hope." *Social Analysis* 1 (48): 126–35.
Rao, Anupama. 2009. *The Caste Question: Dalits and the Politics of Modern India.* Berkeley: University of California Press.
Raimon, S. 2006. *Selected Documents on Vaikom Satyagraha.* Trivandrum: Kerala State Archives Department/Government of Kerala.

Rata, Elizabeth. 2003. "Late Capitalism and Ethnic Revivalism: A 'New Middle Age'?" *Anthropological Theory* 3: 43.

Rege, Sharmila. 2006. *Writing Caste, Writing Gender: Dalit Women's Testimonios.* Delhi: Zubaan Books.

Robins, Steven. 2003. "Whose Modernity? Indigenous Modernities and Land Claims after Apartheid." *Development and Change* 34 (2): 265–85.

Rodriguez, Valerian, ed. 2002. *The Essential Writing of B. R. Ambedkar.* Oxford: Oxford University Press.

Roseberry, William. 1989. *Anthropologies and Histories: Essays in Culture, History and Political Economy.* New Brunswick: Rutgers State University.

———. 1994. "Hegemony and the Language of Contention." In *Everyday Forms of State Formation: Revolution and the Negotiation of Rule,* edited by G. Joseph and D. Nugent. Durham: Duke University Press.

Routledge, Paul. 2003. "Voices of the Damned: Discursive Resistance amidst Erasure in the Narmada Valley, India." *Political Geography* 22 (3), 243–70.

Roy, Arundhati. 1997. *The God of Small Things.* New York: Random House.

———. 2009. "The Heart of India Is Under Attack." The Guardian, 30 September. www.guardian.co.uk/commentisfree/2009/oct/30/mining-india-maoists-green-hunt.

———. 2010. "The Trickledown Revolution." Outlook India.com, 20 September. Accessed 10 January 2016.http://www.outlookindia.com/article.aspx?267040.

Roy, Srirupa. 2007. *Beyond Belief: India and the Politics of Postcolonial Nationalism.* Durham: Duke University Press.

Sandbrook, Richard, Marc Edelman, Patrick Heller, and Judith Teichman. 2007. *Social Democracy in the Global Periphery: Origins, Challenges, Prospects.* Cambridge: Cambridge University Press.

Sanyal, Kalyan. 2007. *Rethinking Capitalist Development: Primitive Accumulation, Governmentality and Post-Colonial Capital.* London: Routledge.

Saradamoni, K. 1980. *Emergence of a Slave-Caste: The Pulayas of Kerala.* Delhi: People's Publishing House.

Sarkar, Sumit. 1983. *Modern India, 1885–1947.* New Delhi: Macmillan.

———. 1997. "The Decline of the Subaltern in Subaltern Studies." In *Writing Social History,* 82–108. Delhi: Oxford University Press India.

Schulze, Brigitte. 2004. *Feminist Cinema Culture: A Forum for Cooperation and Communication.* Http: http://www.femcinecult-kerala.uni-trier.de

Scott, James C. 2009. *The Art of Not Being Governed: An Anarchist History of Upland Southeast Asia.* New Haven: Yale University Press.

Schneider, Jane and Reyna Rapp. 1995. *Articulating Hidden Histories: Exploring the Influence of Eric R. Wolf.* Berkeley: University of California Press.

Shah, Alpa. 2006. "The Labour of Love: Seasonal Migration from Jharkhand to the Brick Kilns of Other States in India." *Contributions to Indian Sociology* 40 (1): 91–118.

———. 2007. "The Dark Side of Indigeneity? Indigenous People, Rights and Development in India." *History Compass* 5 (6): 1806–32.

———. 2010. *In the Shadows of the State: Indigenous Politics, Environmentalism, and Insurgency in Jharkhand, India.* Durham: Duke University Press.

Shah, Apoorna. 2010. "Putting the Kerala Model to Rest." American Enterprise Institute Working Paper Series on Development Policy. Accessed 10 January 2016. Http://www.aei.org/docLib/Putting-Kerala-Model-Rest-September-10.pdf

Shani, Ornit. 2007. *Communalism, Caste and Hindu Nationalism: The Violence in Gujarat.* Cambridge: Cambridge University Press.

Shore, Chris. 2010. "Beyond the Multiversity: Neoliberalism and the Rise of the Schizophrenic University." *Social Anthropology* 18 (1): 15–29.

Sider, Gerald. 2003. *Living Indian Histories: Lumbee and Tuscarora people in North Carolina.* Chapel Hill: University of Carolina Press.
Singh, Kumar Suresh. 2002. *People of India: Kerala.* New Delhi: Affiliated East-West Press.
———, ed. 1989. *Jawaharlal Nehru, Tribes and Tribal policy.* Calcutta: Anthropological Survey of India.
Singh, Kumar Sanjay. 2001. *The dark clouds and the silver lining: Adivasi struggle in Kerala.* New Delhi: Kalpana Printing House.
Sinha, A. C. 2004. "Colonial Anthropology vs Indological Sociology: Elwin and Ghurye on Tribal Policy in India." In *Between Ethnography and Fiction: Verrier Elwin and the Tribal Question in India,* edited by T. B. Subba and Sujit Som. New Delhi: Orient Longman.
Sinha, Surajit. 2002. "Tribal Solidarity Movement in India: A Review." In *Social Movement and the State,* edited by Ghanshyam Shah. London: SAGE.
Sissons, Jeffrey. 2005. *First People: Indigenous Cultures and their Futures.* London: Reaktion Books.
Sivaramakrishnan, Kalyanakrishnan. 1999. *Modern Forests: Statemaking and Environmental Change in Colonial Eastern India.* Stanford: Stanford University Press.
Skaria, Ajay. 1999. *Hybrid Histories: Forests, Frontiers and Wildness in Western India.* OUP India.
Smith, Gavin. 2004. "Hegemony: Critical Interpretations in Anthropology and Beyond." *Focaal* 2004 (43): 99–120.
Sonntag, Selma. 2005. "Self-Government, Indigeneity and Cultural Authenticity: A Comparative Study of India and the United States." In *Indigeneity in India,* edited by Bengt Karlsson and Tanka Subba. London: Kegan Paul.
Speed, Shannon. 2008. *Rights in Rebellion: Indigenous Struggle and Human Rights in Chiapas.* Stanford: Stanford University Press.
Sreekumar, K. K., and Govindan Parayil. 2002. "Contention and Contradictions of Tourism as Development Option: The Case of Kerala, India." *Third World Quarterly* 23 (3): 529–48.
———. 2006. "Interrogating Development: New Social Movements, Democracy, and Indigenous People's Struggles in Kerala." In *Kerala: The Paradoxes of Public Action and Development,* edited by J. Tharamangalam, 215–57. New Delhi: Orient Longman.
Srinivas, M. N. 1962. *Caste in Modern India and Other Essays.* Bombay: J. K. Publishers.
Steur, Luisa. 2005. "'On the Correct Handling of Contradictions': Liberal-Culturalism in Indigenous Studies." *Focaal* 46: 169–76.
———. 2009. "What's Left? Land Expropriation, Socialist 'Modernizers,' and Peasant Resistance in Asia." *Focaal* 54: 67–73.
———. 2015. "Theorizing Thervoy: Subaltern Studies and Dalit Praxis in India's Land Wars." In *New Subaltern Politics: Reconceptualizing Hegemony and Resistance in Contemporary India,* edited by Alf Nilsen and Srila Roy, 228–249. Oxford: Oxford University Press.
Sundar, Nandini. 2008. *Subalterns and Sovereigns: An Anthropological History of Bastar (1854—2006).* Oxford: Oxford University Press.
———, ed. 2009. *Legal Grounds: Natural Resources, Identity, and the Law in Jharkhand.* Oxford: Oxford University Press.
Surendran, C. P. 2006. *An Iron Harvest.* New Delhi: Roli Books.
Surjeet, Harkishnan Singh. 1998. *March of the Communist Movement in India.* Calcutta: National Book Agency.
Swaan, Abram de. 1997. "Widening Circles of Disidentification." *Theory, Culture and Society* 14 (2): 105–22.
Sylvain, Renee. 2002. "'Land, Water and Truth': San Identity and Global Indigenism." *American Anthropologist* 104 (4): 1974–85.
Tarrow, Sidney G. 1998. *Power in Movement.* Cambridge: Cambridge University Press.
Teltumbde, Anand. 2010. "Rethinking Strategies for the Dalit Movement: A Concept Note for Discussion." *Dalit Bulletin* (April) 10–18.

Thachil, Tariq. 2008. "Poor Choices: De-Alignment, Development and Dalit/Adivasi Voting Patterns in Indian States." *Contemporary South Asia* 16 (4): 441–64.
Thapar, Romila. 2008. *The Aryan: Recasting Constructs.* Gurgaon: Three Essays Collective.
Thompson, E. P. 1965. "Peculiarities of the English." In *The Socialist Register,* edited by R. Miliband and J. Saville, 311–62. London: Merlin Press.
———. 1970. *The Making of the English Working Class.* London: Penguin Books.
Thurston, Edgar. 1909. *Castes and Tribes of Southern India.* 7 Volumes. Madras: Government Press.
Tilly, Charles. 2001. "Relational Origins of Inequality." *Anthropological Theory* 1 (3): 355–72.
Tsing, Anna. 2004. *Friction: An Ethnography of Global Connection.* Princeton: Princeton University Press.
———. 2007. "Indigenous Voice." In *Indigenous Experience Today,* edited by Marisol de la Cadena and Orin Starn, 33–68. Oxford: Berg.
United Nations. 1975. *Poverty, Unemployment and Development Policy: A Case Study of Selected Issues with Special Reference to Kerala.* New York: United Nations.
Uyl, Marion den. 1994. *Invisible Barriers: Gender, Caste and Kinship in a Southern Indian Village.* Utrecht: International Books.
Verrier, Elwin. 1959. *A Philosophy for NEFA.* Shillong: North-East Frontier Agency.
Wallerstein, Immanuel. 1987. "The Construction of Peoplehood: Racism, Nationalism, Ethnicity." *Sociological Forum* 2 (2): 373–88.
———. 2004. *World-Systems Analysis: An Introduction.* Durham: Duke University Press.
Walton, John. 1984. *Reluctant Rebels: Comparative Studies of Revolution and Underdevelopment.* NY: Columbia University Press.
Whitehead, Judy. 2007. "Sunken Voices: Adivasis, Neo-Gandhian Environmentalism and State-Civil Society Relations in the Narmada Valley 1998–2001." *Antropologica* 49 (2).
Williams, Michelle. 2008. *The Roots of Participatory Democracy: Democratic Communists in South Africa and Kerala, India.* New York: Palgrave, Macmillan.
Wilmsen, Edwin. 1989. *Land Filled with Flies: A Political Economy of the Kalahari Desert.* Chicago: Chicago University Press.
Wolf, Eric. 1966. *Peasants.* New Jersey: Prentice Hall.
———. 1982. *Europe and the People without History.* Berkeley: University of California Press.
———. 1990. "Facing Power, Old Insights, New Questions." *American Anthropologist* 92(3) : 586–596.
Xaxa, Virginius. 1999. "Tribes as Indigenous People of India." *Economic and Political Weekly* 34 (51): 3589–96.
Yashar, Deborah. 2005. *Contesting Citizenship in Latin America: The Rise of Indigenous Movements and the Postliberal Challenge.* Cambridge: Cambridge University Press.
Zachariah, Mathew, and R. Sooryamoorthy. 1994. *Science for Social Revolution? Achievements and Dilemmas of a Development Movement—The Kerala Sastra Sahitya Parishad.* London: Zed Books.

# INDEX

## DISLOCATIONS

**General Editors:** August Carbonella, *Memorial University of Newfoundland,* Don Kalb, *Central European University & Utrecht University,* Linda Green, *University of Arizona*

The immense dislocations and suffering caused by neoliberal globalization, the retreat of the welfare state in the last decades of the twentieth century, and the heightened military imperialism at the turn of the twenty-first century have raised urgent questions about the temporal and spatial dimensions of power. Through stimulating critical perspectives and new and cross-disciplinary frameworks that reflect recent innovations in the social and human sciences, this series provides a forum for politically engaged and theoretically imaginative responses to these important issues of late modernity.

**Volume 1**
*Where Have All the Homeless Gone?: The Making and Unmaking of a Crisis*
Anthony Marcus

**Volume 2**
*Blood and Oranges: Immigrant Labor and European Markets in Rural Greece*
Christopher M. Lawrence

**Volume 3**
*Struggles for Home: Violence, Hope and the Movement of People*
Edited by Stef Jansen and Staffan Löfving

**Volume 4**
*Slipping Away: Banana Politics and Fair Trade in the Eastern Caribbean*
Mark Moberg

**Volume 5**
*Made in Sheffield: An Ethnography of Industrial Work and Politics*
Massimiliano Mollona

**Volume 6**
*Biopolitics, Militarism, and Development: Eritrea in the Twenty-First Century*
Edited by David O'Kane and Tricia Redeker Hepner

**Volume 7**
*When Women Held the Dragon's Tongue and Other Essays in Historical Anthropology*
Hermann Rebel

**Volume 8**
*Class, Contention, and a World in Motion*
Edited by Winnie Lem and Pauline Gardiner Barber

**Volume 9**
*Crude Domination: An Anthropology of Oil*
Edited by Andrea Behrends, Stephen P. Reyna, and Günther Schlee

**Volume 10**
*Communities of Complicity: Everyday Ethics in Rural China*
Hans Steinmüller

**Volume 11**
*Elusive Promises: Planning in the Contemporary World*
Edited by Simone Abram and Gisa Weszkalnys

**Volume 12**
*Intellectuals and (Counter-) Politics: Essays in Historical Realism*
Gavin Smith

**Volume 13**
*Blood and Fire: Toward a Global Anthropology of Labor*
Edited by Sharryn Kasmir and August Carbonella

**Volume 14**
*The Neoliberal Landscape and the Rise of Islamist Capital in Turkey*
Edited by Neşecan Balkan, Erol Balkan, and Ahmet Öncü

**Volume 15**
*Yearnings in the Meantime: 'Normal Lives' and the State in a Sarajevo Apartment Complex*
Stef Jansen

**Volume 16**
*Where Are All Our Sheep? Kyrgyzstan, A Global Political Arena*
Boris Petric, translated by Cynthia Schoch

**Volume 17**
*Enduring Uncertainty: Deportation, Punishment and Everyday Life*
Ines Hasselberg

**Volume 18**
*The Anthropology of Corporate Social Responsibility*
Edited by Catherine Dolan and Dinah Rajak

**Volume 19**
*Breaking Rocks: Music, Ideology and Economic Collapse, from Paris to Kinshasa*
Joe Trapido

**Volume 20**
*Indigenist Mobilization: Confronting Electoral Communism and Precarious Livelihoods in Post-Reform Kerala*
Luisa Steur